KT-529-911

Children's Personal and Social Development

Sharon Ding and Karen Littleton

The Open University

Blackwell
Publishing

Copyright © 2005 The Open University

First published 2005 by Blackwell Publishing Ltd in association with The Open University

The Open University
Walton Hall, Milton Keynes
MK7 6AA

Blackwell Publishing Ltd:

350 Main Street, Malden, MA 02148-5020, USA
9600 Garsington Road, Oxford OX4 2DQ, UK
550 Swanston Street, Carlton, Victoria 3053, Australia

For further information on Blackwell Publishing please visit our website:
www.blackwellpublishing.com

Library of Congress Cataloguing in Publication Data has been applied for.
A catalogue record for this title is available from the British Library.

Edited, designed and typeset by The Open University.

Printed and bound in the United Kingdom by The Alden Group, Oxford.

ISBN 13: 978-1-4051-1694-7 (paperback)

ISBN 10: 1-4051-1694-3 (paperback)
1.1

P4/07

Children's Personal and Social Development

This publication forms part of an Open University course ED209 *Child Development*.
Details of this and other Open University courses can be obtained from the Student
Registration and Enquiry Service, The Open University, PO Box 197, Milton Keynes,
MK7 6BJ, United Kingdom: tel. +44 (0) 870 333 4340, email general-enquiries@open.ac.uk

Alternatively, you may visit the Open University website at http://www.open.ac.uk where
you can learn more about the wide range of courses and packs offered at all levels by The
Open University.

To purchase a selection of Open University course materials visit http://www.ouw.co.uk,
or contact Open University Worldwide, Michael Young Building, Walton Hall, Milton
Keynes MK7 6AA, United Kingdom for a brochure. tel. +44 (0)1908 858785;
fax +44 (0)1908 858787; email ouwenq@open.ac.uk

Contents

Foreword

This book has been made possible by the contributions of many of our colleagues, and we would like to thank them for the substantial part they have played in making it a text that we feel very proud of. First of all we would like to thank the team of editors: Julia Brennan, Bridgette Jones and Margaret Mellor. Their careful and detailed reading has resulted in changes which have greatly improved readability and clarity for our readers. We have greatly valued the opportunity to work with our knowledgeable and supportive consultant authors: Robin Banerjee, Martyn Barrett, Michael E. Lamb, Charlie Lewis and Sinead Rhodes. The book has been strengthened by the quality of their contributions. Our critical reader, Jackie Abell, provided much useful critique and support, as did the Child Development Course Team at The Open University. Iris Rowbotham has managed the project efficiently and supportively throughout, and Stephanie Withers' secretarial skills have also been invaluable. We would also like to thank Shereen Karmali, the proofreader; Jonathan Davies and Sian Lewis, the book designers; Janis Gilbert, the illustrator; and Nikki Tolcher, the compositor.

Sharon Ding

Karen Littleton

Introduction: children's personal and social development

Sharon Ding

1 Changing approaches to child development

This book focuses on one of the most important areas in developmental psychology – that of children's personal and social development. Interest in this topic has increased significantly over recent years. This is partly due to a greater understanding within society that children's relationships, both with adults and with other children, can have a fundamental effect on children and on the adults they become. Patterns of child-rearing are changing – more children experience the separation of their parents, life in a stepfamily or lengthy periods of time in childcare. These have a profound influence on children's experiences of relationships and on their sense of identity.

There have also been some changes in the way that psychologists view the social and personal development of children. This has seen a move away from considering children as passive individuals whose development is predetermined and influenced by the actions of others. Instead, children are viewed as active participants in their own development. They negotiate their own place in their social worlds, and construct their own understandings, rather than having them merely 'passed on' by more experienced members of society. Alongside this view of children as active meaning-makers in their own social worlds is a belief that cognitive, social and personal development do not happen in parallel, but are inextricably linked together in the developmental process. The active nature of children's involvement in their own development means that both individual and social processes are brought to bear to enable children to function in the complex environment within which they exist.

2 The structure of this book

Chapter 1 covers the topics of parenting and attachment. The early relationships that children form with their caregivers have long been of interest to psychologists because they have been seen as extremely powerful in influencing development. Some of the history of this work is described, beginning with early pioneering work on children's attachment to their mothers, and moving through more recent work on parent–child relationships throughout childhood and into adolescence and adulthood. The theme of the mutual dependence and close linkage between cognitive, personal and social development is developed through the concept of the 'internal working model'. This is a set of expectations constructed from a model of the child's own self, a model of 'other selves' and a model of the relationship between these two. Children use these expectations to help them to respond appropriately to new situations. In this way, personal and social understandings are used to construct a working knowledge of the child's environment.

One reason for the interest in children's relationships is the belief that early relationships have a formative influence on children's development and their subsequent mental health. Chapter 2, however, demonstrates how the issues surrounding the origins of disturbed behaviour in childhood are often much more complex. It is argued that psychological development – including disturbed development – is best understood in terms of a complex, continuous transaction between individual and social processes.

Until relatively recently, as indicated in Chapter 1, the majority of research has focused on children with their primary caregivers (usually their mothers). However, there is now a growing area of study which concentrates on children's relationships with their siblings and peers. Chapter 3 takes this as its topic and focuses on the nature and developmental significance of interactions between children. It highlights the complexity of children's social worlds, and considers the processes through which children build ongoing relationships with each other.

The first three chapters in this book cover different aspects of children's relationships with others. Chapter 4 introduces a change of focus – it is the first of four chapters which consider how a child's sense of his or her own identity develops. However, this change of focus does not mean that children's relationships are put to one side. Instead, the mutual dependency of social and personal development is again underlined – children's interactions and relationships with others have a crucial impact on their sense of their own identity. The study of identity development began with work with infants and young children. It looked at how babies come to see themselves as separate from other individuals, and how this understanding develops into a more elaborate knowledge of their personal characteristics and their experiences and actions. Chapter 4 introduces some of this classic work.

Some of these theories are then developed in Chapter 5, which looks at the development of gender identity. It reviews some of the main theories which have contributed to the understanding of identity, and calls for an integration of these theories into a coherent view of gender development as involving both cognitive and social aspects. In particular, it emphasizes the reciprocal relationship between the two. Features in the social environment influence children's views of and knowledge about gender. These in turn guide their behaviour in that social environment, thereby influencing the social environment itself.

Chapter 6 introduces a relatively new area of research in developmental psychology– that of the sense of national identity. New technologies and increasing mobility are transforming our national identities and how they grow and change, and developmental psychologists are building up an understanding of these processes. The chapter reviews research in this area using some of the theories which were introduced in Chapter 5. However, it concludes that, as yet, there is no adequate explanation for the large variabilities across and within countries in the development of national identity and it suggests that more work needs to be done on the influence of social context, such as family, school and the mass media. Yet again, the close interlinkage between the social and the personal is highlighted.

It is becoming increasingly evident that identity cannot be considered independently from the social context in which it develops. This theme was introduced in Chapter 5 and developed in Chapter 6. Chapter 7 continues with the topic, by looking at children and young people as consumers of material goods. By emphasizing external signals of maturity, such as appropriate music and clothing, this chapter questions the notion of development as a series of natural phases which children pass through in a largely predefined fashion. It focuses on childhood as a time when individuals learn the next set of age-appropriate behaviours by observing others, and comparing their own behaviour to that of their peers and of older individuals. Children demonstrate that they are 'growing up' by using new, more mature behaviours learned by comparison with other individuals in their social world.

The book ends with an integrative chapter. This identifies common themes arising from the topic areas discussed in the book, such as parenting or gender identity. For example, considerations about the universality of research outcomes which have been obtained primarily in Western industrialized contexts are highlighted. The chapter emphasizes that care must be taken not to over-generalize findings from a particular society at a particular time. This concern also applies to more generally held views about identity and relationships. In the West, identity development is seen as a pathway towards becoming an independent, self-aware adult. However, it is important to bear in mind that beliefs such as these are not common in every cultural context. Methodological challenges, such as difficulties in interpreting children's behaviour, are also discussed. Boisterous behaviour such as chasing and 'fighting' could be described as either aggressive or playful. How can we be sure that our interpretation of behaviours such as these is valid and consistent?

By drawing on examples from the earlier chapters to inform issues such as those mentioned above, Chapter 8 provides an overarching conceptual framework which helps to locate some of the key themes of the book.

Chapter 1
Parenting and attachment

John Oates, Charlie Lewis and Michael E. Lamb

Contents

Learning outcomes

After you have studied this chapter you should be able to:

1   discuss what 'being a parent' means in terms of beliefs about parenting and child development;
2   explain the relevance of animal studies to the understanding of attachment in humans;
3   define and illustrate the concept of the internal working model;
4   describe the main types of infant attachment and understand how they are assessed;
5   discuss the ways in which parental behaviour may affect infant attachment and how child behaviour may affect parents;
6   describe Baumrind's theory of parenting styles;
7   define and illustrate the three categories of adult attachment style;
8   discuss the links between infant and adult attachment;
9   recognize that there is substantial social and cultural variation in parenting and its effects.

1   Introduction

This chapter is about parenting and its effects on child development. Given the focus of this book on the social, emotional and personal aspects of child development, this chapter concentrates on the development of attachment theory, its applications to the ways in which parents behave with their children and the implications for subsequent development. It also explores how these in turn affect a person's capacity to in due course be a parent themselves, to a new generation. Forming relationships with other people is an important, core process that runs through the various topics that this book explores. Attachment theory is proving to be a most productive framework for posing interesting questions about this process and it has stimulated, as a consequence, a massive body of research in recent years (Cassidy and Shaver, 1999).

1.1 What is a parent?

In its most limited, biological sense, being a parent is simply the business of contributing a set of chromosomes to a fertilized egg, thus becoming a 'biological parent'. In addition, for a woman, there are then a further 9 months of pregnancy during which time her body supports the development of the foetus to term delivery.

But in everyday talk about parenting, much more than this is usually implied. The biological part is just the beginning. Typically, parenting is thought of as involving a long-term commitment to nurturing an infant into a child, into an adolescent and then onward into adult life.

Most people expect men and women to fulfil different roles in parenting, beyond the obvious differences in relation to pregnancy and the potential to breastfeed the infant. Both fathers and mothers are also commonly considered to have important and complementary roles in supporting the healthy physical and psychological development of their children. The way these roles play out, however, varies a great deal from country to country, from one neighbourhood to another, and even between one family and another. They also change over time – being a parent today is different from what it was 50, let alone 150 years ago.

The idea of a 'parent', then, is actually in large part a culturally, socially and historically specific set of expectations about what sorts of behaviours are appropriate to the 'raising of children', based on a set of notions about how particular forms of parenting lead to expected outcomes in child development. The following examples show some of the ways in which beliefs about being a parent have been expressed.

BOX 1

Being a parent

Through Jacqueline I'm realizing so much the importance of that relationship, um, what it does for her and what it does for me. And I think in a lot of ways, this is getting very psychological, but I think it's like coming all the way around, that her relationship with me is giving me something that perhaps I didn't have when I was younger.

(Kaplan, 1992, p. 89)

What I need. (Yeah.) That's the problem of being a parent. You have to be, you have to be an adult even when you don't want to be an adult. [sigh] And yeah, that's the loss of my freedom. To be childish when I want. Or demanding when I want to be demanding.

(Kaplan, 1992, p. 61)

Views from the BBC Parenting website

You'll need an unlimited supply of love. You may also need a back-up supply for use at 4 a.m., when children are wide-awake or teenagers are still not home.

Your sense of humour will grow – especially when answering the door to the postman with tomato sauce for hair gel or dressed as batman.

Wisdom and patience will always be helpful – knowing when to just listen and when to step in.

You'll find you need to do three or more things at once.

You'll develop a love of all things messy and realise it's a good day when you can see the carpet through the layer of toys or teenagers' clothes.

You'll feel like you could do better! A normal part of parenting is the constant worry that you may not be getting it right.

You'll possess healing powers – remember there is a magical quality to your kiss and calm words which can soothe cuts, bruises and disappointments.

Sources: Kaplan, 1992, p. 89, p. 61 and BBC Parenting Website, 2004.

1.2 The importance of parents

In popular culture, parenting is widely thought of as an essential contribution to the development of personality – that is to say all the characteristics of one's emotional, relational life and its individuality. The specific qualities of relationships between parents and their children are commonly held to account for both positive and negative outcomes of the development of personality through the lifespan. Successful people often praise the support and guidance of their parents in their 'formative years'. Conversely, in cases of criminal behaviour, poor, perhaps abusive parenting during childhood is often cited as a contributory cause. Given this commonly held belief in the power of parents to affect their children for good or ill, it is not surprising that developmental psychologists have taken the influence of parents on children's development as one of the key questions to be addressed.

From most psychological perspectives, parents are seen as the primary agents who constrain, organize and structure their children's experiences and personalities. For example, behaviourists see the reward contingencies provided by parents as 'shaping' their children's behaviour; social behaviourists see imitation of parents' behaviour by children as a primary means of new behaviour being learned, with parents serving as 'models'; social constructivists see parents as potentially 'scaffolding' their children's development and psychodynamic theorists offer accounts of how the child's internal world takes form through the incorporation of aspects of relations with parents.

Inter-generational transmission
A process whereby patterns of behaviour, attitudes, beliefs and other variables may to some degree pass from parents to children, to the children's children and on through further generations.

The generally held notion that parents can pass on their problems to their children, and public concern at the way this may serve to perpetuate society's inequalities and disadvantages, has led to the idea of 'intergenerational transmission' becoming a core concept for much research in this area.

In part, such research has been driven by a public agenda that sees early intervention as a potential means of ameliorating some of the more troubling behaviours of our times (such as vandalism, theft, child abuse, violence and drug misuse) and reducing the social costs associated with these.

A dominant concern is that poor parenting results in children lacking the key skills that they need to adequately raise their own children to be able to function as well-adjusted members of society. Thus an important objective for this area of research is to identify the factors and processes that support good parenting and the intergenerational transmission of successful and positive behaviours and relationships.

Activity 1

Allow about
10 minutes

Beliefs about the effects of parenting

This activity will help you to explore your own beliefs about the effects of parenting.

Consider the following list of behaviours. For each one, write down what first comes to your mind as the reason(s) why a young person or adult might indulge in this sort of behaviour.

> Use of illegal drugs
> Being helpful and friendly to others
> Petty theft
> Artistic pursuits
> Bullying
> Sport
> Vandalism
> Charity work

When you have done this, go through your list again and highlight those which included parenting as a contributory factor.

Comment

Clearly there may be many influences on these behaviours, parenting being just one. And each individual case will have its own unique set of influences. But the general point is that many people believe that parenting can have significant effects on children's subsequent behaviour.

In responding to Activity 1 you probably also started to think about different aspects of parenting and the ways in which these might affect a child's development. Perhaps you felt that drug misuse becomes more attractive to young people if they are not getting enough affection from their parents and striving for peer acceptance instead, that altruism is encouraged in families where relationships are caring, or that bullying happens to children who are abused at home? These sorts of ideas about cause and effect are in fact complex and represent the starting points for asking meaningful questions about the specific features of parenting that significantly affect a child's subsequent development and how these developmental effects come about. As we shall show later in this chapter, most developmental processes associated with parenting are more complex than simple, one-way cause–effect relationships.

Summary of Section 1

- Parenting is generally considered to involve a long-term commitment to raising a child.
- The meaning of parenting is a social and cultural construction, based on beliefs about the influence of parenting on child development.

2 Animal studies

2.1 Infancy and dependency

One of the striking, distinguishing features of human development as opposed to the development of other animals is the long period of dependency of children on their caregivers. This dependency is absolute at first. An infant's very survival depends on the presence of some other person who can provide the infant's basic needs for warmth, shelter and food. The psychoanalyst Winnicott insightfully wrote that 'there is no such thing as a baby ... if you set out to describe a baby, you will find you are describing a *baby and someone*. A baby cannot exist alone, but is essentially part of a relationship' (Winnicott, 1964, p. 88), highlighting the universal truth that existence itself starts in the context of a providing relationship.

Of course this sort of dependency is not unique to humans; most other species of animals need a period of feeding, protection and care during the early part of their lives. A scientific interest in this aspect of biology was one of the features of ethologists' research during the first half of the twentieth century.

Ethology
The scientific study of the behaviour of organisms and the ways in which particular behaviours confer adaptive success by aiding survival.

Two ethologists, Lorenz and Tinbergen, played a key role in identifying such behaviours in different species. Lorenz is best known for his identification of the phenomenon of 'imprinting' in those species of birds, such as ducks and geese, where the young remain close to the mother for some time after hatching. He found that these young birds 'imprint' on any moving object in their immediate environment during a 'critical period' shortly after hatching happens, that is, they become 'attached' to the moving object, showing a strong tendency to follow it and stay close to it. Lorenz succeeded in imprinting young greylag geese on himself by being there at this critical period (see Figure 1).

Figure I Mother goose?

It became clear from this area of research that the formation of some sort of bond between young animals and their parents was important for many species and this idea was also explicitly seen as relevant to human development.

Extrapolating from these sorts of findings to humans is clearly not a straightforward matter; the bonding of young to parent varies tremendously among different species. Nevertheless, in the 1950s, many people, notably the psychiatrist Bowlby, did make the conceptual leap to hypothesizing about a biological basis for human bonding and posed some interesting questions about the nature of the attachments between human infants and their parents.

2.2 Basic needs and bonding

But is it simply the assuring of basic physical survival that human infants need, or is the relationship itself also important? A classic set of studies with young monkeys by Harlow (1958) was carried out in the 1950s to explore this question.

The results of this research played a major part in stimulating thinking about the nature of human relationships and particularly the factors that are important in mother–infant care. These experiments also highlighted some of the processes by which early parenting affects children's development.

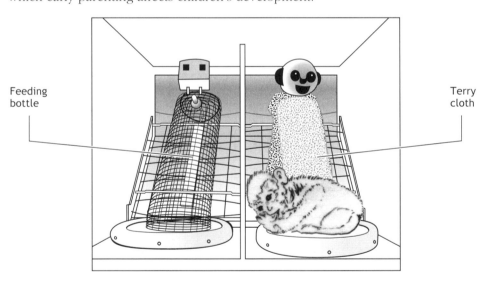

Feeding bottle

Terry cloth

Figure 2   An infant macaque monkey chooses the 'cloth mother' rather than the 'wire mother'.

Harlow separated macaque infant monkeys from their mothers at birth and reared them in isolation cages. He found that close, frequent attention from human carers led to higher survival rates than care by captive natural mothers and that the infant monkeys learned to come to their human carers for food and comfort, in a way reminiscent of imprinting. He also noticed that the infants often clung to the cloth pads that were used to cover the bases of the cages and they protested when these pads were removed for cleaning. Interested in what features were important to this sort of bonding, and recognizing that comfort, like food, was important to these monkeys, Harlow put various sorts of objects in the infant monkeys' cages. He found that even a simple wire mesh cone was often used as a refuge to cling to when the infants were frightened, and that this helped to boost survival rates. Covering the cone with cloth helped even more. Harlow then raised infant monkeys in isolation with only two simple 'mother surrogate' models available to them. In a key experiment, one of these 'mothers' was made from wire mesh and had an attached milk bottle from which the monkey could feed. The other 'mother' had a soft towelling surface but did not deliver any food.

Harlow's initial results were striking: the infant monkeys overwhelmingly preferred to cling to the 'cloth mother' rather than the 'wire mother' and when they were frightened, they almost always went straight to the cloth mother and held tightly to it – in spite of the fact that only the wire mother was their source of food. As the infants got older, these preferences increased rather than decreased. Furthermore, when these infant monkeys were put into an unfamiliar environment (a new room) the presence of their cloth mother greatly reduced their panic reactions: if the cloth mother was available, the infants would use it as what Harlow called a 'base for operations', exploring the new room and its objects while periodically returning to cling to the mother surrogate. These findings were taken as strong evidence that there is another factor, stronger even than the provision of the basic necessity of food, which determines how macaque infants become attached to one object rather than another. Crucially, when Harlow moved the milk source to the cloth mother, this seemed to have no effect on the amount of clinging to 'her'. Harlow had found that a bond with an object could provide security in the face of threat. What he called 'contact comfort' had emerged as being at least as significant as the basic need for nourishment.

While the macaque infants who grew up with the cloth mothers had a good survival rate, all was not well in their development. When they were later brought into contact with other macaques, their social behaviour was seriously disturbed to the extent that they were rarely able to mate successfully. Clearly 'contact comfort' was still not enough to ensure adaptive success, that is, the passing on of genes. Harlow found that some improvement in these poor outcomes could be gained if the cloth-mothered macaques had opportunities to socialize with other young macaques during their development.

2.3 From greylag geese and macaques to humans

This research with animals brought to the fore a series of concepts that has proved to be of great value in understanding human development. It is not so much that a direct parallel can be drawn between the behaviours of birds and monkeys and those of humans, but rather that the organizing ideas provoke questions which have helped to focus theory-building and research. The most important of these questions are as follows.

- Does a human mother–infant bond form very early on, perhaps shortly after birth, as a form of imprinting?
- Is there a 'critical' period for forming such bonds?
- Can infants bond with anyone or does it have to be the mother?
- What features of parenting are important for attachment?
- Does early parenting affect later life?

Harlow's work, and the work of the other animal researchers such as Lorenz, were keystones in the foundations of a major line of research with humans and their early relations. A central figure in this tradition is Bowlby, whose work over four decades from 1940 established a strong, elaborated and productive theory, around the central concept of 'attachment'. Bowlby, inspired by the ethological research, took its findings and explored their value for understanding human behaviour.

Summary of Section 2

- Many animal species show a biological propensity for infants to bond with parents, although this is expressed in varied and different ways in different species.
- Early bonding has survival value in nature.
- For primates, comfort and security are significant factors in bonding, in addition to the need for sustenance.
- Ethological studies of bonding in other animal species led to an interest in the significance of bonding for human development.

3   Attachment theory

What emerged clearly from the work of ethologists and resonates with common beliefs about human attachment is that something special can happen early in an individual's development whereby certain specific objects come to have an exceptional significance. Close contact with these objects is used as an important source of comfort and support at times of stress and the absence of these attachment objects at such times can lead to distress and anxiety. The ways in which these attachments form and their consequences for later development have been the subject of study by many theorists and researchers under the umbrella term of 'attachment theory'. In this section we will review and analyse the main theoretical concepts.

3.1 Objects of attachment

The word 'object' is being used here in a broad sense to include human beings as well as other sorts of comfort objects. While not all children do so, many make use of objects like favourite feeding bottles or a comfort blanket to which they develop a strong attachment. Winnicott (1953) described such attachments as involving 'transitional objects'. He argued that such attachments represent a developmental stage whereby the infant makes use of an object over which they have control to deal with and move on from their early attachment to the mother, who is less under the infant's control. In both cases, attachment to the mother and attachment to a transitional object, the significant point is that they are attachments to specific, single objects.

Figure 3 A child using his comfort blanket.

3.2 Internal working models

A central premise of attachment theory is that infants learn about ways of relating from these early relationships with their attachment objects and build up a set of expectations about themselves in relation to others. On the basis of these first experiences they build what has been termed an 'internal working model' (IWM). This means that infants can approach new situations with some prior ideas about how they can cope in the face of threat. This IWM has three elements: a model of the self, a model of 'the other' and a model of the relationships between these (Bowlby, 1969, 1973, 1988; Bretherton, 1990, 1991, 1993).

For example, one infant might have a father as the primary carer who is quite devoted and, as well as being with the infant most of the time that they are awake, is also very responsive to the infant's distress. This infant will thus be likely to construct an IWM in which self is seen as capable of calling for comfort when needed and as worthy of receiving comfort. The model of other will represent an expectation that comfort will be given when needed and that the other will show concern for the infant's state. The relationship part of this IWM will include an expectation of satisfactory resolution of crises, with mutual communication.

By contrast, another infant may have a carer who spends a lot of time in a self-absorbed state with a generally low mood. This infant may spend long periods of time alone, or with an emotionally unavailable carer, where distress goes unacknowledged. When infant distress is responded to, it may sometimes be that the carer feels the distress as being invasive and the infant is handled roughly as a result. On other occasions, the infant's distress may trigger a need in the carer for them to be cared for and the carer will seek to reverse roles. In this situation, the infant's IWM will have an ambivalent model of self, as sometimes worthy of attention, but not always; as sometimes receiving comfort, but at times also expected to give comfort when distressed. The model of other will be similarly confused, between availability, ignoring and rejecting aspects. The relationship model will also have multiple expectations. So an infant in this latter situation will have an IWM that is less able to generate accurate predictions of what will happen in the case of distress. The following activity will help you better understand the concept of IWMs and how the theory might work in practice.

Activity 2   Different contexts, different IWMs?

Allow about 5 minutes

This activity will help you to better understand the concept of IWM.

For the following situations, consider what sort of IWMs the infants are likely to develop. For each situation, consider the model of self, the model of other and the model of relationship that are likely to be formed.

Vignette 1
An infant who is one of a pair of identical twins, with a single parent who is not working and struggles on a low income.

Vignette 2
An infant who is an only child with two working parents who share caring roles but also have an au pair who cares for the infant during the day.

Vignette 3
An infant with an illness that necessitates long periods in hospital with painful treatments that require periods of isolation.

Vignette 4
An infant in a nomadic ethnic group where all adults take shared responsibility for the care of infants.

Comment

In none of these vignettes are we suggesting that there are inevitably positive or negative outcomes; rather, we are encouraging you to consider the differences in expectations about self, other and relating that might arise in each. We would also stress that much depends on the quality of relatedness between parent and infant; warm, supportive relationships can be formed even in the most adverse circumstances. Comments on each vignette follow.

Vignette 1
There are two elements to consider in this vignette; the twins and the parent's situation. With respect to the twin element, the twins are going to experience the division of parental attention between them, hence their IWMs are likely to contain expectations that sometimes attention will be available and sometimes not. Thus, compared with the situation for a single child, each twin will probably be able to tolerate waiting for attention. The fact of low income in itself might only be relevant if it means that the parent is self-absorbed in the problems that

low income might cause. This might then lead to each infant's IWM also including an expectation of the other as not always being emotionally available. But the fact of having a single parent can also contribute to a more unified view of self, since the reactions of the other are more likely to be consistently predictable than for two or more carers. The presence of the other twin might add some expectation of companionship and empathy from a peer to each infant's IWM.

Vignette 2

An only child will not have the twins' experiences of peer companionship that could contribute to their IWMs and, in the vignette described, is likely to develop an IWM that has multiple facets, representing the relationships with each of the parents and the au pair. To the extent that these differ from each other, the infant may also develop a more diversified sense of self.

Vignette 3

The infant in hospital might come to associate pain with relating to others, thus the IWM might incorporate fearful feelings around relating. There is a possibility that the isolation and lack of contact with parents could lead to a view of self as unworthy and that relating to others is rarely and unpredictably possible. However, the risks that attachments to parents may be damaged during hospitalization of children are better recognized nowadays, as is the need to foster and maintain supportive relationships with parents and nursing staff.

Vignette 4

In a nomadic ethnic group, the infant's IWM is likely to hold an expectation that care will be available no matter who is turned to. To the extent that the different members of the group relate in different ways to the infant, the image of self may become somewhat diffuse and varied. This sort of caring environment can still lead to an infant feeling secure in relations with others, but in a contrasting way to the single parent–infant bond situation.

Thus IWMs are formed from infants repeatedly experiencing particular sorts of relationships with their carers. The crucial point is that IWMs persist onwards into childhood and beyond. The argument goes that these expectations about self, other and relationships are carried onwards and outwards to subsequent interactions with other people, providing a template to make initial sense of new encounters:

> No variables, it is held, have more far-reaching effects on personality development than have a child's experiences within his family: for, starting during his first months in his relations with his mother figure, and extending through the years of childhood and adolescence in his relations with both parents, he builds up working models of how attachment figures are likely to behave towards him in any of a variety of situations; and on those models are based all his expectations, and therefore all his plans, for the rest of his life.
>
> (Bowlby, 1973, p. 369)

Thus, Bowlby set out this central tenet of attachment theory, and this now serves as a springboard to the topics that are considered in the rest of this chapter. Bowlby was based at the Tavistock Clinic, London, among a group of developmental psychologists, psychiatrists and other mental health professionals focusing on parenting and its effects, setting out the basis of attachment theory in the 1950s.

Activity 3

Allow about
10 minutes

IWMs and new relationships

This activity should help you to begin to think about how IWMs formed during infancy might affect later relationships.

For each of the four infant vignettes outlined in Activity 2, consider how the IWM that the infant formed might influence the quality of a first romantic attachment when the infant becomes a teenager.

Comment

Again, we emphasize that the suggestions we give on each vignette simply point to possible scenarios as illustrative of particular outcomes out of the many possible.

Vignette 1

As a teenager, this infant's IWM might be a good basis for a single, exclusive attachment, which nevertheless allows for other simultaneous close peer relationships. This teenager might be less well prepared to accept a romantic partner's other close relationships.

Vignette 2

One outcome here might be that the IWM allows for a number of different close relationships, hence the teenager might be more likely to form a relationship with a partner within a small group of very close friends.

Vignette 3

This infant might be somewhat wary of entering a new relationship until reassured that it is safe. There might be some fears of loss and unavailability of the other, but adequate support and care during the hospitalization could well have alleviated that and helped the infant to hold a view of self as worthy of affection.

Vignette 4

Here, the IWM might be most likely to support strong bonds with many members of the community, which is clearly important for a nomadic group. The romantic relationship might only form a small part of the teenager's web of attachments. This vignette brings out the significance of the context within which attachments form and operate.

3.3 What Bowlby did and didn't say

Theoretical ideas about early attachment tend to touch us more deeply than some other psychological theories, since we are often drawn by them to reflect on our own early experiences and how they have affected us, for good or ill. Add to this the forthright nature of Bowlby's thinking and writing, and the controversial nature of his theory becomes easier to understand. It is unfortunate that Bowlby's attachment theory has often been inaccurately criticized by academic commentators for things that he didn't actually state, so it is worth briefly reviewing the important aspects of what he *did* say. Although Bowlby believed that healthy attachment in infants is indeed based on relatively long-term, stable relationships with carers, he did not see a single attachment (monotropy) as necessarily being the best and only way of achieving this. Indeed, he explicitly recognized that the attachment to a 'father' can complement and support an infant's attachment to their 'mother' and that other people in an infant's social world can also play important roles. He also came to the conclusion that there is nothing sacrosanct about this ongoing care being provided by the biological parents and that it can equally well be provided by other consistently and reliably available people. Indeed, he argued that a variety of attachment objects could lead to a more fully developed IWM, since it would encompass relations with different people, better preparing the child for forming relationships with a wider range of people later on in life.

Although a key feature of Bowlby's view of IWMs was that they are the basis for later relationships, he did not see them as permanently and unalterably fixed during infancy. Contact with a greater variety of people with whom infants can form attachments can actually be a benefit, according to Bowlby, who saw this as a way in which IWMs can be modified and develop. This part of his theory also began to further question the idea that an infant only needs a strong bond with a totally available and responsive biological mother for healthy emotional development.

3.4 'Good-enough' mothering

Bowlby was much influenced by the work of Winnicott, another theorist at the Tavistock Clinic. Winnicott, in his work with mothers and infants, came to see how important it is for a mother to be emotionally available to her infant, and for a 'system' of two-way communication to be built up. At the same time, he did a great deal to challenge the idea of a 'perfect mother'. He strongly believed that an important part of a mother's role is to allow her infant to experience tolerable frustrations. He coined the term 'good-enough mother' to describe a mother who allows just the right amount of delay in meeting an infant's needs to encourage both tolerance of waiting and confidence in ultimate satisfaction (Winnicott, 1964). According to Winnicott, this then leads to a healthy development of independence and sense of self (Winnicott, 1965). He did not believe that a mother was doing the best for her child if her aim was to alleviate all distress, discomfort and frustration at the earliest possible opportunity.

3.5 Separation and reunion

The Robertsons, who also collaborated with Bowlby and Winnicott in the 1950s and 60s, were a husband and wife team and were both social workers. They brought to public attention the distress that children experience when their parents leave them in hospital or if the parents themselves are hospitalized (Robertson and Robertson, 1989). Their work impressed on Bowlby the way in which a child's attachment to a person is reflected in the way they react when they are separated from that person. It was around this time that the term 'separation anxiety' began to be used by developmental psychologists to describe how infants tend to react with distress when separated from their parents, a behaviour which emerges at around 6 months of age and which tends also to coincide with the emergence of a marked fear of strangers. A rather over-simplified idea became current, that the strength of a child's reaction on being separated from their 'attachment figure' is a good index of how 'strongly attached' they are. However, work by another attachment researcher and theorist, Ainsworth, pointed the way to a deeper understanding of appropriate ways to assess a child's attachment and the ways in which attachment can vary from one child to another.

3.6 Attachment classification

Maternal deprivation
The lack of an adequate mother experience in infancy.

Ainsworth, another researcher who spent some years in the early 1950s with Bowlby, initially examined the effects of 'maternal deprivation' on children's development (Ainsworth, 1962). In 1954, she left for Africa, and moved attachment theory forward through her observations of 28 mothers and their children in Uganda. She noted that, although there were some important differences in how children behaved when they were separated from their mothers, it was during *reunions* after separations that differences between children's behaviour were most evident. She kept in touch with Bowlby, and reported that she had identified three different types of attachment: secure, insecure and absent. She later moved to Baltimore in the United States, and spent a long period closely observing and recording the behaviour of two further samples of infants and their mothers. It was during this time that she clarified her attachment categories by sub-dividing the insecure classification into two. She also developed a standard method for assessing attachment in infants aged around 1 year old, the *Strange Situation*, which has become a 'gold standard' laboratory technique for attachment research (Ainsworth *et al.*, 1978), now widely used to study the influences on attachment and its developmental consequences.

The procedure, as shown in Box 2, has eight episodes, designed to expose infants to increasing amounts of stress in order to observe how they organize their attachment behaviours around their parents when distressed by being in an unfamiliar environment, by the entrance of an unfamiliar adult, and by brief separations from the parent.

BOX 2

The Strange Situation

This assessment is carried out in an observation laboratory, with video cameras recording the behaviour of mothers and their infants. The laboratory contains two easy chairs, a play area, and a set of toys.

1 After a mother and infant have settled, a stranger enters and sits quietly on the free chair.

2 After an interval, the stranger starts talking with the mother, and after a while, starts to play with the child.

3 Then, a little later, the mother gets up and leaves the room.

4 The stranger stays and tries to interact with the child.

5 After a period, the mother then re-enters. The stranger leaves.

6 After a further interval, the mother leaves again, leaving the child alone.

7 After a period, the stranger enters, offers comfort to the child if necessary, and tries to play with the child.

8 The mother returns, the stranger leaves, and mother and child remain in the room for a few more minutes.

The video-recording of the whole session is then coded by trained observers.

According to attachment theory, infants who have formed a good attachment to one or both parents should be able to use them as secure bases from which to explore the novel environment, because their IWMs contain representations of available parent figures. The stranger's entrance should lead infants to inhibit exploration and draw a little closer to their parents, at least temporarily. The parent's departure should lead infants to attempt to bring them back by crying or searching, and to less exploration of the room and toys. Following the parent's return, infants should seek to re-engage in interaction and, if distressed, perhaps ask to be cuddled and comforted. The same responses should occur, with somewhat greater intensity, following the second separation and reunion. In fact, this is how about 65 per cent of infants, studied in a number of different countries, behave in the Strange Situation (van IJzendoorn and Kroonenberg, 1988) although there is substantial variation in this figure both within and between countries. Following the definitions developed by Ainsworth and her colleagues, these infants' relationships are classified as securely attached (Type B) because their behaviour conforms to theoretical predictions about how babies should behave in relation to their primary caregivers if they have established a good attachment.

In contrast, some infants seem unable or unwilling to use their parents as secure bases from which to explore, and they are called insecure. Some insecure infants are distressed by their parents' absence, and behave ambivalently on reunion, both seeking contact and interaction and angrily rejecting it when it is offered. These infants are conventionally labelled insecure-resistant or ambivalent (Type C). They typically account for approximately 15 per cent of infants (van IJzendoorn and Kroonenberg, 1988). Other insecure infants seem little concerned by their parents' absence. Instead of greeting their parents on reunion, they actively avoid interaction and ignore their parents' bids. These infants are said to show insecure-avoidant attachments (Type A) and they typically constitute about 20 per cent of infants (van IJzendoorn and Kroonenberg, 1988). Main and Solomon have also described a fourth group of infants whose behaviour is 'disoriented' and/or 'disorganized' (Type D; Main and Solomon, 1990). These infants simultaneously show contradictory behaviour patterns, and incomplete or undirected movements, and they seem to be confused or apprehensive about approaching their parents. In some cases these infants appear to have been maltreated by their parents, but the causes of disorganized attachment are still not clear and research continues on this topic.

3.7 Attachment and internal working models

According to attachment theory, these types show the main forms that a child's internal working model can take:

- A child with a Type A attachment has a rather troubled attachment to her parent. She is often not upset at separation, and tends not to get close to her parent even when they are reunited after a separation. Often, she turns away from, rather than towards, the parent. She seems to expect the parent's response to be inappropriate and the relationship to be difficult, and she seems to lack a solid sense of herself as worthy of affection.

- A child with a Type B attachment has an image of his parent as a secure base, who is available for comfort. He also has an image of himself as worthy of his parent's attention and love, and can gain some comfort from this when separated, having confidence that his parent will return. His reactions to separation do not show panic; he has some capacity to contain them in the knowledge of his parent's availability. He is able to use his parent for comfort, and shows pleasure at reunion. He has an untroubled expectation of closeness and warmth between people, and this is also shown in his being able to accept some contact with the stranger.
- A child with a Type C attachment is likely to show distress at the separation, suggesting that her parent's presence is important to her. She seems to lack a firm belief that her parent will return, or that her parent will be able to comfort her effectively on return, and fails to use her parent as a source of comfort at reunion. She is not easily able to comfort herself, nor does she seem to feel herself worthy of affection from her parent. She rejects the stranger's attempts to console her. Her expectation seems to be a pessimistic one, that upset cannot be eased by another.
- In Type D, disorganized behaviours show a child being unable to 'know what to do'; there seems to be lack of solid expectations or consistent strategies. The child may seem to be somewhat hesitant about contact, not quite sure whether it is something to be sought or not. There is little obvious goal-seeking in the behaviour. The child may tend to turn to himself for comfort. He seems somewhat 'dazed' or confused.

Evidently, each type of attachment is associated with a different IWM of self, other and the relationship. The child whose behaviour is predominantly disorganized seems to lack a coherent IWM to structure their behaviour. Following Bowlby's theory that a child's IWM will affect how they approach new relationships, someone with a secure attachment, for example, might approach a relationship with a degree of confidence that the other will respond positively, while someone with an insecure ambivalent attachment may be more likely to be hesitant, ambivalent and rather wary. Avoidant attachment is likely to be associated with a lack of motivation to relate to others. Insecure children with disorganized attachment-related behaviours are likely to find it hard to approach new relationships in consistent ways; they may 'launch' an attempt at relating but then fail to follow it through, for example. Attachment type is believed to have important effects on a child's subsequent development, which are explored later in this chapter.

Summary of Section 3

- Attachment theory has been developed by a number of theorists to explain the nature of parent–infant bonding.
- A core concept is that of 'internal working model' (IWM).
- The IWM of a person includes a representation of self, of other and of the relationship between the two.
- IWMs serve to organize behaviour towards other people.
- People can have more than one IWM, which can change through life.
- Infant attachment can be classified into two main types, secure and insecure, using a standardized laboratory assessment known as the Strange Situation.
- Insecure attachments can be sub-divided into two main types; avoidant (Type A) or ambivalent (Type C). Children who show highly disorganized attachment-related behaviours can be classed as a further insecure group (Type D).
- Key figures include Bowlby, Winnicott, the Robertsons and Ainsworth.

4   Influences on attachment

Attachment theorists have emphasized the role played by infant–parent interactions in shaping these patterns of attachment behaviour. There is general support for the notion that sensitive parenting – that is, nurturant, attentive, non-restrictive parental care – and harmonious infant–parent interactions are associated with secure (Type B) infant behaviour in the Strange Situation, and this appears to be generally true of infants in those cultures so far studied (de Wolff and van IJzendoorn, 1997; Posada *et al.*, 1999; Thompson, 1998). The parents of infants who behave in either insecure-avoidant (Type A) or insecure-ambivalent (Type C) fashions are more likely to over- or under-stimulate, they may fail to make their behaviours contingent on infant behaviour and appear cold or rejecting, and sometimes act ineptly.

RESEARCH SUMMARY I

Attachment and maternal behaviour

Vondra *et al.* (1995) studied 95 mothers and their 12-month-old infants. In a laboratory situation, they video-recorded each mother and infant participating in three different activity episodes, followed by a rest and snack period, and then a Strange Situation assessment. In the first episode the mother completed some questionnaires at one end of the room for 3 minutes while the infant was in a highchair at the other end. Mothers' and infants' interactions were video-recorded and coded to yield scores for appropriate, insufficient and intrusive maternal behaviour. For the second episode, mothers continued to complete the questionnaires, but with the infant free to roam around the room, which contained no playthings. Video-recordings of this episode were coded and scored as for the first episode. The third activity consisted of a series of four teaching tasks; putting wooden blocks in a box, playing a toy xylophone, stacking plastic rings and playing with the levers on an activity box. Video-recordings of this episode were coded using scales (Ainsworth *et al.*, 1978) assessing sensitivity/insensitivity and co-operation/independence, in addition to coding the incidence of angry behaviour on the part of the mother. The scores on these various scales were combined so as to classify mothers into one of three groups: sensitive, controlling or unresponsive.

The results showed that the infants' attachment classifications could be reasonably well predicted from the mothers' group classifications. Sensitive mothers tended to have infants with secure attachments (Type B), controlling mothers' infants were most likely to be avoidant (Type A) and unresponsive mothers tended to have ambivalently attached (Type C) infants.

Because there is a great deal of variability in associations between parental behaviour and attachment classifications, it is difficult to identify precisely what aspects of parental behaviour are important. Some studies identify warmth but not sensitivity, some patterning of stimulation but not warmth or amount of stimulation, and so forth. There is general agreement, however, that insecure-avoidant (Type A) attachments are associated with intrusive, over-stimulating, rejecting parenting, whereas insecure-ambivalent (Type C) attachments are linked to inconsistent, unresponsive parenting (Belsky, 1999; de Wolff and van IJzendoorn, 1997).

Although the associations with disorganized (Type D) attachments are less well established, Type D attachments are more common among abused and maltreated infants and among infants exposed to other pathological caregiving environments (Lyons-Ruth and Jacobvitz, 1999; Teti *et al.*, 1995) and may be consequences of parental behaviours that infants find frightening or disturbing (Main and Hesse, 1990; Schuengel *et al.*, 1999). It has also been suggested that genetic factors may be implicated in disorganized attachment, but the evidence here is not yet clear (Lakatos *et al.*, 2002; Bakermans-Kranenburg and van IJzendoorn, 2004).

4.1 Parent–infant interactions

One aspect of parenting behaviour that appears to be linked to attachment security is the expression of emotion and emotional responses by both parents and infants.

RESEARCH SUMMARY 2

Emotional communication and attachment

30 video recordings of Strange Situations, gathered in a longitudinal study of Canadian children, were analysed (Goldberg et al., 1994). They were selected to ensure that 10 secure, 10 insecure-avoidant and 10 insecure-ambivalent relationships were included. The three groups were matched for infant gender, age at testing, and parent age, occupation and education. The analysis of the videotapes focused on recording and coding emotional events in the infants' experience (smiles, whines, cries, etc.), and on mothers' responses to these events.

First, it was found that insecure-ambivalent infants showed the highest frequencies of emotional events, followed by secure infants, with insecure avoidant infants showing the fewest. There were also significant differences in the relative proportions of different types of emotional events: secure infants showed roughly equal proportions of positive, neutral and negative events, avoidant infants engaged in few negative events, and ambivalent infants showed high levels of negative emotion.

Taking into account these differing proportions of infants' emotions, the mothers of secure infants responded most frequently to their infants' emotions, and to all types of emotional events. Mothers of ambivalent infants responded rather less frequently overall, but a higher proportion of their responses were to negative affect; they rarely responded to positive emotions. Mothers of avoidant infants responded least often, and particularly infrequently to their infants' negative emotions.

To summarize, secure infants showed a full range of emotions and their mothers responded to all of these; the dyads showed rich, full emotional exchanges. It could be said that the infants were learning that all emotions are 'valid' in relationships.

The avoidant infants showed few emotions, and were especially muted in showing negative emotions. Their mothers were similarly unresponsive, especially to the very few negative emotions their infants showed. These infants seemed to be learning to suppress emotionality in general, and particularly to suppress negative feelings.

The ambivalent infants showed a lot of distress, and their mothers responded especially to these displays. Ambivalent infants seemed to be learning that negative emotions get attention; that these are the 'valid' emotions in the relationship.

The results in Research summary 2 show clearly how mothers' differential sensitivity to their infants' emotional communications, and to the positive and negative emotions, could be an important factor leading to infants developing different types of internal working models of relationships. This supports Ainsworth's fundamental observations made during her pioneering studies (Ainsworth, 1969).

4.2 Infants, mothers and fathers

Typically, in two-parent families, infants form attachments to each of their parents. For example, Fagot and Kavanagh (1993) found that both mothers and fathers reported that their experience of interacting with insecurely attached infants was less pleasant, and both tended to become less involved in interactions with insecurely attached boys, a factor that may help to explain the greater likelihood of behaviour problems among boys. Once both mothers and fathers are brought into consideration, the complexity of the causes and effects increases substantially, since the quality of marital relationships has consistently been found to be linked with parent–child relationships and child outcomes (Gable *et al.*, 1994). One study found that infants who showed more negative emotionality early in the first year tended to become more positive when they had active, sensitive and happily-married mothers, whereas some infants became more negative when their fathers were dissatisfied with their marriages, were insensitive and were uninvolved in their children's lives (Belsky *et al.*, 1991). In a study of 20 month olds, Easterbrooks and Goldberg (1984) found that the children's adaptation was promoted by the amount of paternal involvement and the quality or sensitivity of their fathers' behaviour.

Lamb and others (Lamb *et al.*, 1985; Thompson, 1998) have emphasized that predictions from Strange Situation behaviour are far from perfect, regardless of which attachment type is concerned. Rather, the predictive relationship between Strange Situation behaviour in infancy and subsequent child behaviour is found only when there is stability in caregiving arrangements and family circumstances which maintain stability in patterns of parent–child interaction. This raises the interesting question: is the prediction over time attributable to individual differences in the quality of early infant–parent attachments or is it attributable to the continuing quality of child–parent interactions over time? The latter would imply that the quality of early relationships was predictively valuable, not because it caused later differences directly, but because it was associated with later differences in the quality of relationships that in turn support continuing differences in the child's behaviour. Such a pattern of findings would suggest that stability in attachment is a consequence of stability in parent–child interactions rather than in some inner feature of the child's personality, and some evidence has been found that supports this notion (Belsky and Fearon, 2002).

4.3 Mind-mindedness

Theory of mind
The understanding that other people have minds which inform their behaviour.

Bretherton *et al.* (1981) and Fonagy and Target (1997) have suggested that the understanding that other people have mental states depends on first developing a representation of self, as happens in the internal working model. Fonagy and Target suggest that this 'reflective function' serves as a basis for later social understanding, emerging as a natural consequence of generalizations from the early attachment relationship.

RESEARCH SUMMARY 3

Maternal mind-mindedness and attachment

Meins and her colleagues (2001) carried out a study of 71 mothers and their infants. When the infants were 6 months old, the mothers' behaviour and talk with them during a 20-minute free-play episode, with a range of toys available, were video-recorded. As well as coding for maternal sensitivity using Ainsworth's scale (Ainsworth *et al.*, 1971), the recordings were analysed to find out the proportions of mothers' utterances and behaviours that made clear references to their infants' mental states. When the infants were aged 12 months, Strange Situation assessments of infant security were carried out. It was found that the mothers of infants who were assessed as securely attached had used substantially more mental state references in the first set of sessions at age 6 months. Although the 6-month sensitivity codings also predicted attachment security, the mental state reference measures were more powerful, suggesting that parents' communication styles may be a crucial aspect of the transmission of attachment.

Describing parents who treat their children as 'persons' with thoughts and feelings as 'mind-minded', Meins has argued that such a parent tends to 'treat her infant as an individual with a mind, rather than merely as a creature with needs that must be satisfied' (Meins *et al.*, 2001, p. 638), exposing infants and toddlers to more talk about psychological constructs. From this perspective, exposure to mental state language and secure attachment are highly intertwined. Meins and colleagues (2002), in a subsequent study of 57 mother–infant pairs, looked at mothers' mind-mindedness when the infants were 6 months old. They also collected data on how well these infants were subsequently able to perform on a range of tasks assessing the capacity to think about other people's beliefs (so-called 'theory of mind' tasks). They found that the more mothers' language made reference to and comments about their 6-month-old infants' minds the better was the children's performance on the theory of mind tasks at age 4. This highlights the way in which social understanding can be acquired while children learn about and within social relationships (Carpendale and Lewis, 2004).

Summary of Section 4

- Parental sensitivity and emotional communication are emerging as important factors in attachment formation in infants.
- Both fathers' and mothers' behaviour affects attachment formation.
- The development of attachment is not a simple one-way, cause–effect process; infants affect parents just as parents affect infants.
- Stability in infant attachment type over time may be due in part to stable environmental factors such as caregiving style.
- As well as sensitivity and emotional communication, parents who treat their infants as 'persons' with their own thoughts and feelings may contribute to secure attachment.

5   Baumrind's model of parenting styles

The research described so far, utilizing the concepts of IWM and qualities of attachment, has proved very productive. But there have also been other approaches to understanding how parenting affects child development. One of the most influential of these originated in the work of Baumrind and her colleagues, who began in the 1960s to examine the associations between specific child-rearing patterns and particular child outcomes (Baumrind, 1967, 1971, 1973, 1975, 1991; Baumrind and Black, 1967). These researchers distinguished four patterns of parenting, which they labelled authoritarian, authoritative, permissive, and nonconformist. According to Baumrind, authoritarian parents value obedience and forceful imposition of the parents' will, permissive parents believe that parents should be non-intrusive but available as resources, whereas nonconformist parents, although opposed to authority, are less passive and exert more control than permissive parents (Baumrind, 1975). Between the extremes represented by authoritarian and permissive parents fall authoritative parents, who are warm, encourage independence, and attempt to shape their pre-schoolers' behaviour using rational explanation.

According to Baumrind, authoritative parents are sensitive to and facilitate their children's changing sense of self. Furthermore, by allowing themselves to learn from their children, authoritative parents maximize their positive impact, teaching their children, as authoritarian and permissive parents do not, that social competence emerges within a context of interpersonal give-and-take. Although authoritative parents strive to foster independence, they also inculcate a value system characterized by conformity to cultural and societal norms by balancing the use of both reasoning and punishment.

Authoritative parents value self-assertion, wilfulness, and independence, and foster these goals by assuming active and rational parental roles. Baumrind (1967, 1973) argued that the children of authoritative parents become socially responsible because their parents clearly communicate realistic demands that are intellectually stimulating, while generating moderate amounts of tension.

5.1 Mothers, fathers and cultural influences on parenting styles

Researchers who have set out to explore differences and similarities in mothers' and fathers' approaches to parenting have produced inconclusive findings. Baumrind's analysis underscores the need to study parents' philosophies of child-rearing, but she has not explored why parents adopt the strategies they do. Studying the parents of 305 Australian pre-schoolers, Russell and his colleagues (2003) found that mothers were more likely to identify with the authoritative style of parenting whereas fathers were more likely to describe themselves as either authoritarian or permissive. Parents were also more often identified with the authoritarian perspective when the child under discussion was a son. These patterns suggest that it is important to consider the children's impact on the parents' child-rearing beliefs as well as the reasons why mothers and fathers may have differing philosophies, since these may well be coloured by the divergent roles they assume in the family. This assertion however needs to be explored empirically in a wide variety of cultural and sub-cultural settings.

Many researchers have confirmed Baumrind's original conclusion that firm and responsive parenting can promote greater co-operation, less delinquency and higher social and cognitive competence in children. However, further research into comparisons of different cultural contexts has also complicated the picture. In African-American families, for example, authoritarian parenting, particularly if associated with physical punishment, may not increase the level of behaviour problems, suggesting that the pattern of findings reported by Baumrind is culture-specific (Baumrind, 1973). In addition, Baumrind has yet to document the developmental processes by which authoritative parents facilitate their children's socialization.

However, other researchers have greatly enriched our understanding of socialization processes (Bugental and Goodnow, 1998), with researchers such as Patterson (1976, 1982) documenting the processes by which parents shape their children's behaviour and children shape their parents' behaviour. For example, some parents unwittingly train their children to use negative gestures manipulatively while others fail to extinguish their children's undesirable behaviours and may even foster conduct problems (Andrews and Dishion, 1994). Conduct disordered teenagers also elicit coercive behaviour from adults (Anderson *et al.*, 1986) and these insights have been useful in the development of intervention programmes designed to help parents exercise more effective control over their children's and adolescents' behaviour.

MacKinnon-Lewis and her colleagues (2001) have also built on Patterson's work, demonstrating that the behaviour of both parents and children is affected by their expectations or attributions about one another, and that both attributions and behavioural tendencies are influenced by the parent–child dyad's history of interactions. Studies such as these illustrate the role of cognitions in family socialization; values and beliefs are increasingly viewed as both motivators and interpretive lenses through which parents and children of all ages view one another, and analysis of the cognitive facets of parent–child socialization is increasingly prominent (Bugental and Goodnow, 1998). These findings also show eloquently the inadequacy of simple cause–effect models of child development that see parental behaviour having direct and wholly predictable effects upon children. Instead, transactional models (Sameroff and Fiese, 2000) are needed to capture the complexity of the multiple influences involved. Such models highlight the mutual effects that children and adults have on modifying each other's behaviour, hence affecting the child's developmental environment.

Summary	of Section 5

- Baumrind identified four styles of child-rearing; authoritarian, permissive, authoritative and non-conformist.
- Some research has suggested that authoritative parenting results in more positive child outcomes.
- This research has also highlighted the two-way influence of children on parents and vice versa.
- Transactional models are needed to capture the complexity of parent–child relationships and influences.

6   Parent–child relationships and later child development

SG

Many theorists have examined the changing nature and function of parent–child relationships, reasoning that these develop in ways that require continued co-ordination and integration as maturing individuals adapt to their changing social contexts (Greenberg *et al.*, 1990; Sroufe, 1996). While internal working models continue to be formed during and after early childhood, maintaining continuity in individual developmental pathways, there exists wide variation across individuals in the degree to which working models reflect the individual's own experiences, as well as his or her cognitive, linguistic, and behavioural skills (Bowlby, 1973).

The IWM construct has become central to explanations of the role played by attachment relationships in children's social relationships and individual psycho-social functioning. Main *et al.* (1985) suggested that emotional openness in discussing imagined parent–child separations and conversations with parents reflected aspects of children's mental representations of relationships with their parents. Specifically, children who were securely attached at 12 months provided accounts that appeared more coherent, elaborate and emotionally open when they were 6 years old, whereas those children who were insecurely attached at 12 months were more likely to offer sad, irrational, or bizarre responses later, or else were completely silent. Furthermore, in using a story completion task, Cassidy (1988) found that children who behaved securely in a Strange Situation assessment at around 12–18 months of age represented themselves positively in interviews and were better able to acknowledge less than perfect aspects of the self than children who behaved insecurely.

Story completion task
This is a form of assessment where the first part of a story is presented and the participant is asked to generate the rest of the story.

6.1 Links between infant attachment and adult attachment

According to attachment theory, if IWMs do indeed show some persistence in their effects after childhood, each type of infant attachment would be expected to be associated with a particular type of adult attachment. One prediction of attachment theory is that there will be continuities across generations in attachment styles. Main and others (George *et al.*, 1985; Main and Goldwyn, 1994) developed the Adult Attachment Interview (AAI) to assess an adult's ability to integrate early memories of their relationships with their parents into overarching working models of relationships. According to Main, these working models fall into one of three categories, with adults classified as *dismissing* of their attachment relationships, *autonomous* (free to evaluate their early attachment relationships), or *preoccupied* with their attachment relationships.

BOX 3

Adult Attachment Interview narrative types

A *dismissing* narrative is one in which the person asserts that what happened in their childhood is not important. They may say, for example, 'my father shut me up in the cellar when I was naughty, but I didn't really mind, and anyway, it's in the past now. No, I didn't get upset, it didn't bother me at all. In fact, I've forgotten about it'. The person gives the impression that personal relationships are not of much significance. The narrative is sparse, with little detail, and events and people are recalled in a rather bland, unemotional way, even where the content suggests that emotions would have been felt. The past is not described as having an influence on the self.

An *autonomous* narrative is one in which the person acknowledges the importance of relationships to them, both in the present and during their childhood and talks freely and in some depth about past and present attachments. Richly described examples are given of both positive and negative experiences, and the person shows a capacity to integrate these. Insight is shown into others' motives and feelings, and into influences on the self.

A *preoccupied* narrative is lengthy, and without a clear structure. The link from one statement to another is often not apparent; points may be repeated. The person acknowledges the significance of past experiences, but does not seem to have resolved these and moved on from them. Past events are talked about with feeling; the person seems to re-experience the feelings in the interview. The person seems to be stuck or 'enmeshed' in unresolved issues from the past.

Activity 4   *Infant attachment and adult attachment*

Allow about
5 minutes

This activity will help you consider the possible links between infant and adult attachment.

Look at the following table. Work out which adult attachment type you would expect to be associated with each of the infant attachment classifications discussed in Section 3.6, and write it in the appropriate cell.

Infant attachment classification	Adult attachment classification
Type A insecure-avoidant	?
Type B secure	?
Type C insecure-resistant	?

Comment

A logical set of predictions would be that a Type A infant attachment would be associated with a dismissing adult attachment type; that a Type B infant attachment would lead to an autonomous adult attachment type; and a Type C infant attachment would go with an enmeshed adult attachment type.

A good way to test out these theoretical predictions would be to conduct some longitudinal research, lasting for at least 17 years so that the children, first seen at 1 year old for Strange Situation assessment, could be followed into early adulthood. It would be necessary to carry out Strange Situation assessments with a selected sample of infants and to then assess their adult attachment classification when they reached young adulthood.

▲

Another approach to testing such hypotheses is to assess adults' adult attachment types and to ask them to give retrospective accounts of their early childhood experiences. The intention could be to use these retrospective accounts to assess the adults' infant attachment classifications.

▼

Activity 5

Allow about
5 minutes

Problems with retrospective studies

This activity will help you to understand the methodological problems with retrospective studies of attachment.

A simple research project could be to carry out a set of adult attachment classifications with a group of adults, and ask them also to recall how they behaved with their parents when they were separated and reunited, when they were young children. Can you think of any problems with the design of this suggested study?

Comment

One major problem would be that the two measures (adult attachment and retrospective infant attachment style) would be 'confounded'. In other words, because the adult attachment classification is based on narrative accounts of early childhood experiences, it is highly likely that it will correspond with an infant attachment classification simply because that also has to be based on the person's recall of his or her childhood experience. A person is likely to recall their childhood experiences in consistent ways. We would not be able to distinguish between 'real' correspondence and a false positive result arising simply from a person's tendency to give consistent accounts. Without independent evidence, it is hard to establish whether consistency between different aspects of childhood experiences recalled by the same person is real or to some extent reconstructed. For these reasons longitudinal research is preferable.

▲

Several longitudinal studies on attachment were started in the 1980s, and these are now beginning to deliver results. One such, the Bielefeld longitudinal study, has been tracking the development of children in 49 families in Germany (Zimmerman, 2000). Forty-four children, whose attachment security was assessed when they were between 12 and 18 months of age, were later assessed for adult attachment type classification at 16 years of age. Information was also systematically collected on the occurrence of various 'life events', such as divorce and death or illness of parents, in the intervening period between the two assessments. It was found that the Strange Situation type classification (SST) was not a good predictor of the adolescents' adult attachment type; what emerged as a significant influence was, instead, the life events, particularly divorce and serious parental illness, which had happened during childhood. However, another study (Hamilton, 1994) of 30 adolescents in California, did find a strong correspondence between SST and adult attachment classification. This study also collected data on intervening events and experiences. A careful analysis of these data showed that the correspondence was largely found for children whose family circumstances had remained stable over the 16-year period between the SST and the adult attachment assessment. This was true for both secure and insecure type classifications on the two measures. Those children who changed from a secure to insecure (or vice-versa) classification were much more likely to have experienced major changes in their family circumstances.

Taking these two sets of results together suggests that there is some support for the link between infant and adult attachment status, but that life events are also a potent factor in influencing adult attachment type. In a stable childhood, SST can predict adult attachment, but in a less stable 'trajectory' through childhood, other events can have both positive and negative effects.

6.2 Adult attachment's influence on infant attachment

It has been much easier for researchers to look at the converse aspect of the SST–adult attachment type link – the way that a mother's adult attachment type might be associated with their infant's SST. Many studies have been carried out looking at how mothers with different adult attachment classifications behave towards their infants, and what types of attachment their infants show. Three consistent findings have emerged from these studies:

1   Mothers' adult attachment typing *is* predictive of their infants' SST types, particularly for secure attachment. But the prediction is not 100 per cent accurate; for secure versus insecure classifications it is reasonably strong, but for the two types of insecure attachment, it is weaker.

2   Adult attachment typing is also to some extent predictive of how mothers behave towards their infants: secure mothers are more likely to behave sensitively towards their infants, responding to their bids for attention, comfort and communication. Autonomous adults appear more sensitively responsive to their infants than do adults in the dismissive and preoccupied groups, and their children are more likely to be securely attached

(van IJzendoorn, 1995). For example, ratings of British mothers' and fathers' AAI narratives of their attachments to their own parents, collected during the pregnancy, predicted the security of their infants' attachments to them (Fonagy *et al.*, 1991; Steele *et al.*, 1996).

3   As noted earlier, sensitive parenting is itself predictive of infant attachment, but it is again only a relatively weak predictor. However, it does seem to have an association with infant attachment that is not wholly explained by the relation between adult attachment and sensitivity noted in the previous point. These latter findings are drawn from a large-scale meta-analysis of attachment research (van Ijzendoorn, 1995) which led to the idea of an as yet unexplained 'transmission gap' highlighting the fact that the factors contributing to the intergenerational transmission of attachment are still not wholly identified nor are their modes of action fully understood.

Meta-analysis
A method of 'analysis of analyses' which uses statistical techniques to identify underlying effects from the results of a number of different studies of the same topic.

Summary of Section 6

- The concept of IWM underpins the definition of three types of adult attachment: dismissing, autonomous and preoccupied.
- Adult attachment classifications have been based on ratings of responses in a standardized Adult Attachment Interview (AAI).
- Infant attachment type is associated with subsequent adult attachment type.
- Parental adult attachment type appears to have an effect on infant attachment security.
- The process of intergenerational transmission of attachment is now better understood.
- Life events affect the course of attachment development.

7   Adolescence

Adolescence is the time of transition from being a child of parents to potentially becoming a parent of children. If attachment is indeed transmitted from one generation to the next, then it would be expected that adolescents would show some effects of the parenting that they had received. The Adult Attachment Interview (AAI) has also been used as a way of exploring the development of attachment in adolescence. According to Kobak and Sceery (1988), adolescents rated as secure or autonomous adult attachment types are rated by their peers as being more resilient, less anxious, and less hostile. These adolescents reported little distress and high levels of social support, whereas adolescents rated as dismissive were rated low on resilience and high on hostility by their peers, with whom they had distant relationships. Adolescents in the preoccupied group were viewed as less resilient and more anxious by their peers, and they reported higher levels of personal distress and family support than those in the dismissing group. Steinberg (1990) has suggested that securely attached adolescents may be more likely than dismissive or preoccupied adolescents to successfully maintain healthy relationships with their parents.

These studies on the associations between individual IWM and parent–child relationships suggest that secure children, adolescents and adults see attachment figures as well as themselves as primarily good, though not perfect. They are also able to communicate with ease, tend to have flexible interpersonal styles, express empathy for others and discuss attachment relationships coherently without idealizing them.

According to psychoanalysts, close relationships with parents can become especially difficult for children to handle in early adolescence and, as a result, behavioural manifestations of emotional attachment are highly likely to be suppressed. These hypotheses laid the groundwork for research on qualitative and functional transformations in parent–child relationships during a child's adolescence. Research in Western industrial cultures suggests that children shift their dependence from parents first to same-sex and then to opposite-sex peers, while continuing the processes of self-differentiation and individuation which become major themes of development in adolescence (Grotevant, 1998). The biological changes associated with puberty also foster change and promote distance between parents and children in early adolescence (Hill and Holmbeck, 1987; Steinberg, 1988, 1990; Collins, 1991). Among both human and non-human primates, the parent–child relationship is increasingly marked by self-assertion, distance and conflict as children develop. Steinberg (1987) found that early maturing sons and daughters reported more conflict with their mothers than later maturing children, although these processes may take a different form and have different meaning in mother–child and father–child relationships. The effects of puberty are frequently confounded with the effects of other age-related changes such as moving up in school systems (Collins and Russell, 1991; Simmons and Blyth, 1987), but whatever their relative importance, the biological, social and cognitive changes associated with puberty all make early adolescence a critical transitional period during which youngsters are expected to consolidate their knowledge of the norms and roles of adult society and, at least in Western industrialized societies, begin to become emotionally and economically independent of their parents (Grotevant, 1998).

Baumrind (1991) noted that parents of adolescents tend to use increasingly complex variations of the basic patterns described above when faced with the unique challenges and changes characteristic of the adolescent period. She concluded that:

> Adolescents' developmental progress is held back by directive, officious, or unengaged practices and facilitated by reciprocal, balanced interaction characteristic of both authoritative and democratic parents. Directive parents who are authoritarian generate internalizing problem behaviours and are less successful at curtailing drug use. Directive parents who are not authoritarian effectively curtail adolescents' drug use but do not promote positive competence.

(Baumrind, 1991, p. 753)

Summary of Section 7

- Adolescence typically marks a change in a young person's attachment objects from parents to peers.
- Baumrind's theory suggests that authoritative parenting may help the transition from childhood to adulthood.

8 Diversity in family patterns and relationships

Despite the multicultural nature of contemporary societies, most information on the socio-emotional development of children has been derived from studies of white, middle-class North Americans and Europeans. Ethnocentricity in developmental psychology has limited the generalizability and universality of developmental principles and norms, while restricting our understanding of the variations in human behaviour and experiences across cultures and sub-cultures (Lamb, 1999, 2004). It is all too easy to make assumptions about the similarities and differences between family types and members of different ethnic groups. Social scientists may assume, for example, that most households comprise two adults living with their children, although such households are in the minority (Rapoport and Rapoport, 1975).

Because socio-economic and socio-cultural factors appear to have such a powerful effect on the processes and outcomes of socialization (Parke and Buriel, 1998), there have been increasing demands by social scientists to include culture and cultural experiences as critical variables in research on human development. The significance of socio-cultural factors is evident in research on parental disciplinary styles. Steinberg and Darling (1994; Steinberg *et al.*, 1995), for example, found that although authoritative rearing was always beneficial or at least not harmful and that disengaged parenting was always harmful or at least not beneficial, the impact of parenting style varied across socio-cultural groups. Authoritative parenting was beneficial and neglectful parenting was disadvantageous for European American and Hispanic American youth, for example, but authoritarian parenting was more advantageous for Asian American adolescents and more disadvantageous for European American adolescents than for adolescents in the other groups.

Few researchers have compared parent–adolescent relationships in different countries. Kroger (1985) found that American, New Zealand and British adolescents all had similar attitudes towards parental authority. Although American girls of all ages felt more favourably about their parents, girls in New Zealand, who had positive attitudes towards their parents in early adolescence, became less positive as they grew older. Meanwhile, Feldman and her colleagues

(Feldman and Rosenthal, 1991; Feldman *et al.*, 1991), found that, although Hong Kong Chinese adolescents reported more misbehaviour and expected to achieve behavioural autonomy later than the Australian and American young people, levels of misconduct and expectations of behavioural autonomy were related in similar ways to family environments and adolescent values in both Chinese and Western cultures. More studies of this sort may be especially informative as we seek to distinguish the effects of broad cultural factors from the effects of parental socialization strategies.

Summary of Section 8

- There is substantial diversity in parenting and its effects in different cultures.
- Further research is needed to find out whether it is possible to separate universal effects of parenting from specific cultural factors.

9 Conclusion

This chapter has introduced some central topics in the field of research into parenting and its effects on children's development.

Because attachment theory, first developed by Bowlby and colleagues in the 1950s, continues to be a fruitful basis for research, this has been one focus of the chapter. We have shown how the forms that attachments can take between parents and children have been explored and clarified in an ongoing, extensive area of study. The influences that parents can have on young children's attachment and the consequences for their relationships later in their lives have begun to be identified. Other important lines of research, notably those initiated by Baumrind in the 1960s, have similarly found consistencies between different styles of parenting and differences in child outcomes. It has also become evident that parents' and children's expectations, and the ways in which each interpret the other's behaviour, are key elements in these processes.

As a result of these areas of research, the pattern of the interplay among child characteristics, parental behaviour and context in the development of children's attachments is becoming clearer, but at the same time is being shown to be far from simple.

Given the complexity of the cause and effect relationships in parenting and child development, and the ways in which these are intimately bound up with social, economic and cultural contexts, it is going to be important for future research in this area to explore how these processes operate in ethnic groups around the world. There are many different perspectives on what count as 'good' outcomes for child development, and there are many different ways in which parents behave towards their children within these perspectives. Broadening research to take advantage of these differences will help in gaining a clearer understanding of the underlying processes involved.

References

Ainsworth, M. S. (1962) 'The effects of maternal deprivation: a review of findings and controversy in the context of research strategy', in *Deprivation of Maternal Care: a reassessment of its effects*, Public Health Papers, no. 14, Geneva, World Health Organisation.

Ainsworth, M. D. S. (1969) 'Object relations, dependency, and attachment: a theoretical review of the infant–mother relationship', *Child Development*, vol. 40, pp. 969–1025.

Ainsworth, M., Bell, S. M. and Stayton, D. J. (1971) 'Individual differences in the strange situation behaviour of one-year-olds', in Schaffer, H. R. (ed.) *The Origins of Human Social Relations*, pp. 17–57, New York, Academic Press.

Ainsworth, M. D. S., Blehar, M. C., Waters, E. and Wall, S. (1978) *Patterns of Attachment*, Hillsdale, NJ, Lawrence Erlbaum Associates.

Anderson, K. E., Lytton, J. and Romney, D. M. (1986) 'Mothers' interactions with normal and conduct-disordered boys: who affects whom?', *Developmental Psychology*, vol. 22, pp. 415–19.

Andrews, D. W. and Dishion, T. J. (1994) 'The microsocial structure underpinnings of adolescent problem behavior', in Ketterlinus, R. D. and Lamb, M. E. (eds) *Adolescent Problem Behaviors: issues and research*, pp. 187–207, Hillsdale, NJ, Lawrence Erlbaum Associates.

Bakermans-Kranenburg, M. J. and van IJzendoorn, M. H. (2004) 'No association of the dopamine D4 receptor (DRD4) and -521 C/T promoter polymorphisms with infant attachment disorganization', *Attachment and Human Development*, vol. 6, pp. 211–19.

Baumrind, D. (1967) 'Child care practices anteceding three patterns of preschool behavior', *Genetic Psychology Monographs*, vol. 75, pp. 43–88.

Baumrind, D. (1971) 'Current patterns of parental authority', *Developmental Psychology Monographs*, vol. 4, pp. 1–103.

Baumrind, D. (1973) 'The development of instrumental competence through socialization', in Pick, A. (ed.), *Minnesota Symposium on Child Psychology*, vol. 7, pp. 3–46, Minneapolis, University of Minnesota Press.

Baumrind, D. (1975) *Early Socialization and the Discipline Controversy*, Morristown, NJ, General Learning Press.

Baumrind, D. (1991) 'Parenting styles and adolescent development', in Lerner, R. M., Petersen, A. C. and Brooks-Gunn, J. (eds), *Encyclopedia of Adolescence, vol. 2*, pp. 746–58, New York, Garland Publishing.

Baumrind, D. and Black, A. E. (1967) 'Socialization practices associated with dimensions of competence in preschool boys and girls', *Child Development*, vol. 38, pp. 291–327.

BBC Parenting website (2004) 'Being a Parent' [online] http://www.bbc.co.uk/parenting/ [Accessed March 2004].

Belsky, J. (1999) 'Interactional and contextual determinants of attachment security', in Cassidy, J. and Shaver, P. (eds), *Handbook of Attachment: theory, research, and clinical applications*, pp. 249–64, New York, NY, The Guilford Press.

Belsky, J. and Fearon, R. M. P. (2002) 'Early attachment security, subsequent maternal sensitivity, and later child development: does continuity in development depend upon continuity of caregiving?', *Attachment and Human Development*, vol. 4, pp. 361–87.

Belsky, J., Fish, M. and Isabella, R. (1991) 'Continuity and discontinuity in infant negative and positive emotionality: family antecedents and attachment consequences', *Developmental Psychology*, vol. 27, pp. 421–31.

Bowlby, J. (1969) *Attachment and Loss: Vol. 1., Attachment*, New York, NY, Basic Books.

Bowlby, J. (1973) *Attachment and Loss: Vol. 2., Separation: anxiety and anger*, New York, NY, Basic Books.

Bowlby, J. (1988) *A Secure Base: parent–child attachment and healthy human development*, New York, NY, Basic Books.

Bretherton, I. (1990) 'Open communication and internal working models: Their role in the development of attachment relationships', in Thompson, R. A. (ed.), *Socioemotional Development*, pp. 57–114, Lincoln, NE, University of Nebraska Press.

Bretherton, I. (1991) 'Pouring new wine into old bottles: the social self as internal working model', in Gunnar, M. R. and Sroufe, L. A. (eds), *Self Process and Development: minnesota symposia on child psychology*, vol. 23, pp. 1–41, Hillsdale, NJ, Lawrence Erlbaum Associates.

Bretherton, I. (1993) 'From dialogue to internal working models: the co-construction of self relationships', in Nelson, C. A. (ed.) *Memory and Affect in Development: minnesota symposia on child psychology*, vol. 26, pp. 237–63, Hillsdale, NJ, Lawrence Erlbaum Associates.

Bretherton, I., McNew, S. and Beeghly-Smith, M. (1981) 'Early person knowledge as expressed in gestural and verbal communication: when do infants acquire a theory of mind?', in Lamb, M. E. and Sherrod, L. R. (eds) *Infant Social Cognition*, pp. 333–73, Hillsdale, NJ, Erlbaum.

Bugental, D. B. and Goodnow, J. S. (1998, 5th edn) 'Socialization processes', in Damon, W. and Eisenberg, N. (eds), *Handbook of Child Psychology: Vol. 3: Social, emotional and personality development*, pp. 289–463, New York, NY, Wiley.

Carpendale, J. I. M. and Lewis, C. (2004) 'Constructing an understanding of mind: the development of children's social understanding within social interaction', *Behavioural and Brain Sciences*, vol. 27, pp. 79–96.

Cassidy, J. (1998) 'Child–mother attachment and the self in six-year-olds', *Child Development*, vol. 59, 121–34.

Cassidy, J. and Shaver, P. R. (1999) *Handbook of Attachment: theory, research and clinical applications*, New York, NY, The Guilford Press.

Collins, W. A. (1991) 'Shared views and parent–adolescent relationships', in Paikoff, R. L. (ed.), *Shared Views in the Family During Adolescence: new directions for child development*, vol. 51, pp. 103–10, San Francisco, Jossey-Bass.

Collins, W. A. and Russell, G. (1991) 'Mother–child and father–child relationships in middle childhood and adolescence: a developmental analysis', *Developmental Review*, vol. 11, pp. 99–136.

de Wolff, M. S. and van IJzendoorn, M. H. (1997) 'Sensitivity and attachment: A meta-analysis on parental antecedents of infant attachment', *Child Development*, vol. 68, pp. 571–91.

Easterbrooks, M. A. and Goldberg, W. A. (1984) 'Toddler development in the family: impact of father involvement and parenting characteristics', *Child Development*, vol. 55, pp. 740–52.

Fagot, B. I. and Kavanagh, K. (1993) 'Parenting during the second year: effects of children's age, sex and attachment classification', *Child Development*, vol. 64, pp. 258–71.

Feldman, S. S. and Rosenthal, D. A. (1991) 'Age expectations of behavioral autonomy in Hong Kong, Australian, and American youth: the influence of family variables and adolescents' values', *International Journal of Psychology*, vol. 26, pp. 1–23.

Feldman, S. S., Rosenthal. D. A., Mont-Reynaud, R., Leung, K. and Lau, S. (1991) 'Ain't misbehavin': adolescent values and family environments as correlates of misconduct in Australia, Hong Kong, and the United States', *Journal of Research on Adolescence*, vol. 1, pp. 109–34.

Fonagy, P. and Target, M. (1997) 'Attachment and reflective function: their role in self-organization', *Development and Psychopathology*, vol. 9, pp. 679–700.

Fonagy, P., Steele, H. and Steele, M. (1991) 'Maternal representations of attachment during pregnancy predict the organization of infant–mother attachment at one year of age', *Child Development*, vol. 62, pp. 891–905.

Gable, S., Crnic, K. and Belsky, J. (1994) 'Coparenting within the family system: influences on children's development', *Family Relations*, vol. 43, pp. 380–86.

George, C., Kaplan, N. and Main, M. (1985) *'Adult attachment interview'*, unpublished manuscript, University of California, Berkeley.

Goldberg, S., MacKay-Soroka, S. and Rochester, M. (1994) 'Affect, attachment and maternal responsiveness', *Infant Behaviour and Development*, vol. 17, pp. 335–39.

Greenberg, M. T., Cicchetti, D. and Cummings, E. M. (eds) (1990) *Attachment in the Preschool Years: theory, research, and intervention*, Chicago, University of Chicago Press.

Grotevant, H. D. (1998, 5th edn) 'Adolescent development in family contexts', in Damon, W. and Eisenberg, N. (eds), *Handbook of Child Psychology: Vol. 3: Social, personality, and emotional development*, pp. 1097–149, New York, NY, Wiley.

Harlow, H. F. (1958) 'The nature of love', *American Psychologist*, vol. 13, pp. 573–685.

Hamilton, C. E. (1994) 'Continuity and discontinuity of attachment from infancy through adolescence', *Child Development*, vol. 71, pp. 690–94.

Hill, J. and Holmbeck, G. N. (1987) 'Familial adaptation to biological change during adolescence', in Lerner, R. M. and Foch, T. (eds) *Biological–psychological Interactions in Early Adolescence: a life-span perspective*, pp. 207–23, Hillsdale, NJ, Lawrence Erlbaum Associates.

Kaplan, M. M. (1992) *Mother's Images of Motherhood*, London, Routledge.

Kobak, R. and Sceery, A. (1988) 'Attachment in late adolescence: working models, affect regulation, and representation of self and others', *Child Development*, vol. 59, pp. 135–46.

Kroger, J. (1985) 'Relationships during adolescence: a cross-national study of New Zealand and United States teenagers', *Journal of Adolescence*, vol. 8, pp. 47–56.

Lakatos, K., Nemoda, Z., Toth, I., Ronai, Z., Ney, K., Sasvari-Szekely, M. and Gervai, J. (2002) 'Further evidence for the role of the dopamine D4 receptor gene (DRD4) in attachment disorganization: interaction of the III exon 48 bp repeat and the -521 C/T promoter polymorphisms', *Molecular Psychiatry*, vol. 7, pp. 27–31.

Lamb, M. E. (1999) 'Parental behavior, family processes, and child development in nontraditional and traditionally understudied families', in Lamb, M. E. (ed.) *Parenting and Child Development in 'nontraditional' families*, pp. 1–14, Mahwah, NJ, Lawrence Erlbaum Associates.

Lamb, M. E. (2004) 'Developmental theory and public policy: a cross-national perspective', in Goelman, H., Marshall, S. K. and Ross, S. (eds), in *Multiple Lenses Multiple Images: perspectives on the child across time, space and disciplines*, (pp. 122–46), Toronto, University of Toronto Press.

Lamb, M. E., Thompson, R. W., Gardner, E. L. and Charnov, E. L. (1985) *Infant–Mother Attachment: the origins and development significance of individual differences in Strange Situation behavior*, Hillsdale, NJ, Lawrence Erlbaum Associates.

Lyons-Ruth K. and Jacobvitz, D. (1999) 'Attachment disorganization: unresolved loss, relational violence, and lapses in behavioral and attentional strategies', in Cassidy J. and Shaver P. (eds) *Handbook of Attachment: theory, research, and clinical applications*, pp. 520–54, New York, NY, The Guilford Press.

MacKinnon-Lewis, C., Volling, B. L., Lamb, M. E., Hattie, J. and Baradaran, I. (2001) 'A longitudinal examination of the associations between mothers' and children's attributions and their aggression', *Development and Psychopathology*, vol. 13, pp. 69–81.

Main, M. and Goldwyn, R. (1994) *'Adult attachment classification system'*, unpublished manuscript, University of California, Berkeley.

Main, M. and Hesse, E. (1990) 'Parents' unresolved traumatic experiences are related to infant disorganized attachment status: is frightened and/or frightening parental behavior the linking mechanism?', in Greenberg M. T., Cicchetti, D. and Cummings, E. M. (eds) *Attachment in the Preschool Years: theory, research, and intervention*, pp. 161–84, Chicago, University of Chicago Press.

Main, M. and Solomon, J. (1990) 'Procedures for identifying infants as disorganized/disoriented during the Ainsworth Strange Situation', in Greenberg, M. T., Cicchetti, D. and Cummings, E. M. (eds) *Attachment during the preschool years: theory, research and intervention*, pp. 121–60, Chicago, University of Chicago Press.

Main, M., Kaplan, N. and Cassidy, J. (1985) 'Security in infancy, childhood, and adulthood: a move to the level of representation', in Bretherton, I. and E. Waters, E. (eds) *Growing Points of Attachment Theory and Research. Monographs of the Society for Research in Child Development*, 50, pp. 66–104.

Meins, E., Fernyhough, C., Fradley, E. and Tuckey, M. (2001) 'Rethinking maternal sensitivity: mothers' comments on infants' mental processes predict security of attachment at 12 months', *Journal of Child Psychology and Psychiatry*, vol. 42, pp. 637–48.

Meins, E., Fernyhough, C., Wainwright, R., Das Gupta, M., Fradley, E. and Tuckey, M. (2002) 'Maternal mind-mindedness and attachment security as predictors of theory of mind understanding', *Child Development*, vol. 73, pp. 1715–26.

Parke, R. D. and Buriel, R. (1998, 5th edn) 'Socialization in the family: ethnic and ecological perspectives', in Damon, W. and Eisenberg. N. (eds) *Handbook of Child Psychology: Vol. 3 Social, emotional, and personality development*, pp. 463–552, New York, NY, Wiley.

Patterson, G. R. (1976) 'The aggressive child: victim and architect of a coercive system', in Hamelynch, L. A., Handy, L. C. and March, E. J. (eds), *Behavior Modification and Families*, pp. 267–316, New York, Brunner/Mazel.

Patterson, G. R. (1982) *Coercive Family Processes*, Eugene, OR, Castalia Press.

Posada, G., Jacobs, A., Carbonell, O. A., Alzate, G., Bustamante, M. R. and Arenas, A. (1999) 'Maternal care and attachment security in ordinary and emergency contexts', *Developmental Psychology*, vol. 35, pp. 1379–88.

Rapoport, R. and Rapoport, R. N. (1975) *Leisure and the family life cycle,* London, Routledge and Kegan Paul.

Robertson, J. and Robertson, J. (1989) *Separation and the Very Young*, London, Free Association Press.

Russell, A., Hart., C. H., Robinson, C. C. and Olsen, S. F. (2003) 'Children's sociable and aggressive behaviour with peers: a comparison of the U.S. and Australia, and contributions of temperament and parenting styles', *International Journal of Behavioral Development*, vol. 27, pp. 74–86.

Sameroff A. J. and Fiese, B. H. (2000, 2nd edn) 'Models of development and developmental risk', in Zeanah, C. H. Jr. (ed.) *Handbook of Infant Mental Health*, pp. 3–13, New York, NY, The Guilford Press.

Schuengel, C., Bakermans-Kranenburg, M. J. and van IJzendoorn, M. H. (1999) 'Frightening maternal behavior linking unresolved loss and disorganized infant attachment', *Journal of Consulting and Clinical Psychology*, vol. 67, pp. 54–63.

Simmons, R. G. and Blyth, D. A. (1987) *Moving into Adolescence: the impact of pubertal change and school context*, New York, Aldine De Gruyter.

Sroufe, L. A. (1996) *Emotional Development*, Cambridge, Cambridge University Press.

Steele, H., Steele, M. and Fonagy, P. (1996) 'Associations among attachment classifications of infants, mothers and fathers', *Child Development*, vol. 67, pp. 542–555.

Steinberg, L. (1987) 'Impact of puberty on family relations: effects of pubertal status and pubertal timing', *Developmental Psychology*, vol. 23, pp. 451–60.

Steinberg, L. (1988) 'Reciprocal relations between parent–child distance and pubertal maturation', *Developmental Psychology*, vol. 24, pp. 122–28.

Steinberg, L. (1990) 'Interdependence in the family: autonomy, conflict, and harmony in the parent–adolescent relationships', in Feldman, S. S. and Elliott, G. (eds) *At the Threshold: the developing adolescent*, pp. 255–76, Cambridge, MA, Harvard University Press.

Steinberg, L. D. and Darling, N. E. (1994) 'The broader context of social influence in adolescence', in Silbereisen, R. K. and Todt, E. (eds) *Adolescence in Context*, pp. 25–45, New York, NY, Springer-Verlag.

Steinberg, L., Darling, N. E. and Fletcher, A. C. (1995) 'Authoritative parenting and adolescent development: an ecological journey', in Moen, P., Elder, G. H. and Luscher, K. (eds) *Examining Lives in Context*, pp. 423–66, Washington, DC, American Psychological Association.

Teti, D. M., Gelfand, D. M., Messinger, D. and Isabella, R. (1995) 'Maternal depression and the quality of early attachment: an examination of infants, preschoolers and their mothers', *Developmental Psychology*, vol. 31, pp. 364–76.

Thompson, R. A. (1998, 5th edn) 'Early sociopersonality development', in Damon, W. and Eisenberg. N. (eds) *Handbook of Child Psychology: Vol. 3: Social, emotional, and personality development*, pp. 25–104, New York, NY, Wiley.

van IJzendoorn, M. H. (1995) 'The association between adult attachment representations and infant attachment, parental responsiveness, and clinical status: a meta-analysis on the predictive validity of the Adult Attachment Interview', *Psychological Bulletin*, vol. 113, pp. 404–10.

van IJzendoorn, M. H. and Kroonenberg, P. M. (1988) 'Cross-cultural Patterns of Attachment: a meta-analysis of the Strange Situation', *Child Development*, vol. 59, pp. 147–56.

Vondra, J. I., Shaw, D. S. and Kevenides, M. C. (1995) 'Predicting infant attachment classification from multiple, contemporaneous measures of maternal care', *Infant Behavior and Development*, vol. 18, pp. 215–25.

Winnicott, D. W. (1953) 'Transitional objects and transitional phenomena', *International Journal of Psychoanalysis*, vol. 34, pp. 89–97.

Winnicott, D. W. (1964) *The Child, the Family and the Outside World*, Harmondsworth, Penguin Books.

Winnicott, D. W. (1965) *The Family and Individual Development*, London, Tavistock Publications.

Zimmerman, P., Becker-Stoll, F., Grossman, K., Grossman, K. E., Scheurer-Englisch, H. and Wartner, U. (2000) 'Longitudinal attachment development from infancy through adolescence', *Psychologie in Erziehung und Unterricht*, vol. 47, pp. 99–117.

Chapter 2
Disturbed and disturbing behaviour

Martin Woodhead, Sinead Rhodes and John Oates

Contents

Learning outcomes

After you have studied this chapter you should be able to:

1 analyse the concepts of 'normal' and 'disturbing' behaviour, and highlight the issues surrounding the identification of psychological difficulties;

2 describe research on the incidence of psychological difficulties, including some issues surrounding attempts to evaluate their stability, and to introduce the concept of risk factors;

3 understand the potential contribution of maternal behaviour, attitudes and mental state to the development of difficulties within the context of wider family and social factors;

4 understand the role of fathers in relation to disturbed relations and conflict in children;

5 understand the interaction between maternal and paternal factors;

6 recognize the role of children in the development of disturbed behaviour – in particular, the way child temperament can interact with parental responsiveness;

7 discuss the relevance of a transactional model for describing these parent–child processes;

8 explain the relevance of vulnerability, resilience, protective mechanisms, gateways and amplifiers in the context of studies of behavioural difficulties.

1 Introduction

The previous chapter examined the role of attachment in social development and considered whether insecure attachments contribute to the development of psychological difficulties. In this chapter we shall focus directly on children whose development becomes a cause for concern. Their behaviour may become challenging and difficult, they may appear isolated, anxious and fearful, or they may seem unhappy or disturbed. We shall be looking at the characteristics of these problems, at some of the explanations that have been offered about how they arise, and at the assumptions that underlie the judgements that we as adults make of children as 'a problem', 'abnormal', 'pathological', 'maladjusted' or 'disturbed'.

The first activity introduces four children who have been referred to a clinical psychologist and raises questions about how, if at all, their behaviour is 'a problem'.

Activity 1

Allow about
25 minutes

Thinking about disturbed development

This activity will develop your critical skills when reading about children with behavioural problems.

Below there are four case studies which introduce children who have been referred to a clinical psychologist. Read the case studies and then consider the questions that accompany each one.

Noel, aged 9

Noel has had behavioural problems. Noel's mother and father, Deirdre and Christy, separated 18 months prior to the referral after Deirdre found out Christy was having an affair. Noel's conduct problems had become worse in the last year when he and his mother Deirdre and sister Kate moved in with Deirdre's boyfriend (Des) and his two sons (Barry and Tom). Noel stole and destroyed a number of toys belonging to Barry and Tom. He scratched Des's car with a Stanley knife and recently exploded fireworks in his darkroom, destroying about £500 worth of equipment. The separation of Noel's parents had occurred suddenly without a long period of overt conflict. Noel idolized his father and liked his new partner Molly.

(Adapted from Carr, 1999, p. 881)

- Do you think Noel's behaviour constitutes a 'problem'?
- What do you think may be the cause(s) of Noel's problems?
- Whose problem is it: a problem for Noel, a problem for Deirdre, Des or Christy, or is there a problem in the relationship between Noel and the adults involved?

Nora, aged 9

Nora was referred because of her fear of the dark. She wanted to go on a camping trip with the Brownies but was frightened because she would have to sleep in complete darkness. At home she always slept with her light on. Her developmental history was unremarkable and she had never experienced a traumatic incident in the darkness.

(Adapted from Carr, 1999, p. 413)

- Do you think Nora's behaviour constitutes a 'problem'?
- What do you think might be the cause of this type of problem?

Margie, aged 10

Margie was referred because of excessive tearfulness in school which had been gradually worsening over a number of months. She was worried about many routine daily activities and responsibilities. She worried about doing poorly at school, that she had made mistakes which would later be discovered, that her friends wouldn't like her, and that her parents would be worried about the way she did her household jobs. Margie was the eldest of four children and the only girl in the family. Both of her parents showed symptoms of anxiety when interviewed and her mother had been treated with medication for anxiety over a number of years. The parents' chief concern was about Margie's tearfulness, which they viewed as unusual. Her worries and fears they saw as quite legitimate.

(Adapted from Carr, 1999, p. 416)

- Do you think Margie's behaviour constitutes a problem?

- What do you think are the causes of the problems in this case?

- Are these problems located in Margie, her parents or the relationship between them?

- What do you think is the likelihood of Margie continuing to have problems later in childhood?

Timmy, aged 6

Timmy was referred for assessment because his teachers found him unmanageable. He was unable to sit still in school and concentrate on his school work. He left his chair frequently and ran around the classroom shouting. Even with individual tuition he could not apply himself to his school work. He also had difficulties getting on with other children. They disliked him because he disrupted their games. He rarely waited for his turn and did not obey the rules. Timmy came from a well-functioning family. The parents had a very stable and satisfying marriage and together ran a successful business. Their daughter, Amanda, was a well-adjusted and academically able 8 year old. Timmy's parents were undoubtedly committed to him and although they were careful not to favour the daughter or to punish Timmy unduly, there was a growing tension between each of the parents and Timmy. They were continually suppressing their growing irritation with his frenetic activity, disobedience, shouting and school problems.

(Adapted from Carr, 1999, p. 369)

- Do you think Timmy's behaviour constitutes 'a problem'?

- When do problems experienced when growing up justify labels like 'disturbed'?

- Do you think this is Timmy's problem, a problem for his parents, or is there a problem in the relationship between them?

Comment

This activity provides an introduction to many of the issues to be examined in this chapter. To help clarify your initial responses we offer the following brief contrast between two perspectives. As you read them, consider how each perspective represents a different set of answers to the questions posed in this activity.

Perspective 1 (medical model): Adherents to the first perspective might describe the problems in terms of 'disorders', thereby locating them firmly within the child, as part of the child's psychological make-up. The emphasis of this approach is on describing symptoms, making a diagnosis and prescribing treatment, which might include drugs or psychotherapy offered to an individual child in the setting of a child and adolescent mental health department. This medical model dominated the field during the middle decades of the twentieth century, but was subsequently the subject of much criticism. It is not difficult to see why. Emotional and behavioural difficulties are not like medical conditions. In some cases, of course, there may be an underlying neurological problem, chromosomal abnormality or psychiatric disorder, but in many more cases there are no clear-cut organic causes. Even when a child is born with or develops an identifiable disorder, the expression of that disorder in emotional and behavioural difficulties is the product of developmental processes that take place in the context of social relationships, at home, at school and so on.

Perspective 2 (social environment model): The second perspective is wary of putting labels like 'disturbed' onto the child. The child's problems are thought more likely to reflect 'disturbed' patterns of parental care. Whereas in the medical model the child is the focus of explanation, in this social environment model the attention is on such issues as impoverished home circumstances, inadequate or abusive parental care, or a lack of discipline at school. Bowlby's theory of maternal deprivation is a good illustration of this perspective, which was highly influential in the 1950s in the construction of post-war social policy on the functions of the family, and especially the role of women, as mothers, in promoting children's mental health. The emphasis of intervention within this perspective would be on support and training for parents or on the placement of children in a therapeutic community in which a more stable social environment can be constructed to support their development. As a last resort, the emphasis of intervention within this perspective would focus on taking children into care.

In the sections that follow we shall argue that neither the medical model nor the social environment model can provide a satisfactory account of the development of disturbed behaviour on its own. While a narrow emphasis on psychological disorders solely within the child is in most cases inappropriate, explanations that single out particular features of the child's social environment can be equally misleading. Psychological development comprises a complex, continuous transaction between individual and social processes. This is as true of disturbed as it is of typical development. Simplistic attempts to attribute causes to either the 'child' or the 'environment' make little sense. The challenge is to understand the interrelationships between these sources of influence.

Activity 2   *Disturbed and disturbing behaviour*

Allow about 5 minutes

This activity will help you consider the meanings of the terms 'disturbed' and 'disturbing behaviour'.

Think about your own understanding of the source of children's difficulties. Is it about young children whose behaviour is being disturbed? Or is it about young children whose behaviour is disturbing to others? Could it be about both?

Comment

The phrase 'disturbed and disturbing behaviour' is deeply ambiguous, and intentionally so. It has multiple meanings which are difficult to hold simultaneously in mind. One reading suggests a compassionate view, that of the child as a victim whose behaviour is the product of external forces, perhaps inadequate or abusive parenting. But another reading reverses the perspective, producing an image of the child as the cause of the problem, someone whose difficult behaviour needs to be contained and modified. Each view reflects a different aspect of the relationship between children and their social world.

A major goal of this chapter is to highlight these multiple meanings of 'disturbed' and 'disturbing' through a consideration of relevant theory and research. We hope that by the time you reach the end of this chapter you will be able to offer a partial resolution to these ambiguities.

Summary of Section 1

- This chapter is about the concepts, causes and progress of disturbances in young children's emotional, social and behavioural development.
- Our perspective is that children with developmental difficulties are both disturbing to, as well as disturbed by, family, school and society.
- Children can be troublesome as well as troubled; disorderly as well as disordered.
- Attempts to attribute the cause of a problem to either 'the child' or their 'environment' are too simplistic. The challenge is to understand how different sources of influence interact.

2 Problem behaviour

In this section we shall look at some examples of attempts to measure the characteristics and prevalence of disturbed behaviour in young children. Our attention will be focused on the more common social, emotional and behavioural difficulties that have no obvious organic root. So we shall not be considering those generally quite severe conditions that are associated with recognized clinical disorders – such as chromosomal abnormalities, metabolic disorders or the autistic spectrum of disorders (Barker, 1995). We shall start with issues of diagnosis. What constitutes 'a problem'?

2.1 Everyday difficulties or problem behaviour?

In a leading textbook of clinical child psychology, Herbert argues that:

> Childhood signs of psychological abnormality are, by and large, manifestations of behavioural, cognitive and emotional responses common to all children. Their quality of being dysfunctional lies in their inappropriate intensity, frequency and persistence.

> (Herbert, 1991, p. 13)

In other words, whether a child's behaviour is identified as a problem becomes a judgement about where to draw the line between typical and atypical development and health and pathology. But the problems of assessment are more complicated than this. Expressions of difficulty are also inherently unstable, and are associated with developmental issues related to particular age groups, as the following activity will help make clear.

Activity 3

Allow about
10 minutes

Developmental stage or psychological disturbance?

This activity will highlight the importance of considering the role of age in behavioural difficulties.

Think about the following list of 'problems' of early childhood: first, as they might be described by the parents of a 1-year-old child; then as they might be described by the parents of a 5 year old. How might parental concerns and professional advice about the possibility of psychological disturbance be affected by consideration of the child's age?

> bed wetting;
>
> temper tantrums;
>
> night waking;
>
> clinging to parents.

Comment

Knowing a child's age is crucial to making judgements about the appropriateness of their behaviour. Take the example of 'clinging to parents'. The clinging 1-year-old child might be seen as a having a strong attachment whereas the 5 year old showing the same behaviour might be viewed as over-dependent. In other words, the criteria for emotional or behavioural disturbance need to take account of not only the severity of the difficulties presented by a child, but also the developmental expectations for that age group. The Kiddie Schedule for Affective Disorders and Schizophrenia (K-SADS), a semi-structured clinical interview commonly used in modern clinical practice for assessment of disturbing behaviour, specifies ages after which behaviour is deemed developmentally inappropriate (Ambrosini, 2000). For example, the section which assesses the presence of separation anxiety disorder includes a question which asks the parent 'has your child followed you around ... after the age of 4?'.

These complexities of assessment apply to all clinical work and especially to larger-scale research. Most assessments of childhood difficulties carried out within the context of research have been based on rating scales of children's behaviour completed by parents, teachers and/or clinicians. Two rating scales commonly used in modern clinical practice are the Strengths and Difficulties Questionnaire (SDQ) (Goodman, 1997) and the Child Behaviour Checklist (CBCL) (Achenbach, 1991), which was developed in America. The CBCL is a 113-item standardized rating scale for both parents and teachers. By way of illustration, eight items are reproduced in Table 1.

Table 1   **Extracts from the Child Behaviour Checklist**

STATEMENT	0	1	2
to be completed by **PARENTS**	Not true	Somewhat or sometimes true	Very true or often true
10 Can't sit still, restless or hyperactive			
21 Destroys things belonging to his/ her family or others			
22 Disobedient at home			
30 Fears going to school			
45 Nervous, high strung or tense			
48 Not liked by other kids			
82 Steals outside the home			
102 Underactive, slow moving, or lacks energy			

Source: © Achenbach, 1991.

The items in the scale have been found to reflect eight reasonably stable, broad dimensions of children's behavioural difficulties: withdrawn, somatic (bodily health) complaints, anxious/depressed, social problems, thought problems, attention problems, delinquent behaviour, and aggressive behaviour. They indicate how 'extreme' a child rates on each of the eight dimensions. These dimensions are often regarded as falling into two broad categories: 'internalizing' and 'externalizing' difficulties. The tendency is for the latter to be associated more with boys and the former more with girls. While recognizing that both types of difficulties are clearly significant for the children, families and others involved, this chapter is primarily concerned with 'externalizing' difficulties. Bearing in mind the concerns already raised about the complexities of identifying 'problems' and different ways of assessing them, we turn now to a consideration of how prevalent they are in different populations and how differences in prevalence may help us to understand the role of cultural and social factors.

Internalizing difficulties Emotional problems such as depression or anxiety.
Externalizing difficulties 'Acting-out' problems such as aggression or vandalism.

2.2 Issues of measurement

Activity 4

Allow about
10 minutes

Three studies of disturbed or disturbing behaviour

This activity will raise your awareness of different methods of assessment applied to disturbed behaviour.

We have briefly summarized below the findings of three major studies, two British and one from New Zealand, that have assessed the extent of disturbed development in children.

* What do you conclude about how widespread these problems are in the different countries?

* What difficulties are there in drawing conclusions from these studies?

Study 1: The Dunedin Multidisciplinary Health and Development Study

The Dunedin Multidisciplinary Health and Development Study is one of the biggest ongoing, longitudinal studies of development. The study is following the progress of a representative 1972 birth cohort of 1,000 New Zealand men and women from age 3 onwards. Its most positive strength is its minimal attrition rate – 96 per cent of the original sample took part in the assessments at age 26. This study reported that the prevalence of disorder in children aged 11 years old was 17.6 per cent (Anderson *et al.*, 1987; Arsenault *et al.*, 2000). Sex differences were reported, with a sex ratio of 1.7:1 (boys to girls).

Study 2: The National Child Development Study

The National Child Development Study followed the progress of a cohort of British children born in 1958. To date six follow-ups have been made with the most recent conducted in 2000 (age 42). Teacher assessments when the children were 7 years old indicated that 22 per cent were showing some symptoms of maladjustment and 14 per cent were considered to present serious problems. This study also found, in common with other research, that levels of maladjustment were higher in boys than girls and more common in children from lower-income families (Ferri, 1993).

Study 3: The British Child Mental Health Survey

In 1999, the Office for National Statistics carried out a survey of the mental health of British 5–15 year olds, who were recruited through child benefit records. This survey utilized a standardized diagnostic interview (Development and Well-Being Assessment), and questionnaire data from the SDQ referred to earlier. It was reported that approximately 10 per cent of children had clinically significant psychiatric impairments. The proportion of children with mental disorders was greater among boys (11 per cent) than girls (8 per cent) (Meltzer *et al.*, 2000).

Comment

These studies provide valuable information about the incidence of disturbed behaviour in children, especially because they draw attention to the variations in levels of difficulty associated with the age of the child, their gender and social background. However, statistics like these must be treated with extreme caution. There can be no direct comparison between the percentages reported in the three studies. Their methods of assessing problems were different, in terms of both the kinds of problems assessed and the source of the assessment (parents at home, teachers at school, psychologists at clinics and so on). For example, the Dunedin study seems to report a higher prevalence (17.6 per cent) than the British studies. On closer inspection however, it is apparent that differences in the way the studies have classified disorders has influenced these figures. The Dunedin study reports that pervasive disorders – reported by more than one source, for example, parent and teacher – had an overall prevalence of 7.3 per cent.

▲

Increasingly, clinicians and researchers are standardizing the assessment of emotional and behavioural problems, but while criteria may become dictated by convention, in the final analysis there is no universal standard for behaviour and social integration, nor any clear set of rules that define children with behavioural problems. To take the case of Achenbach's CBCL, the rating of items reflects the expectations that particular schools place on particular children at particular ages, not the behaviour of children in any absolute sense. In other words, children's behavioural disturbance is normatively defined, where normality comprises a wide variety of ways of functioning which fit within broad boundaries of social or moral acceptability for particular age groups. Children are said to present problems when their behaviour falls outside the range of tolerance and age-appropriateness. That range may be more or less wide depending both on the context and on the attitudes of those making such judgements. To put it bluntly, many children are only seen as having problems when they become a problem to others. So, whose problem is it? Where does the problem reside?

2.3 Context-embedded and normatively defined problems

One way of addressing the questions raised above is to compare the judgements of teachers, parents and others about what constitutes 'a problem'. You may know of cases in which children who have been reported as 'anxious' or 'playing-up' at school seem very different at home, or vice versa. Achenbach *et al.* (1987) collected and analysed the findings of more than 100 systematic studies of the way various parental and professional groups judge children's behavioural problems. From this procedure (technically known as meta-analysis) they concluded that there was only a very modest agreement between these groups. The average correlations were as follows:

$r = +.24$ between parents and mental health workers

$r = +.27$ between parents and teachers

$r = +.34$ between teachers and mental health workers

Furthermore, when the judgements of children's problems made by these adult groups were compared with children's own perceptions of their problems the correlations were even lower.

What do such low levels of agreement mean? One interpretation might be that this is a problem of reliability, that the assessment procedures used were insufficiently sensitive to identify problems clearly, or that the adults lacked sufficient information about the children concerned. This interpretation would point to the limitations of clinical assessment procedures that depend too heavily on a single informant's view. A comprehensive assessment clearly needs to take account of more than one perspective on behavioural problems. With regards to the SDQ, Goodman *et al.* (2000) reported that the predictive value of information provided by parents and teachers depends on the type of disorder. They also found that information from parents is more useful for detecting internalizing disorders while information from teachers is more useful for detecting externalizing disorders. The issue, however, is not simply about improving the reliability of identifying disorders in children. Achenbach *et al.* argue that low correlations highlight a very different interpretation of the issue: one which centres on the relationship between behaviour and social context. There are several respects in which problems can be seen as context-embedded and normatively defined:

- Different contexts offer different opportunities and place different demands on children, in terms of physical setting, social groupings, activities and routines. Children may behave differently in the context of home as opposed to school.
- Standards of behaviour expected of children vary. There are different rules, rituals and regulations, partly related to the age of the child. A child may cope in one situation but not in another.
- Those making the judgements may vary in their expectations of children's behaviour, their tolerance of difficulties and the effectiveness of their approach to maintaining discipline.
- Relationship patterns will differ in various contexts. The characteristics of the caregiver and the characteristics of the child may interact to produce harmony in one setting, but discord in another.

Each of the above factors may modify the expression and identification of disturbed behaviour. Difficulties arise when the behaviour and goals of the child lack 'goodness of fit' with the social environment to which the child is expected to adapt (Chess and Thomas, 1984). Goodness of fit does not apply at just one particular point in time. Each child brings to a given situation an internalized history of experiences, feelings and behaviours evoked by comparable situations in the past (for example, confronting an authority figure, coping with separation, integrating with a peer group). On each occasion there will have been greater or lesser degrees of goodness of fit. In short, any particular 'problems' that a child might present need to be understood in terms of the demands of the context, the history of similar experiences faced by the child, and the history of the adult who finds the child's behaviour disturbing.

These principles can also be illustrated from a broader cross-cultural perspective. Weisz *et al.* (1993) used a standardized behaviour checklist to compare parents' perception of 'problems' in their 11–15 year olds in Kenya, Thailand and the USA. They found that American parents often reported that their children were disobedient and argumentative, whereas Kenyan parents' concerns often centred on their children's fears and anxieties. Such variations can be interpreted in terms of some combination of variation in child behaviours and parental expectations between the two societies. Weisz *et al.* note that while American children grow up in a relatively more permissive and child-centred atmosphere, Kenyan child-rearing patterns are much more strict and controlling. Boys showed greater levels of externalizing behaviours in all three cultures, a surprising finding since Thai boys receive special training in Buddhist ideals of non-aggressiveness, humility and politeness.

Adopting a cross-cultural perspective has important implications for the clinical assessment of 'disturbed' behaviour. Behaviour that is adapted to one social or cultural context may be maladjusted in another. The concept of 'ecological adaptiveness' (Bronfenbrenner, 1979; Bronfenbrenner and Morris, 1998) recognizes that social adjustment solutions to the tasks of growing up may vary at cultural, sub-cultural and individual levels.

We can summarize the arguments so far in terms of the issues raised in Activity 1. For most emotional and behavioural difficulties there is no clear-cut boundary between health and pathology. The diagnosis of a 'problem' will depend on who is making that judgement and in what context. It will also depend crucially on issues to do with the age and maturity of the child, since some difficulties are linked to specific developmental issues. In summary, 'problems' are defined through the relationship between children, their social context and the beliefs of the adults who make the judgement.

Given these caveats, we turn next to look more closely at data on how many children appear to be affected by developmental problems, the extent to which these persist during their childhood and beyond, and the risk factors that appear to be involved.

2.4 Prevalence of developmental problems

The Dunedin Multidisciplinary Health and Development Study referred to earlier is one of the largest current longitudinal studies of development which reported that the overall prevalence of disorder in children aged 11 years was approximately 17 per cent (Anderson *et al.*, 1987). The most common were attention deficit disorders (problems in staying 'on-task'), conduct-oppositional disorders (defiance of requests and directions, confrontational and challenging behaviour) and separation anxiety disorders (distress and fear around separation). The least prevalent were depression and social phobia (fear of social interactions). Figures for the more common problems are summarized in Table 2. The final column of the table shows how many of these had been referred in the previous 2 years, thus indicating also what percentage had been referred earlier and were more long-term problems.

Table 2   **Incidence of behavioural disorders at age 1**

Group	Total number	Number of boys	Number of girls	Number of children referred between 9 and 11 years old (%)
Attention deficit disorder (ADD)	28	22	6	12 (43)
Conduct-oppositional	43	28	15	10 (23)
ADD+ conduct-oppositional	15	15	0	2 (13)
Anxious-phobic	36	10	26	8 (22)
Multiple	14	11	3	8 (57)
Total with disorder	136	86	50	40 (29)
No disorder	646	333	313	54 (8)

Source: Anderson et al, 1987.

Note the differences between girls and boys in the diagnosis of behavioural problems.

2.5 Continuity and stability of behaviour difficulties

A further important issue is the degree of stability in children's problems. Do children who are regarded as having behavioural or emotional dysfunction at the pre-adolescent stage have clear difficulties from early in development? Are such problems evident from the age children first started school or even earlier? After all, parents expressing concern are often greeted with the reassuring advice: 'Don't worry, it's only a phase – they'll grow out of it'.

Using data from the Dunedin sample, White *et al.* (1990) found that antisocial behaviour is stable from pre-school age to adolescence in some children in the sample and Bates *et al.* (2003) found that there was continuity of aggressive behaviours from early childhood through to adolescence. Boys were found to follow one of three paths: a majority of boys exhibit little to no physical aggression throughout childhood (53 per cent). A small group of boys (9 per cent) exhibit consistently high levels of physical aggression. The remainder (38 per cent) exhibit a low but constant level of physical aggression. Girls showed similar stability with regards to aggressive behaviour, although they followed one of two rather than three paths. The majority of the sample (57 per cent) showed little physical aggression over time, while the remaining 43 per cent engaged in a moderate level of physical aggression that declined gradually over time.

This suggests that conventional wisdom about children growing out of their problems does not apply so well to the most disturbing cases. A significant number of children in the Dunedin sample who showed high levels of physical aggression at age 6 were subsequently involved in delinquency in adolescence (Bates *et al.*, 2003), although this was more consistent for boys than girls. This suggests another way of approaching the question of whether behaviour difficulties are transient or enduring. The question now becomes whether there is continuity in a deeper sense, perhaps as problems expressed at one stage of development in one way become transmuted into later development and are expressed in a different way.

Many of the children in the Dunedin sample who were diagnosed with a disorder met criteria for several disorders. The overlap of disorders was examined in the Dunedin sample and it was found that the category with the fewest single disorders, representing the most overlapping category, was for depression. Only three of the fourteen children identified as depressed met criteria for depression only (Anderson *et al.*, 1987). The other type of problem that appears to cluster most with other problems is that of conduct and/or oppositional disorder.

2.6 Risk factors

It is now widely accepted that there are multiple risk factors associated with problem behaviour (Liu *et al.*, 1999). Five factors in particular have been emphasized in the literature.

1   Social background: data from the Dunedin study revealed that children who exhibited antisocial behaviour were more likely to come from families of low social status (Henry *et al.*, 1993).

2   Parental attitudes to the child: parental attitudes towards children have been found to be important predictors of children's behaviour. In the Dunedin sample, it was found that 'parental agreement on discipline', which was measured when children aged 5, was one of the most significant predictors of antisocial behaviour in adolescence (Henry *et al.*, 1993).

3   Mother's mental state: many studies have reported a relationship between maternal mental illness and children's mental health outcomes. For example, Oyserman *et al.* (2002) found that children whose mothers were rated as having more psychiatric symptoms had higher levels of anxiety and depressive symptoms when assessed as adolescents. Maternal mental illness influenced the mental health of adolescents even after other factors such as family context and parenting style were taken into account.

4   Father's behaviour: although historically there has been little focus on the role of paternal behaviour – and indeed the role of the father in general – there is now a growing body of evidence suggesting an important role of the father's behaviour in predicting children's problem behaviours. A recent study by Jaffee and colleagues (2003) reported that fathers' antisocial behaviours are associated with conduct problems in their children.

5   Marital relationship and interaction between maternal and paternal factors: these two risk factors are inextricably linked. It is well recognized that in

addition to parents independently shaping children's behaviour, the interaction of maternal and paternal factors can also influence children. The quality of parents' marital relationship can directly influence children's behaviour. Liu *et al.* (1999) found, in a Chinese sample, that poor marital relations of the parents was one of the most significant risk factors for the development of later behaviour problems in children. Indeed, children whose parents' marital relationship was classed as 'very poor' (assessed by a self-administered questionnaire) were twelve times more likely to develop behavioural difficulties. Data from the Dunedin sample showed that antisocial behaviour in adolescence (Henry *et al.*, 1993) was strongly associated with divorce and separation of parents. In addition, there is a second more indirect effect of parental behaviour on children which arises from the interaction of maternal and paternal factors. For example, Fagan and Barnett (2003) found that mothers may play a significant role in determining paternal involvement with their children. They found that some mothers restrict and exclude fathers from spending time with their children, which they called 'gatekeeping', based on these mothers' views of the fathers' competence as parents.

Activity 5   Risk factors in problem behaviour

Allow about
10 minutes

This activity will develop your ability to assess information and make judgements about how risk factors interact and contribute to problem behaviour.

Reflecting on the list of five risk factors above, consider carefully the processes through which social, marital and parenting variables might influence the development of behavioural disturbance.

Comment

You may have found that the research findings above offer considerable insight into the way social factors are associated with problem behaviour. But great caution needs to be exercised when drawing conclusions about the causal processes through which these factors might be operating. First, we do not have data for a comprehensive set of measures of social background and family process; other, unmeasured, variables might be more strongly associated with disturbance. Second, we are dealing with very different kinds of measure, from socio-economic indicators that are relatively far removed from the symptoms of behaviour problems to ratings of parental attitude that seem closely linked to parental judgements about problem behaviour. Third, these various measures are not statistically independent. For a complete picture we need to know about the interactions involved – for example, the interactions between marital disharmony and parental hostility. Fourth and most important, these are only associations; the patterns of causation are unclear. One of the most controversial and widely debated issues in developmental psychology is that of cause and effect – the extent to which parenting shapes children's behaviour (parent factors) and how factors related to the child, for example temperament, influence parental behaviour (child factors). It is for this reason associations are best described in terms of 'risk factors'.

For the rest of this chapter we shall be looking in more detail at some of the risk factors identified by these research studies. Our treatment of this major topic is necessarily selective, and is designed to stimulate your thinking about the complex range of pathways to disturbed behaviour. We shall be concentrating on research into parental attitudes, mothers' mental states, fathers' behaviours, parents' marital relationships and the interaction of maternal and paternal factors. In the next section we shall expand on the theme of the contribution that the young child's family and social environment can make to the development of difficulties, especially in the case of antisocial/externalizing disorders. Then, in Section 4, we shall turn to the question of what influence characteristics of the child might have on the development of these disorders.

Summary of Section 2

- The emphasis of this chapter is on psychological problems that do not appear to originate in recognized neurophysiological disorders.
- Rating scales are widely used to assess these kinds of disturbed behaviour, completed by parents, teachers and others.
- Precise classification of problems and measurements of their incidence are not straightforward. Problems are context-embedded and normatively defined.
- A major issue is how far problems are transient or enduring. This can be looked at in terms of the continuity and the clustering of problems.
- Risk factors associated with problem behaviour include (i) social background; (ii) parental attitudes to the child; (iii) mother's mental state; (iv) father's behaviour; (v) marital relationship and interactions between maternal and paternal factors.

3 Parents' roles in problem behaviour

We often hear comments in the media and everyday life such as 'I blame it on their parents' in relation to children who are misbehaving. There is an enduring cultural belief that the proper focus for an explanation of aberrant human behaviour lies within early childhood and the home environment, especially in the quality of parenting. This belief draws attention away from the role that children themselves might play in their problems (thereby reinforcing ideas of childhood innocence and perfection), and it also draws attention away from a collective social responsibility for the welfare of children (and their parents). Most importantly, this belief is not just a feature of a particular ideology; it has become a foundation stone for some psychological theories about the processes of typical and disturbed development.

In an influential article, Kessen (1979) examined the way modern Western faith in the objectivity of scientific psychology has been grafted onto cultural beliefs about child development that reflect a particular society and culture. Writing in the American context, he argued that two cultural beliefs, the importance of good mothering and the critical influence of early experiences on development, have been combined with a third belief, that mothers are responsible for their children's welfare, to produce a powerful weapon of social control.

> ... if a social problem is not repaired by modification of the child's first years, the problem is beyond repair. The working of the postulate has produced ways of blaming mothers that appear in all theoretical shapes.

(Kessen, 1979, p. 819)

Kessen is warning us to beware of ideologies that masquerade as psychological knowledge, a caution that it is important to bear in mind when considering research into links between mother–child relationships and the development of disturbed behaviour.

It is important to stress that we are not arguing that parental behaviour in and of itself causes emotional and behavioural problems in children. The causal process is altogether more complex than that. Indeed, one of the reasons for paying attention to mothers' behaviours, attitudes and mental states and fathers' antisocial behaviours is that it can provide a bridge to a discussion of other risk factors, including those associated with the child.

3.1 Maternal sensitivity

Many studies have suggested that disturbed/disturbing behaviour in children can be related to difficulties in the relationship with their mothers, which may reflect the mothers' mental states (Murray and Stein, 1991; Garver, 1997; Wakschlag and Hans, 1999; Halligan *et al.*, 2004). In particular, the concept of maternal sensitivity (Ainsworth, 1993) has been developed to describe an aspect of parenting that has been found in many studies to have strong associations with infants' formation of attachments (DeWolff and von IJzendoorn, 1997).

Figure 1   What is sensitive parenting?

Maternal sensitivity

To examine the effects of an aspect of maternal sensitivity, a study by Murray and Stein (1991) introduced a temporary experimental disruption to normal patterns of maternal behaviour and observed the impact on infants who were 1–2 months old. Mothers were invited to bring their infants to the laboratory and engage in face-to-face communication. Murray then studied the impact of three different conditions of disruption to communication:

Condition 1. During a period when the mother was actively involved with her infant, the experimenter distracted the mother by initiating a conversation so that the mother ceased to engage with her infant's communications.

Condition 2. The mother was asked to continue to face her infant, but remain still and adopt a blank, unresponsive facial expression.

Condition 3. By introducing a delay into a video-link, normal forms of maternal responsiveness were rendered out of phase with the infant's behaviour, so that the mother's expressions were no longer synchronized with the infant's.

There is an important distinction between disruptions which are a normal part of everyday communication ('natural perturbations', as in Condition 1) and those which violate the infant's expectations about relationships ('unnatural perturbations', as in Conditions 2 and 3). In Condition 1 infants typically quietened and watched the communication between mother and experimenter. Even though the mother changed her behaviour markedly, turned her face away from her infant and altered her speech patterns, the infants showed no distress. By contrast, in Condition 2 a blank expression typically provoked a strong reaction from the infants, who initially attempted to engage their mother's attention, frowning and thrashing their arms about, and later became passively self-absorbed. The mismatches of timing between infant initiatives and maternal responses in Condition 3 caused confusion in the infants, who typically made short darting glances at the mother's face before turning away, becoming avoidant, self-absorbed and often distressed.

Although this set of findings clearly shows that maternal responsiveness is important to infants, the concept of maternal sensitivity has been criticized by researchers as being too general and not specified clearly enough (Meins *et al.*, 2001; Raval *et al.*, 2001). Meins has pointed in particular to an important component of sensitivity being mothers' 'mind-mindedness' – a capacity to understand what might be in the infant's mind – and has shown that this is indeed associated with attachment (Meins *et al.*, 2002).

Outside the laboratory, mothers' sensitive responding to their infants can be affected by several factors. One in particular, postnatal depression, has received a substantial amount of research attention. In a longitudinal study of a large number of women and their infants, Murray (1992) found that 18-month-old infants whose mothers had earlier suffered bouts of postnatal depression were much more likely to be assessed as 'insecurely attached' in the 'Strange Situation'. This effect was particularly evident for the boys in the sample. Insecure attachment has been consistently linked with psychological difficulties (Greenberg *et al.*, 1993; Sund and Wichstrom, 2002).

Murray also found that the children of depressed mothers were more often reported to have temper tantrums, eating difficulties, to suffer sleep disturbance and to be overly clinging, suggesting the possibility that infant temperament may also be causing problems.

A feature of Murray's research is that it points to the processes through which mothers' mental states may be influencing their infant's development. Murray video-taped interactions between a sub-sample of mothers and infants throughout the 18-month period. Analyses of maternal speech during play with children at 2 months of age showed that depressed mothers were less responsive to their infants. Also, their speech more often reflected the personal experiences with which they were preoccupied than it reflected their infant's needs and they were more likely to show hostility to their infant's behaviour (Murray and Stein, 1991).

However, researchers in this area do not generally believe that there is a simple causal relationship between depression, responsiveness and child disturbance. Not all depressed mothers develop difficulties in their relationships with their offspring (Cox *et al.*, 1987). Furthermore, in America, Zahn-Waxler *et al.* (1990) found that some depressed mothers appeared able to maintain a responsive style of care towards their child despite their preoccupations.

For a fuller picture, maternal depression needs to be understood as part of a network of risk factors impinging on the developmental process. For example,

Cox *et al.* (1987) reaffirm the central significance of a mother's wider relationship difficulties for her mental state and her relationship with her children. Depression is strongly associated with marital disharmony and a long history of attachment problems. A much higher percentage of the depressed women in Cox's sample reported that they themselves had experienced poor relationships with their own parents, with less warmth and harsher discipline, as well as a high incidence of separations and disruptions, and more emotional and schooling difficulties as children. They also reported having married younger, having had their first child younger than mothers in the control group, and they perceived marital disharmony as a major cause of their depression. Once these wider sets of variables are taken into account, the inappropriateness of thinking in terms of maternal mental state (or any other single variable) as a sole cause of disturbed behaviour becomes apparent. Indeed, an alternative view would be that the mother's depression, the child's disturbance and the difficulties in their relationship are all the effects of deeper, longer-standing problems of social stress and family discord.

The network of factors associated with maternal depression represents only one pathway to disturbed behaviour, albeit a pathway which can be associated with the development of insecure attachments in infancy and may result in longer-term relationship and behaviour difficulties. A second pathway, which has been most extensively elaborated by Patterson (1982, 1986), traces the origins of antisocial behaviour to harsh and inconsistent discipline, and ineffective parental control strategies which unwittingly reinforce the child's negative, coercive behaviour.

3.2 Mothers' attitudes

In our discussion of maternal sensitivity we mainly concentrated on behaviour in disturbed relationships. But the parties to a relationship are not just behaving towards each other. They are thinking about each other. In the terminology of attachment theory (as discussed in Chapter 1), each has an internal working model of the relationship. In other words, the cognitive as well as the social and emotional dimensions of the relationship need to be taken into account. This is especially true of the mother, who may be trying to make sense of her child's behaviour, as well as reflecting on her sense of adequacy as a mother. The child is also beginning to construct expectations of his or her caregiver's behaviour and attitude (Stern-Bruschweiler and Stern, 1989). For example, a large-scale Australian longitudinal study (Bor *et al.*, 2003) found that mothers who had negative attitudes towards their infants at 6 months old were more likely to report behaviour problems when their children were 5 years old, especially for boys. The following example sheds further light on how this sort of process might be operating.

RESEARCH SUMMARY 2

The significance of parents' attitudes to their children's behaviour

Dadds and colleagues (2003) investigated parental attributions about the causes of their children's behaviour in 'abuse-risk' parents (selected on the basis of risk of child abuse and referral to a clinic for assistance with management of difficult behaviour of their child) and a 'non-clinic' group who had no significant parenting problems or problem behaviour in their children. The children of the parents in both groups were aged between 2 and 6 years. The research focused on the mothers' beliefs about the causes of their children's difficult behaviour.

The main findings were based on observations of two sets of video clips. The first set was of the behaviour of each parent interacting with their own child. This was based on a 15-minute semi-structured interaction where the mothers were instructed by the researchers to interact with their child on three tasks:

1   free play;
2   directing the child through the completion of a puzzle; and
3   instructing the child to help her to clean and tidy up the toys in the room.

Dadds and colleagues found that the abuse-risk mothers attributed the positive behaviour of their own child more to external causes than did the non-clinic mothers.

The second set of video clips involved eight 1-minute scenarios of an unfamiliar 3-year-old girl in her home and showed clearly negative, positive and ambiguous behaviour. The girl was from a family who had presented for help with managing her behaviour. The abuse-risk mothers rated the child's behaviour as significantly more negative across all scenarios. Even for the positive scenarios which showed the child happily playing with her mother, the abuse-risk mothers judged the child to show some signs of naughty behaviour. The abuse-risk mothers attributed more negative behaviour to factors internal to the child when viewing both their own child and the unfamiliar child. This finding supports past research which has suggested that high abuse-risk mothers and mothers of children who show problem behaviours tend to view negative child behaviour as arising from child characteristics while positive child behaviour is perceived as a result of situational influences (Stratton and Swaffer, 1988).

Research with high-risk groups thus shows how negative maternal beliefs about a child may feed into a vicious circle of perceptions, behaviours and responses. However, there is a limitation to this research, namely that it focuses on only one party to the relationship, the adult.

For a complete account, we also need to consider the contribution of the child's beliefs about and perceptions of the mother. American research by MacKinnon-Lewis *et al.* (1992) illustrates this point very clearly and builds on the model of pathways to antisocial behaviour elaborated by Patterson (1982). In this model, weak parenting skills are believed to encourage the child to become non-compliant to parental requests and to make unreasonable (coercive) demands on parents and other members of the family. The growing negative attention given to the child's inappropriate behaviours combines with a failure to reward positive behaviours to produce an escalating cycle of parent–child conflict.

MacKinnon-Lewis *et al.* extended Patterson's analysis beyond the behavioural to the cognitive and emotional aspects of relationships. They studied 104 mother–son pairs. First, the boys (aged 7–9 years) were interviewed individually on a standardized procedure designed to elicit their beliefs about their mother's intentions and reactions in potential conflict or discipline situations. They were told a series of stories about a boy (with whom they were invited to identify) and his mother. In each case, the boy behaved in a way that might be construed by a parent as 'naughty'. The mother's disciplinary response was left ambiguous, and the child was invited to give his interpretation of the mother's actions, his understanding of her intentions and his likely response to them. The child's response to each story was then scored on a five-point scale of perceived maternal attitude (ranging from hostile to positive). Second, mothers were interviewed about their response to a series of equivalent hypothetical stories in which the child's behaviour was ambiguous, but could be construed as provocative. Mothers were asked about the boy's intentions, and again these were scored on a scale of perceived child attitude (from hostile to positive).

Mother–son interactions were then video-recorded during 20-minute sessions in which they were invited to play two games: one highly competitive; the second demanding close co-operation. These interactions were later analysed in terms of the frequency of positive, negative and neutral behaviours by mother and son. It was found that there was a strong association between mothers' and sons' perceptions of each other's hostile intent. These perceptions were also closely linked to the negativity of their behaviours towards each other. In other words, the aggressive interactions between mothers and sons were being sustained, at least in part, by mutual, negative, affective interpretations of each other's behaviour. Most significantly, children's beliefs about their mother's hostility appeared to be influential, over and above their actual hostility, in fuelling children's negative behaviour. Having said that, this research still leaves many questions unanswered about the interrelationships between cognition, feelings and behaviour in the genesis of disturbed relationships between parents and their children.

3.3 The role of fathers

Historically, researchers have focused almost exclusively on mothers when examining family influences on children's behaviour. Over the last decade or so a number of studies have examined the role of fathers. A study conducted in the United States by the National Institute of Child Health and Development (NICHD) Early Child Care Research Network (NICHD, 2000) found that paternal caregiving activities were predicted by a number of factors (see Research summary 3).

RESEARCH SUMMARY 3

The role of fathers in caregiving

A NICHD study reported that fathers' caregiving activities are predicted by factors associated with the father, the marital relationship of the parents, and the child.

Fathers: fathers' child-rearing beliefs, working hours, personality and age predicted fathers' caregiving activities. Fathers were more likely to assume caregiving responsibilities if they had more positive personalities and were younger. They also assumed more caregiving responsibilities when they contributed lower proportions of family income and were employed for fewer hours.

Mothers: mothers' working hours and age predicted fathers' caregiving activities. Fathers were more involved in caregiving activities when mothers were employed for more hours and were younger.

Marital relationships: marital intimacy predicted father's caregiving activities with fathers more involved in caregiving activities when mothers reported more intimate marriages.

Children: the age and gender of children predicted fathers' caregiving activities. Fathers increased the level of their caregiving responsibilities between the 6th and 15th months of their children's development and this was relatively stable thereafter. Fathers assumed more caregiving responsibilities for sons than for daughters.

The NICHD study conducted further analyses to identify which factors would predict fathers' sensitivity during play. Both socio-demographic and fathers' characteristics were found to predict paternal sensitivity. Fathers who were older, who endorsed less traditional child-rearing beliefs, and who reported more marital intimacy were more sensitive during the play interactions. Paternal sensitivity was also higher in households in which family income was lower. Paternal sensitivity did not appear to be predicted by maternal sensitivity.

Much of the research which has explored fathers' roles in shaping children's behaviour has focused on the relationship between antisocial behaviour in fathers and children's development. There is now strong evidence that there is a significant relationship between the two (DeKlyen et al., 1998; Margolin and Gordis, 2000; Jaffee et al., 2003). The link between high levels of antisocial behaviour in fathers and children's behavioural difficulties may be mediated by a range of family problems including social and economic disadvantage (Fergusson et al., 1995), violence (Margolin and Gordis, 2000), and alcohol and drug problems (Fergusson and Horwood, 1999).

Absence or low involvement of the father has been shown to be associated with poor outcomes for children (Scott, 1998; Carlson and Corcoran, 2001). In a series of studies, Flouri and Buchanan (2002, 2003) used the British National Child Development Study sample to look at the relationship between father involvement at age 7 and children's mental health and delinquency at age 16. They reported that father involvement at age 7 protected against psychological maladjustment in adolescents from disrupted families (Flouri and Buchanan, 2003). Specific gender differences were reported in both studies. For boys early father involvement protected against later delinquency as measured by the child's history of trouble with the police (Flouri and Buchanan, 2002), and, for girls, father involvement at age 16 protected against subsequent psychological distress (Flouri and Buchanan, 2003). No evidence was found to suggest that such impact of father involvement varied with the level of maternal involvement. Lamb (1997) suggests that negative outcomes arising from absent fathers may be a result of the remaining parent (most often the mother) receiving little social support, pre- and post-divorce marital conflict, and perceptions of abandonment by children. However, the relationship between a father's absence and difficult behaviours in their children may be more complex as explored in Research summary 4.

RESEARCH SUMMARY 4

The effect of a father's absence

Jafee et al. (2003) conducted a study with 1,116 twin pairs of 5 years of age and their parents who were enrolled in the Environmental Risk Longitudinal Twin Study in England and Wales. Their results suggest that a father's absence might actually be favourable if he himself is showing antisocial behaviours. They found that children whose fathers engaged in very high levels of antisocial behaviour and lived with them had significantly greater behavioural problems than children whose fathers had similar levels of antisocial behaviour but did not live at home. The researchers describe the first group as experiencing a double dose of risk for antisocial behaviour. Their results suggest that the quality of fathers' involvement with their children is of high significance for children's development. Many studies have focused only on the amount of father involvement, neglecting the quality of the relationship.

It is important to reaffirm that there are multiple pathways to disturbed behaviour and that maternal and paternal behaviour represent just two among a constellation of social context, family and parental risk factors that have been found to be associated with childhood difficulties. While it is important to recognize the importance of the role of parenting on children's adjustment, we also need to take account of the role of the child in the process. In the final section we will look at how family and parenting variables can interact with the characteristics of the child, and at how, through the way they shape their environment, children can be the 'producers of their own development' (Lerner and Busch-Rossnagel, 1981).

Summary of Section 3

- Much psychological research and theory has been linked to wider cultural beliefs in the responsibility of parents, especially mothers, for child development.
- Experimental studies of disrupted maternal sensitivity illustrate the potential impact of maternal depression on child development.
- Maternal depression can be associated with insecure attachment and early indicators of behavioural difficulties; it can also contribute to a cycle of disturbed relationships.
- Parents and their children develop internal working models, sets of beliefs about each other's actions and intentions, and about their relationship, which can itself feed the growth of disturbed and disturbing behaviour.
- Paternal antisocial behaviour is now known to be associated with children's behavioural difficulties.

4   Children's roles in problem behaviour

4.1   Directions of effect in human processes

Beliefs about the family and parenting as the cause of aberrant child behaviour reflect a 'social environment' perspective, in which the child is seen as the passive victim of circumstances. This perspective also shapes the design of research which has traditionally set out to address questions about the effects of environmental variables on children's development and adjustment.

For some years now scepticism has been growing about the validity of this way of asking questions about cause and effect in children's development. One of the first challengers to convention was Bell (1968), who took the example of a classic study by Sears *et al.* (1957) into the links between parental style and aggressive behaviour in children. Sears *et al.* had reported a close association between these variables. Parents of aggressive children were found to use punitive discipline strategies, but at the same time they also tended to be permissive. By contrast, the parents of non-aggressive children were much less punitive in their discipline, but they had higher expectations of their children's behaviour. How would you interpret these results?

In their report, Sears *et al.* offered a 'social environment' interpretation, arguing that it was the combination of parents' permissiveness and punitiveness that caused their children to become aggressive. This seems plausible enough. After all, a highly permissive style means that children lack clear guidance on appropriate behaviour, and a highly punitive style means that, at the same time, they may have been frustrated by bouts of severe punishment. Bell (1968) offered a very different interpretation. He argued persuasively for reversing the direction of effect, claiming that it was the child's temperamental characteristics that determined how aggressive he or she was, and that parental discipline strategies were an attempt to modify the child's behaviour. So those parents with difficult youngsters got tough with them, while those with compliant offspring had no need to resort to severe methods. More recent research lends support to Bell's focus on the role of the child in influencing parental behaviours (Rutter *et al.*, 1997).

Activity 6   *Reversing the direction of effect*

Allow about
10 minutes

This activity will encourage you to think about the significance of directions of effect in interpreting research findings.

Look back over research summaries 2–4 in Section 3. Might the concept of 'direction of effect' suggest a different interpretation of the evidence on the relationship between the mental state and attitudes of mothers and the disturbed behaviour of children?

Comment

While at first one might expect that in these studies mothers' mental states may be influencing their child's behaviour, it is also plausible that the children's disturbing behaviour may have had a negative effect on their mothers' mental states.

A striking example of unexpected directions of effect is provided in a research study conducted in the USA. Johnston *et al.* (2002) identified a group of boys aged between 7 and 10 years old with problems of restlessness, impulsivity and short attention span. They were video-taped interacting with their mothers in a laboratory playroom with a standardized set of four episodes:

- 4-minute mother–child free play period;
- 3-minute 'parent busy' period where the mother completed questionnaires while their sons sat in a chair;
- a paper-and-pencil period where the mothers instructed their sons to work on either a mathematics or handwriting task;
- a 'clean-up' period where mothers had their sons tidy the materials.

Coders rated the maternal behaviour along seven dimensions: authoritative control, sensitivity of control, responsiveness, positive affect, acceptance of the child, involvement with the child, and no control. Child conduct problems were found to be uniquely and negatively related to maternal responsiveness. Think about how would you explain this association between maternal style and child behaviour? To what extent do you think the negative interactions originate in the mothers' behaviour and attitude?

In summarizing Johnston *et al.*'s study we omitted one piece of information. The 'problem' children had been selected for study because their behaviour over the preceding 12 months met criteria for a clinical diagnosis of 'attention deficit hyperactivity disorder' (ADHD). How does this label alter your view of cause and effect in Johnston's data? By labelling the problem 'ADHD' our attention is redirected to the children's behaviour as 'the cause' of the problem. Another study conducted by Johnston's research group may help us disentangle cause and effect.

In a second study Johnston *et al.* (2000) evaluated the short-term therapeutic potential of the drug Ritalin (Methylphenidate), a stimulant which is commonly prescribed for ADHD (although not without controversy). In children it has the effect of reducing motor activity and improving attention and concentration. Fifty-five children aged between 5 and 15 (and diagnosed as having ADHD) who were already or beginning to take stimulant medication took part in the study. Parents were interviewed twice, and at the first interview were asked to reflect on the child's unmedicated behaviour and at the second interview were asked to reflect on their medicated behaviour. Mothers had different attributions for their children's positive and negative behaviours. Positive social behaviours that occurred when the child was medicated were attributed as being more internal to the child, and more stable than when the child was not medicated. When children were taking medication their mothers gave more positive reactions to their children's positive child behaviours. In contrast, negative problem behaviours when the child was medicated were attributed as less internal to the child, and less stable, than when the child was not medicated. Importantly, mothers reacted less negatively to problem behaviours which occurred when the child was medicated. Clearly, medication not only influenced the child's positive and negative behaviours but also their mother's reactions to this behaviour.

Johnston *et al.*'s research illustrates the dangers of presuming particular directions of causality. In our earlier discussion of environmental risk factors, there was an implicit assumption that these variables were in some sense causing the child's problems. Yet there may be situations where characteristics of the child contribute to family stress, changing parental attitudes and shaping maternal behaviour.

This argument must not be taken too far. The issue is not about whether the direction of effect runs from child to mother or from mother to child; it is about their mutual influence as partners in a relationship. In short, children as well as parents play an active role in the process of development; interactive patterns of influence will apply in all cases. The relative influence of parenting behaviour versus child behaviour will vary, according to the characteristics of the child, the characteristics of the parent and the circumstances affecting both. Their influence may shift as child, parent and circumstances change. Problems may be amplified by new stresses or attenuated by effective intervention and support.

4.2 A transactional model

The picture of how difficult behaviour develops has much in common with a transactional model as elaborated by Sameroff (1991, 1997) and Sameroff and Fiese (2000).

Figure 2   A transactional model (adapted from Sameroff, 1991).

Figure 2 depicts the interrelationship of child and environment over several time intervals. The child is represented by the symbol 'C', their social environment by the symbol 'E'. The young child is actively relating to the environment and being acted upon by the environment, which includes major caregivers. Interactions at time 1 not only modify the way the child behaves at time 2, they also modify the environment for subsequent development. So difficult behaviour at time 1 will modify the way a parent or teacher treats the child at time 2. Transactional processes do not just affect the child in terms of the quality of their interactions; they can also result in a more fundamental change in their environment – for example, in extreme cases, by being excluded from school, taken into care, or referred to special education. The emerging configuration at time 2 will in turn shape child/environment relationships at time 3, and so on.

Activity 7

Allow about 10 minutes

Applying a transactional model

This activity will provide you with experience of applying a transactional model to a particular situation.

Think about the notion of a transactional model in relation to the theme of this chapter, 'What causes disturbed behaviour?'. Alternatively, try applying it to another aspect of development that interests you – for example, achievement in school, or the development of a skill of some kind. In each case, think about the way influences on a child at one point in time can be understood in a longer-term transactional perspective, and make brief notes.

Sameroff (1991) provides the following example:

A complicated childbirth may have made an otherwise calm mother somewhat anxious. The mother's anxiety during the first months of the child's life may have caused her to be uncertain and inappropriate in her interactions with the child. In response to such inconsistency the infant may have developed some irregularities in feeding and sleeping patterns that give the appearance of a difficult temperament. This difficult temperament decreases the pleasure that the mother obtains from the child and so she tends to spend less time with the child. If there are no adults interacting with the child, and especially speaking to the child, the child may not meet the norms for language development and score poorly on pre-school language tests. In this case the outcome was not determined by the complicated birth nor by the mother's consequent emotional response. If one needed to pick a cause it would be the mother's avoidance of the child, yet one can see that such a view would be a gross oversimplification of a complex developmental sequence.

(Sameroff, 1991, p. 174)

With this framework in mind let us turn to other research that has examined the child's role in transactional processes. The children with ADHD in Johnston *et al.*'s research served as an extreme example of the way a specific behavioural disorder can shape the character of the child's interactions with the environment. Other clinically identified disorders, for example, autism, epilepsy or other syndromes and inherited disorders, place caregivers under different adaptive pressures. But many children who develop disturbing behaviour do not suffer from a readily identifiable pathology. Insofar as children influence the course of their own development, this must happen through the impact on caregivers of more subtle individual characteristics, notably their temperament.

4.3 The influence of temperament

The significance of temperament in accounting for individual differences is controversial (Oates and Stevenson, 2005). Quite strong associations have been found between a 'difficult' temperament at 4 or 5 years of age and behavioural difficulties in later childhood – indeed, it is unclear where the line should be drawn between a 'difficult temperament' and 'behaviour disorder' (Chess and Thomas, 1984; Maziade *et al.*, 1989). Findings from The Dunedin Multidisciplinary Health and Development Study, for example, showed that only temperament discriminated between those participants who had committed a violent offence and those that had committed a non-violent offence (Henry *et al.*, 1996). The weight of evidence, however, suggests that a 'difficult' or 'irritable' temperament is best thought of as another risk factor. Vulnerability to relationship difficulties affects boys especially, who (as you have seen in Section 2) are much more likely than girls in Western society to become identified as presenting difficulties during the pre-school years. The evidence points to an underlying bi-directionality and reciprocity between parenting and children's temperament (Gallagher, 2002). Kochanska (1995, 1997) highlighted how maternal behaviour and children's temperament may intricately interact. She reported that fearful, inhibited children were more compliant when gentle low-power discipline was used whereas in fearless children the role of attachment was more significant in determining compliance. Whether a 'difficult' infant becomes a disturbed child appears to depend on the appropriateness of environmental adaptations to that temperament. As noted in Section 2, Chess and Thomas introduced the concept of 'goodness of fit' to describe the transactional relationship between child and environment. As they state, 'goodness-of-fit results when the child's capacities, motivations and temperament are adequate to master the demands, expectations and opportunities of the environment' (Chess and Thomas, 1984, p. 380). However, as Gallagher (2002) argues, joint effects of parenting and temperament are not simply examples of organism–environment interaction; parenting is intrinsically bi-directional and reciprocal.

Figure 3 is an illustration of how child characteristics can interact with environmental features in producing disturbed behaviour.

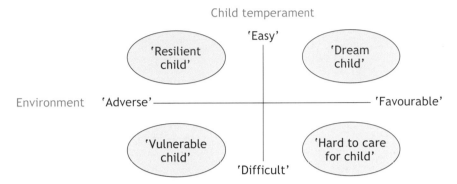

Figure 3   The interaction of child and environmental variables.

In this model difficult temperament is a risk factor, but its impact depends on the caring qualities of the family environment in which the child is growing. Conversely, the relative impact of adverse family experiences depends on the child's ability to adapt and cope with difficulties. This is, of course, a gross over-simplification. Child 'temperament' and 'environment' are not single, bipolar variables, nor are they static in time. Nonetheless, this model indicates the strength of a transactional perspective.

4.4 Protective factors

So far, we have concentrated on risk factors. For a complete picture we also need to consider the factors which may help to protect children from developing disturbed behaviour problems. While some children are, or become vulnerable to disorders, other children who present a slightly different picture of temperament and adversities may be more resilient, suggesting that there may be protective factors that mediate risk factors. To illustrate this theme, we can turn to the issue of intelligence. While the relationship between maternal psychopathology and disturbed behaviour in children is well documented it is also clear that not all children exposed to such risks show disturbed behaviour. Tiet *et al.* (2001) have carried out a series of studies into why some children who are at high risk of maladjustment nevertheless manage to adjust well. They have found that higher IQ protects children whose mothers are psychologically disturbed, suggesting that children with higher IQ may be better able to cope with adverse life events or may be more able to find alternative solutions to problems they encounter. Another study has reported a gender difference in the mediating impact of IQ. Flouri and Buchanan (2002) found that for boys higher IQ protected against later criminality.

The interplay between risk and protective factors is not static. It needs to be understood within a developmental perspective in which children are susceptible to different patterns of influence at different stages and transition points in life. For example, going to nursery or school is often an important gateway through which the 'disturbed' status of a troublesome child becomes confirmed. The particular demands, pressures and expectations for 'good' classroom behaviour (Klein and Ballantine, 1988) often amplify a child's problems of social integration, because of the increased demands on the child to adapt.

A new generation of research is now dedicated to teasing out the interaction of risk factors in longitudinal perspective, guided by concepts such as vulnerability, resilience, protective mechanisms, gateways and amplification (Robins and Rutter, 1990; Rutter and Casaer, 1991; Tiet *et al.*, 2001). Finally in this chapter, we would like to explore some of these themes through research that has traced the interrelationship of temperament with other variables, notably attachment and parental responsiveness, in the generation of disturbance.

4.5 Temperament, attachment, maternal support and difficult behaviour

As you know from Chapter 1, attachment to one or a small number of consistent caregivers is generally recognized as a prerequisite of social adjustment. As was noted in Section 3 of this chapter, insecure attachment is associated with depressed maternal mental state and can be predictive of problem behaviour.

Conventional interpretations of the causes of insecure attachment generally refer to the mother's unavailability, insensitivity or lack of reciprocity. However, there have been some attempts to disentangle the infant's contribution to the process. A study by Waters *et al.* (1980) assessed 100 newborn infants using a neonatal paediatric screening procedure, and followed this up a year later with Ainsworth's Strange Situation procedure (Ainsworth *et al.*, 1978). Those 1 year olds classified as insecurely attached were found to have shown signs of 'irritability' as newborns (in terms of responsiveness, motor immaturity and physiological regulation).

Crockenburg (1981) took the same basic design, as Waters *et al.* but extended it to show how characteristics of the infant interact with qualities of the environment in the production of relationship difficulties. Forty-eight mothers and their infants took part in this study, which involved four sets of measurements:

1   A paediatric assessment made shortly after birth, on which basis the sample was broadly divided into two groups: high irritability and low irritability.
2   Home observations of the way mothers responded to their infant's distress signals, which led to them being classified as high responsive or low responsive.
3   Mother's perceptions of the extent of social support, in relation to stress, given to them by family, neighbours, friends, etc.
4   Security of attachment on the Strange Situation procedure at 1 year of age.

Table 3   Frequency of securely and insecurely attached infants in social support/ irritability sub-groups

Attachment	High irritability		Low irritability	
	Low Support	High Support	Low Support	High Support
Securely attached	2	12	7	13
Insecurely attached	9	1	2	2

Source: adapted from Crockenburg, 1981, p. 862.

Crockenburg's first finding was that the more irritable (that is, vulnerable) infants were less likely to attract responsive care from their mothers, and were in turn more likely to show insecure attachments. But, as Table 3 shows, the impact of irritability was strongly affected by the degree of social support perceived by the mother. This effect did not apply to the low irritability group who were generally securely attached irrespective of support to the mother (that is, they were resilient). In the high irritability group, vulnerability to insecure attachment appears to have been moderated by maternal support, which can be seen as a 'protective factor' for vulnerable infants.

4.6 Multiple pathways in developmental disorders

In this chapter we have looked at some of the pathways to disturbed behaviour that have received attention in recent research. We have concentrated on variables relating to social circumstances, marital relationships, maternal depression, paternal behaviour, parental attitudes and child temperament, as these affect the quality of parent–child relationships in the early years. We have argued against a deterministic view and instead favour a more dynamic, transactional model which acknowledges that problem behaviour is the product of a relationship history between children and their caregivers to which both actively contribute at the level of behaviour, beliefs and feelings. But this is still far from a complete picture, in two key respects.

First, it is arguable that current research is still over-emphasizing the significance of the mother–child relationship at the expense of other relationships. To address this issue, we have referred to some research on fathers' roles and have also emphasized the role of wider relationship difficulties. For example, discord between parents can have serious repercussions for the child. Indeed, Hinde and Stevenson-Hinde (1988) have cogently argued that it is these complex systems of relationships within families, rather than merely the development of children, that should be the starting point for research.

Second, you should not be misled into assuming that, because a child presents social and emotional problems, those problems necessarily originate in a disturbance in their social and emotional development. There are other, quite different, pathways that can feed into the process of becoming disturbed. For example, language disorders are often closely linked to behavioural difficulties (Rutter and Casaer, 1991).

4.7 Gender: a recurring theme

Before concluding this chapter, we would like to highlight a recurrent theme throughout this chapter – gender differences. In several places we have noted risk factors that are greater for boys than girls. Biological and environmental factors may account for the heightened risk for boys of the development of disturbing behaviour, and, like other examples of risk we have discussed throughout this chapter, the transactional approach can contribute to an explanation. A child's gender may interact with parental attitudes and/or behaviour. Berg-Nielsen *et al.* (2003) found that effects of low paternal involvement were heightened for boys. Fathers' lack of contact was also found to be highly associated with anger in their sons. It is likely that socio-cultural effects may also play a role in contributing to such gender differences. Differential expectations of boys and girls may be heightening the risks for the development of specific disturbing behaviours, such as 'externalising' behaviour in boys. As we noted earlier in this chapter, difficulties experienced by girls tend to be expressed more as 'internalizing' problems. While this chapter has given these rather less attention, it is important not to underestimate their significance for children, their families and society.

Summary of Section 4

- Conventional beliefs about the impact of parenting on the child have been modified by re-analyses of directions of effect.
- Studies of the effects of drug therapy on mother–child interaction in children with attention deficit hyperactivity disorder (ADHD) illustrate the potential impact of child variables on the development of disturbed behaviour.
- A transactional model best encapsulates the processes involved in the development of children's psychological difficulties, illustrated by the interaction between infant temperament and environmental support, in terms of 'goodness of fit'.
- The concepts of vulnerability, resilience, protective mechanisms, gateways and amplification have been applied to research into the mutual influence of temperament, maternal responsibility and social support on the security of attachment.
- Gender is a key variable in the study of typical and disturbed development.

5   Conclusion

As we come to the end of this chapter we hope that some of the issues of causality in the study of disturbed and disturbing behaviour have become clearer. Explanations which focus on linear causes, either in the child's social environment or in their own make-up, are a gross over-simplification. Interaction involving a number of risk factors is always the rule. The child is disturbing to others at the same time as they are being and feeling disturbed. Disturbed behaviour is best understood as a spectrum of patterns of troubled and troubling development. At one end of the spectrum the problems may be strongly linked to developmental disorders or a difficult temperament which place extraordinary pressures on even the most well-resourced and well-prepared parents. In the middle of the spectrum is the majority of cases, where there may be a mild developmental issue or irritable temperament, but where behaviour problems and relationship difficulties are also strongly shaped by family factors (discord, maternal depression, negative attitudes, paternal behaviour). These in turn may be amplified by stresses in the social environment (inadequate family support, housing, poverty and lack of access to public services). At the extreme end of spectrum are cases where gross deprivation, neglect, distorted patterns of care or abuse create an adverse environment in which even the most resilient child develops disturbed patterns of adaptation.

References

Achenbach, T.M. (1991) *Manual for the Child Behaviour Checklist 4–18 and 1991 Profile*, Burlington, University of Vermont, Department of Psychiatry.

Achenbach, T. M., McConaughy, S. H. and Howell, C. T. (1987) 'Child adolescent behavioral problems: implications of cross-informant correlations for situational specificity', *Psychological Bulletin*, vol. 102, pp. 213–32.

Ainsworth, M. S. (1993) 'Attachment as related to mother-infant interaction', *Advances in Infancy Research*, vol. 8, pp. 1–50.

Ainsworth, M. D. S., Blehar, M. C., Waters, E. and Wall, S. (1978) *Patterns of Attachment*, Hillsdale, NJ, Lawrence Erlbaum.

Ambrosini, P. J. (2000) 'Historical development and present status of the schedule for affective disorders and schizophrenia for school-age children (K-SADS)', *Journal of the American Academy of Child and Adolescent Psychiatry*, vol. 39, pp. 49–58.

Anderson, J. C., Williams, S., McGee, R. and Silva, P. A. (1987) 'DSM-II Disorders in preadolescent children: prevalence in a large sample from the general population', *Archives of General Psychiatry*, vol. 44, pp. 69–76.

Arsenault, L., Moffitt, T. E., Caspi, A., Taylor, P. J. and Silva, P. A. (2000) 'Mental disorders and violence in a total birth cohort: results from the Dunedin Study', *Archives of General Psychiatry*, vol. 57, pp. 979–86.

Barker, P. (1995) *Basic Child Psychiatry)* (6th edn), Oxford, Blackwell Scientific.

Bates, J. E., Brame, B., Broidy, L. M. *et al.* (2003) 'Developmental trajectories of childhood disruptive behaviors and adolescent delinquency: a six site, cross national study', *Developmental Psychology*, vol. 39, pp. 222–45.

Bell, R. Q. (1968) 'A reinterpretation of the direction of effect in studies of socialization', *Psychological Review*, vol. 75, pp. 81–95.

Berg-Nielsen, T. S., Vika, A. and Dahl, A. A. (2003) 'When adolescents disagree with their mothers: CBCL-YSR discrepancies related to maternal depression and adolescent self-esteem', *Child Care, Health and Development*, vol. 29, pp. 207–13.

Bor, W., Brennan, P. A., Williams, G. M., Najman, J. M. and O'Callaghan, M. (2003) 'A mother's attitude towards her infant and child behaviour five years later', *Australian and New Zealand Journal of Psychiatry*, vol. 37, pp. 748–55.

Bronfenbrenner, U. (1979) *The Ecology of Human Development*, Cambridge, MA, Harvard University Press.

Bronfenbrenner, U. and Morris, P. A. (1998, 5th edn) 'The ecology of developmental processes', in Danon, W. (series ed.) and Lerner, R. M. (vol. ed.), *Handbook of Child Psychology: Vol. 1, Theory*, New York, Wiley.

Carlson, M. J. and Corcoran, M. E. (2001) 'Family structure and children's behavioural and cognitive outcomes', *Journal of Marriage and the Family*, vol. 63, pp. 779–92.

Carr, A. (1999) *The Handbook of Child and Adolescent Clinical Psychology*, London, Routledge.

Chess, S. and Thomas, A. (1984) *Origins and Evolution of Behaviour Disorders*, New York, Brunner Mazel.

Cox, A. D., Puckering, C., Bond, A. and Mills, M. (1987) 'The impact of maternal depression in young children', *Journal of Child Psychology and Psychiatry*, vol. 28, pp. 917–28.

Crockenberg, S. B. (1981) 'Infant irritability, mother responsiveness, and social support influences on the security of infant–mother attachment', *Child Development*, vol. 52, pp. 857–65.

Dadds, M. R., Mullins, M. J., McAllister, R. A. and Atkinson, E. (2003) 'Attributions, affect, and behaviour in abuse-risk mothers: a laboratory study', *Child Abuse and Neglect*, vol. 27, pp. 21–45.

DeKlyen, M., Speltz, M. L. and Greenberg, M. T. (1998) 'Fathering and early onset conduct problems: positive and negative parenting, father-son attachment, and the marital context', *Clinical Child and Family Psychology Review*, vol. 1, pp. 3–21.

DeWolff, M. S. and von IJzendoorn, M. H. (1997) 'Sensitivity and attachment: a meta-analysis on parental antecedents of infant attachment', *Child Development*, vol. 68, pp. 571–91.

Fagan, J. and Barnett, M. (2003) 'The relationship between maternal gatekeeping, paternal competence, mother's attitudes about the father role, and father involvement', *Journal of Family Issues*, vol. 24, pp. 1020–43.

Fergusson, D. M. and Horwood, L. J. (1999) 'Prospective childhood predictors of deviant peer affiliations in adolescence', *Journal of Child Psychology and Psychiatry*, vol. 40, pp. 581–92.

Fergusson, D. M., Lynskey, M. T. and Horwood, L. J. (1995) 'The role of peer affiliations, social, family and individual factors in continuities in cigarette smoking between childhood and adolescence', *Addiction*, vol. 90, pp. 647–60.

Ferri, E. (ed.) (1993) *Life at 33: the fifth follow-up of the National Child Development Study*, London, National Children's Bureau.

Flouri, E. and Buchanan, A. (2002) 'Father involvement in childhood and trouble with the police in adolescence: findings from the 1958 British cohort', *Journal of Interpersonal Violence*, vol. 17, pp. 689–701.

Flouri, E. and Buchanan, A. (2003) 'The role of father involvement in children's later mental health', *Journal of Adolescence*, vol. 26, pp. 63–78.

Gallagher, K. C. (2002) 'Does child temperament moderate the influence of parenting on adjustment?', *Developmental Review*, vol. 22, pp. 623–43.

Garver, D. L. (1997) 'The etiologic heterogeneity of schizophrenia', *Harvard Review of Psychiatry*, vol. 4, pp. 317–27.

Goodman, R. (1997) 'The strengths and difficulties questionnaire: a research note', *Journal of Child Psychology and Psychiatry*, vol. 38, pp. 581–86.

Goodman, R., Ford, T., Simmons, H., Gatward, R. and Meltzer, H. (2000) 'Using the strengths and difficulties questionnaire (SDQ) to screen for child psychiatric disorders in a community sample', *British Journal of Psychiatry*, vol. 177, pp. 534–39.

Greenberg, M. T., Speltz, M. L. and Deklynen, M. (1993) 'The role of attachment in the early development of disruptive behavior problems', *Development and Psychopathology*, vol. 5, pp. 191–213.

Halligan, S. L., Herbert, J., Goodyer, I. M. and Murray, L. (2004) 'Exposure to postnatal depression predicts elevated cortisol in adolescent offspring', *Biological Psychiatry*, vol. 55, pp. 376–81.

Henry, B., Caspi, A., Moffitt, T. E. and Silva, P.A. (1996) 'Temperamental and familial predictors of violent and nonviolent criminal convictions: age 3 to age 18', *Developmental Psychology*, vol. 32, pp. 614–23.

Henry, B., Moffitt, T., Robins, L., Earls, F. and Silva, P. (1993) 'Early family predictors of child and adolescent antisocial behaviour: who are the mothers of delinquents?', *Criminal Behaviour and Mental Health*, vol. 3, pp. 97–118.

Herbert, M. (1991) *Clinical Child Psychology*, Chichester, Wiley.

Hinde, R. A. and Stevenson-Hinde, J. (1988) *Relationships within Families: mutual influences*, Oxford, Clarendon.

Jaffee, S. R., Moffitt, T. E., Caspi, A. and Taylor, A. (2003) 'Life with (or without) father: the benefits of living with two biological parents depend on the father's antisocial behaviour', *Child Development*, vol. 74, pp. 109–26.

Johnston, C., Murray, C., Hinshaw, S. P., Pelham, W. E. Jr. and Hoza, B. (2002) 'Responsiveness in interactions of mothers and sons with ADHD: relations to maternal and child characteristics', *Journal of Abnormal Child Psychology*, vol. 30, pp. 77–88.

Johnston, C., Fine, S., Weiss, M., Weiss, J., Weiss, G. and Freeman, W. S. (2000) 'Effects of stimulant medication treatment on mothers' and children's attributions for the behaviour of children with attention deficit hyperactivity disorder', *Journal of Abnormal Child Psychology*, vol. 28, pp. 371–82.

Kessen, W. (1979) 'The American child and other cultural inventions', *American Psychologist*, vol. 34, pp. 815–20.

Klein, H. A. and Ballantine, J. H. (1988) 'The relationship of temperament to adjustment in British infant schools', *Journal of Social Psychology*, vol. 128, pp. 585–95.

Kochanska, G. (1995) 'Children's temperament, mothers' discipline, and security of attachment: multiple pathways to emerging internalization', *Child Development*, vol. 66, pp. 597–615.

Kochanska, G. (1997) 'Multiple pathways to conscience for children with different temperaments: from toddlerhood to age 5', *Developmental Psychology*, vol. 33, pp. 228–40.

Lamb, M. E. (ed.) (1997) *The Role of the Father in Child Development*, New York, John Wiley.

Lerner, J. M. and Busch-Rossnagel, N. A. (1981) *Individuals as Producers of their Own Development: a lifespan perspective*, New York, Academic Press.

Liu, X., Kurita, H., Sun, Z. and Wang, F. (1999) 'Risk factors for psychopathology among Chinese children', *Psychiatry and Clinical Neurosciences*, vol. 53, pp. 497–503.

MacKinnon-Lewis, C., Lamb, M. E., Arbuckle, B., Baradaran, L. P. and Volling, B. L. (1992) 'The relationship between biased maternal and filial attributions and the aggressiveness of their interactions', *Development and Psychopathology*, vol. 4, pp. 403–15.

Margolin, G. and Gordis, E. B. (2000) 'The effects of family and community violence on children', *Annual Review of Psychology*, vol. 51, pp. 445–79.

Maziade, M., Cote, R., Bernier, H., Boutin, P. and Thivierge, J. (1989) 'Significance of extreme temperament in infancy for clinical status in preschool years', *British Journal of Psychiatry*, vol. 154, pp. 535–43.

Meins, E., Fernyhough, C., Fradley, E. and Tuckey, M. (2001) 'Rethinking maternal sensitivity: mothers' comments on infants' mental processes predict security of attachment at 12 months', *Journal of Child Psychology and Psychiatry*, vol. 42, pp. 637–48.

Meins, E., Fernyhough, C., Wainwright, R., DasGupta, M., Fradley, E. and Tuckey, M. (2002) 'Maternal mind-mindedness and attachment security as predictors of theory of mind understanding', *Child Development*, vol. 73, pp. 1715–26.

Meltzer , H., Gatward, R., Goodman, R. *et al.* (2000) *Mental health of children and adolescents in Great Britain*, London, Stationery Office.

Murray, L. (1992) 'The impact of post-natal depression on infant development', *Journal of Child Psychology and Psychiatry*, vol. 33, pp. 543–61.

Murray, L. and Stein, A. (1991) 'The effects of postnatal depression on mother–infant relations and infant development' in Woodhead, M., Carr, R. and Light, P. (eds) *Becoming a Person*, London, Routledge.

National Institute of Child Health and Development Early Child Care Research Network (2000) 'Factors associated with fathers' caregiving activities and sensitivity with young children', *Journal of Family Psychology*, vol.14, pp. 200–19.

Oates, J. and Stevenson, J. (2005) 'Temperament and development', in Oates, J., Wood, C., and Grayson, A., in *Psychological Development and Early Childhood*, Oxford/Milton Keynes, Blackwell Publishing/The Open University.

Oyserman, D., Bybee, D., and Mowbray, C. (2002) 'Influences of maternal mental illness on psychological outcomes for adolescent children', *Journal of Adolescence*, vol. 25, pp. 587–602.

Patterson, G. R. (1982) *A Social Learning Approach, Vol. 3, Coercive Family Process*, Eugene, OR, Castalia Publishing Company.

Patterson, G. R. (1986) 'The contribution of siblings to training for fighting', in Olweus, M. D. and Radke-Yarrow, M. (eds) *Development of Anti-Social and Prosocial Behaviour*, pp. 235–61, Orlando, FL. Academic Press.

Raval, V., Goldberg, S., Atkinson, L. *et al.* (2001) 'Maternal attachment, maternal responsiveness and infant attachment', *Infant Behaviour and Development*, vol. 24, pp. 281–304.

Robins, L. N. and Rutter, M. (eds) (1990) *Straight and Devious Pathways from Childhood to Adulthood*, Cambridge, Cambridge University Press.

Rutter, M. and Casaer, T. (eds) (1991) *Biological Risk Factors for Psycho-social Disorders*, Cambridge, Cambridge University Press.

Rutter, M., Dunn, J., Plomin, R. *et al.* (1997) 'Integrating nature and nurture: implications of person-environment correlations and interactions for developmental psychology', *Development and Psychopathology*, vol. 9, pp. 335–64.

Sameroff, A. J. (1991) 'The social context of development', in Woodhead, M., Carr, R. and Light, P. (eds) *Becoming a Person*, pp. 61–81, London, Routledge.

Sameroff, A. J. (1997) 'Understanding the social context of early psychopathology', in Noshpitz, J. D., Greenspan, S., Wieder, S. and Osofsky, J.

(eds) *Handbook of Child and Adolescent Psychiatry, Vol. 1*, pp. 224–35, New York, Wiley.

Sameroff, A. J. and Fiese, B. H. (2000, 2nd edn) 'Models of development and developmental risk', in Zeanah, Jr., C. H. (ed.), *Handbook of Infant Mental Health*, pp. 3–19, New York, Guilford Press.

Scott, S. (1998) 'Aggressive behaviour in childhood', *British Medical Journal*, vol. 316, pp. 202–6.

Sears, R. R., Maccoby, E. E. and Levin, H. (1957) *Patterns of Child Rearing*, Evanston, IL, Row Peterson.

Stern-Bruschweiler, N. and Stern, D. N. (1989) 'A model for conceptualizing the role of the mother's representational world in various mother–infant therapies', *Infant Mental Health*, vol. 3, pp. 142–56.

Stratton, P. and Swaffer, R. (1988) 'Maternal causal beliefs for abused and handicapped children', *Journal of Reproductive and Infant Psychology*, vol. 6, pp. 201–16.

Sund, A. M. and Wichstrom, L. (2002) 'Insecure attachment as a risk factor for future depressive symptoms in early adolescence', *Journal of the American Academy of Child and Adolescent Psychiatry*, vol. 41, pp. 1478–85.

Tiet, Q.Q., Bird, H. R., Hoven, C. W., Wu, P., Moore, R. and Davies, M. (2001) 'Resilience in the face of maternal psychopathology and adverse life events', *Journal of Child and Family Studies*, vol. 10, pp. 347–65.

Wakschlag, L .S. and Hans, S. L. (1999) 'Relation of maternal responsiveness during infancy to the development of behaviour problems in high-risk youth', *Developmental Psychology*, vol. 35, pp. 569–79.

Waters, E., Vaughan, B. and Egeland, B. (1980) 'Individual differences in infant–mother attachment relationships at age one: antecedents in neonatal behaviour in an urban, economically disadvantaged sample', *Child Development*, vol. 51, pp. 203–16.

Weisz, J. R., Sigman, M., Weiss, B. and Mosk, J. (1993) 'Parental reports of behavioural and emotional problems among children in Kenya, Thailand and the United States', *Child Development*, vol. 64, pp. 98–109.

White, J., Moffitt, T. E., Earls, F., Robins, L. N. and Silva, P. A. (1990) 'Preschool predictors of boys' antisocial behaviour, with a closer look at the false positives', *Criminology*, vol. 28, pp. 507–53.

Zahn-Waxler, C., Iannotti, R. J., Cummings, E. M. and Denham, S. (1990) 'Antecedents of problem behaviours in children of depressed mothers', *Development and Psychopathology*, vol. 2, pp. 271–91.

Chapter 3
Children's interactions: siblings and peers

Karen Littleton and Dorothy Miell

Contents

Learning outcomes

After you have studied this chapter you should be able to:

1 characterize the nature and developmental significance of sibling and peer interactions;
2 describe some of the ways in which researchers have studied sibling and peer interactions;
3 evaluate research studies, particularly in terms of how behaviour is interpreted and any problems of generalizing findings (e.g. across contexts and cultures).

1   Introduction

The previous two chapters of this book have highlighted the nature and developmental significance of children's relationships with their parents/ caregivers. Such relationships are important contexts for development and it is therefore perhaps not surprising that researchers have paid much attention to relationships between children and their parents or other adult carers. More recently, this research has been complemented by an increased interest in children's relationships and interactions with other children, notably their sisters and brothers (siblings) and their peers.

In this chapter we will introduce you to research that suggests that it is not just parents who influence children's development. As children get older, they interact with an increasingly diverse range of people. They engage in and sustain varied interactions and relationships, including those with other children. We will thus be exploring the developmental significance of sibling and peer relations, asking the question 'What are they important for – psychologically speaking?'.

Partly in reaction to a tradition of research that has placed considerable emphasis on the importance of children's relationships with their parents (particularly their mothers), some contemporary writers have made provocative claims regarding the developmental significance of children's interactions and relationships with other children. Harris (1998) and Pinker (2002), for example, have both argued that parental influences on children have been grossly exaggerated and that it is within the peer group that socialization mainly occurs. We are, however, not concerned with debating which of the relationships that children are involved in are of primary importance in this chapter. The line taken here is that different *kinds* of relationships and interactions can give rise to distinctive experiences and that *each* has developmental significance.

In order to explore the particular nature of what happens when children are relating, researchers often focus on characterizing the detail of their interactions. This enables them to describe the distinctive psychological processes taking place and reflect on the developmental significance of such processes. Examples of research will be presented which, for example, involve the careful analysis of interactions between playmates and siblings. In these studies, researchers are examining how children come to learn how to handle the complexity of social life, for example how to negotiate with others, through their talk and play together. Thus, the work presented in this chapter sees interactions between children as important 'sites for development', with the developmental significance of the processes taking place there needing to be analysed and understood.

There is less emphasis in what we are presenting here on characterizing and understanding the changing nature of children's enduring relationships with each other (e.g. as friends or siblings). Instead, the focus is on what occurs in the day-to-day interactions between children in homes, nurseries, schools, and playgrounds – since it is through such encounters that relationships are built.

2   The nature and features of peer and sibling interactions

In this section we start the exploration of children's relations with other children by characterizing, in general terms, the nature and features of their interactions with others. One way of thinking about the different types of relations in which children engage is to think about how the participants differ in terms of the balance of knowledge and power. In some interactions the individuals have *differing* knowledge and social power – a typical example being when a child interacts with a parent or a teacher. Such interactions are characterized by the *complementarity* of roles – for example, the child asking for help, and the parent or teacher offering it. While the roles of those involved are interwoven, the behaviour patterns demonstrated by each one differ markedly. According to Schaffer (2003) the main function of complementary interactions 'is to provide children with security and protection and to enable them to gain knowledge and acquire skills' (p. 113). By contrast, other interactions can be characterized as being between individuals with *similar* knowledge and social power. They can be characterized by *reciprocal* processes rather than complementary ones. A typical example would be a friendship between same-age peers. It has been suggested that the function of these reciprocal interactions 'is to acquire skills that can only be learned among equals, such as those involving co-operation and competition' (Schaffer, 2003, p. 113).

While not absolute, the distinction between interactions in terms of their complementary and reciprocal features is useful because it helps us to understand some important dimensions along which children's encounters with others can differ. The characterization of interaction in terms of reciprocal and complementary features also applies to sibling relationships. What distinguishes siblings' relationships is that:

Among siblings there is a difference in knowledge and power, yet that difference is not so great that the two children cannot sometimes play and talk together on the same level. It is this combination of features that makes sibling relationships potentially so influential: on the one hand the older child can act as teacher, guide, and model to the younger; on the other hand, however, both children share interest and competence to a sufficient degree to tackle jointly the task of social understanding.

(Schaffer, 1996, pp. 266–7)

Figure I   Two siblings playing.

Different kinds of relations can have different significance for development and learning. Children's interactions with other children are important contexts for development, as it is through such interaction that children learn skills such as how to co-operate and resolve conflict, and share the task of constructing their social understanding. As Dunn has pointed out in her discussion of the differences between children's friendships and their relations with parents and other adults:

The other feature of friendship that is a key contributor to children's growing understanding of the social world is that it marks the beginning of a new independence from parents. Children throughout our evolutionary history, and currently in many cultures other than those of North America and Europe, grow up not in isolated nuclear families, but within a wider world of others, including children – sisters, brothers, playmates, loose-knit gangs of children. This world of other children means opportunities for friendship, enmities, gang life, leaders and followers. It means opportunities for working out the intricate balance of power and status between people, for sharing imaginative experiences, for understanding and manipulating the feelings and ideas of others, for a range of relationships that differ greatly from those of parents-with-children.

(Dunn, 2004)

In this chapter we will consider some of the research work that has investigated children's interactions with other children and what this tells us about children's social skills and their developing social understanding. It is important to note that the interactions we will be discussing take place in wider social contexts – not only of particular relationships (which may vary in intensity from enduring relationships with siblings to interactions with acquaintances and playmates) but also of broader social networks.

Summary of Section 2

- Interactions offer important contexts for children's development, especially in their growth of social understanding.
- Some interactions tend to be characterized by complementarity and others by reciprocity. Interactions with siblings can have features of both forms and are potentially powerful sites for influencing development.

3 Conflicts, disputes and disagreements: playful and real

When caregivers interact with their child they tend to 'scaffold' the interaction, supporting, complementing and extending the child's contributions, perhaps by interpreting their intentions or by adding to or reformulating what she or he says. However, this is not the case with peer interaction. In this situation each child has their own aspirations, motives and intentions and these 'agendas' have to be reconciled with those of others. As Schaffer notes 'though with age these agendas can increasingly overlap, the pressure on the child to acquire the necessary skills for joint interaction is in many respects much greater' (Schaffer, 2003, p. 113). Schaffer is implying here that the nature of children's interactions with other children changes with age. While babies are clearly interested in other children and may gaze intently at them, and perhaps try to touch them, it is from toddlerhood onwards that children's interactions with other children become increasingly complex. Children gradually begin to engage with other children through more reciprocal forms of play, taking notice of each other's behaviour, talking to each other and developing a play scene or game. Yet, as this statement also implies, once children begin to play together more frequently and over a more sustained period of time then there is real 'pressure' on them to develop the skills necessary for initiating, engaging in and sustaining interaction together. We might not often think about it in this way, however, being able to play together is a skilled interactional accomplishment involving sensitivity to others' perspectives as well as negotiation and conflict management skills.

3.1 Play as an interactional accomplishment

To illustrate what we mean when we say that play between children can be seen as a skilled interactional accomplishment, we can look at an example of a pretend play sequence involving play fighting and chasing recorded by Fein (1984). Before looking at this example in detail, however, it is important to think about the way in which researchers like Fein move from observing everyday encounters like this to analysing their nature and significance. Researchers often begin the analytical process by making a detailed transcript of the interaction. While such transcripts allow a relatively detailed examination of joint activity, they nevertheless provide only a partial record. They cannot faithfully reproduce *every* aspect of the interaction, as they do not convey the tone of voice used or the full context of the children's movements and expressions. It is also the case that transcribers will tend to pay attention to different aspects of the talk depending upon their interests, which means that a transcript is already an interpretation of the event it seeks to record. Ochs, in a now classic account of 'Transcription as theory', suggests that: 'transcription is a selective process reflecting theoretical goals and definitions' (1979, p. 44).

Researchers often begin by transcribing the joint activity, although they usually work in their analysis from both the transcript *and* the video or audio record of the interaction, thus allowing a more contextualized interpretation of the material to emerge.

However, in order to communicate their research findings to others through publications, researchers typically rely on extracts from the transcripts alongside their analytic commentary. In this chapter we will be using such extracts and commentary to explore key aspects of children's sibling and peer interactions.

Coming to an extract of transcript like the one below without having seen the original behaviour or viewing the researcher's tapes can be quite daunting at first. It can help to make the interaction seem more vivid and alive if you read it a few times, and perhaps speak it aloud once you have a sense of the overall tenor of the interaction and how events unfold. Try this as you read through the extract of transcript presented in Box 1. Peter and Michael – both 3 ½ years old – are playing a game involving a 'Dracula Monster' and a 'Monster-vanishing Hero' and they are using toy blocks as substitute weapons.

BOX 1

Dracula and the Monster-vanishing Hero

1   Peter: (Swings hat in air, approaches Michael) 'You be Dracula'.

2   Michael: OK (Gets up, extends arms in front of him) 'Grrow!'

3   P: (Points block at Michael) 'Pow!'

4   M: (Falls down)

5   P: (Approaches, points block at Michael) 'Pow!'

6   M: (Stirs slightly while lying down)

7   P: (Starts to put block in pocket)

8   M: (Starts to get up)

9   P: (Points block at Michael) 'Pow!'

10   M: (Falls down)

11   P: (Puts block in pocket)

12   M: (Gets up) 'Now you be Dracula'

13   P: 'Wait, ... I gotta put my cowboy hat on first' (Puts hat on, approaches
14   Michael)

15   M: (Points block at Peter) 'Pow!'

16   P: (Falls down)

17   M: (Points block at Peter) 'Pow, pow, pow, pow!' (Puts block in pocket)
18   'You're dead'; (Leaves)

19   P: 'Hey, aahh!' (Gets up) 'Ah, ahh!'

20   M: (Points block at Peter)

21   P: (Approaches Michael)

22   M: 'Prsh, prsh, prsh, prsh, prsh!'

23   M: (Pushes Peter down, places block in pocket)

23   P: (Falls down)(Gets up) 'Now you be Dracula'

24   M: (Gets toy from shelf) 'No, I ... pow, pow, pow!' (Points toy at Peter)

25   P: 'You be Dracula'

26   M: (Pushes Peter)

27   P: 'Be you like you?'

28   M: 'No, you be Dracula, and you say wow, and I push you down, and I
29   shoot you' (Approaches Peter with block extended in front of him)

30   P: 'The hell you shoot me. No.' (Pushes Michael's arm) 'You ...'

31   M: 'All right' (Lies down)

32   P: (Points block at Michael) 'Pow!'

33   M: (Stirs slightly)

34   P: (Puts block in pocket, puts hat on head)

35   M: (Gets up, points block at Peter) 'Pow, pow, pow!'

36 P: (Points block at Michael) 'Pow!' (Pushes Michael with block and arms
37   extended in front of him)
38 M: (Pushes Peter with arms and block extended in front of him)
39 P: 'Pow, pow!'
40 M: (Falls down)
41 P: (Puts block in pocket)

Source: adapted from Fein, 1984, pp. 136–7

To a casual observer, this play sequence might simply look like two little boys rushing around pretending to shoot each other. But a careful reading of the account offers some interesting observations. It is through this type of line-by-line analysis that a qualitative researcher interested in studying children's interactions would begin to tease out the interactional processes inherent in the apparently simple game. Such an analysis shows how the children are involved in the ongoing negotiation of roles – for example around who is to be Dracula and who is to be the hero (lines 1 and 2; 12 and 13; 23–28).

You will also see that the children instruct each other on how to behave and what to say in their respective roles (lines 23–28). Note that there is a possible moment of tension when Michael suggests that he should shoot Peter (who he has nominated to be Dracula) and begins to approach him with his block extended in front of him (line 29). This suggestion is countered by Peter's reply: 'The hell you shoot me. No' and he pushes Michael's arm away (line 30). This is a pivotal moment in the sequence and one in which the playful fighting had the potential to turn into a physical conflict between the boys. Perhaps because he had sensed this, Michael appears to limit his response, conceding with the words 'all right' and physically lying down (line 31). The boys' play then continues. Michael's reply and associated response is interesting analytically, as it is not completely clear whether he is reacting as 'play' or 'non-play.' This extract thus highlights the multiple levels on which children's communications in play situations are conducted. The psychologist Göncü makes a distinction that is useful in understanding what is going on here, namely the distinction between communication *within* play and metacommunication (i.e. communication *about* play):

> A mutual pretend focus is necessary but not sufficient for social pretend play. It must also be communicated that a pretend play message is to be interpreted as such, rather than as a literal message. Bateson (1955) refers to such communication as metacommunication ... The metacommunication indicates the changing form of interaction from non-play to play ... Used effectively, this metacommunication conveys a desire to have fun by playing with representations.

(Göncü, 1998, pp. 123–4)

Even very young children engaged in pretend play can switch from one level of representation and mode of communication to another – often apparently without effort. Peter and Michael (both only 3½) in their play sequence in Box 1 show a continual shift between *talk about* their play – who is to be which character and particular suggested sequences of action – and *engagement with* and the *acting out* of the details of their pretence. It illustrates the complexity of playful encounters and why they can be considered to be interactional accomplishments.

3.2 The significance of playfighting

Through analysing extracts carefully we can also get a sense of why psychologists think that such encounters are developmentally salient. Commenting on the significance of play-fighting and chasing more generally, Smith *et al.* (1999) argue that important social skills and abilities are developed and practised in such situations:

> the communication skills of encoding and decoding (as in such playful encounters children need to be able to both display and understand play signals);
>
> the ability to regulate emotional display and the strength of physical action (in these boisterous encounters restraint is needed);
>
> turn-taking skills and the ability to understand another person's point of view (for example, as is the case in role reversals and self-limiting behaviour).
>
> (Adapted from Smith *et al.*, 1999, p. 123)

Peter and Michael's Dracula game highlights how at times children's playful interactions can be poised between playful activity and actual conflict between them. While in Peter and Michael's case the play continued, in some cases play-fighting and chasing does become angry and turns into fighting. A field observation of older children by American researchers in a village in Mexico (Juxtlahuaca), which is reproduced in Box 2, illustrates how this transition can happen rapidly.

BOX 2

Juvenal in the playground

Juvenal and several other boys are running around the school playground engaging each other in wrestling. There is much laughter in the wrestling match with the first boy ... In one of the movements, they fall to the ground intertwined. They go rolling around the ground until Juvenal remains on top and stops. While he looks at his opponent, laughing and breathing heavily ... The other boy stands up and begins to run, looking at Juvenal (a chase and capture sequence follows) ... Another boy comes running from the courtyard and grabs Juvenal from behind as if he wants to fight. Juvenal loosens himself, and with a push almost throws him to the ground. He laughs. The two again lock in a struggle, trying to intertwine their legs so that they will both fall to the ground ... The other takes

Juvenal's leg and throws him to the ground. Juvenal gets up. The other boy remains laughing in an expectant attitude. They grab each other again. This time Juvenal throws the other to the ground. The boy hits quite hard upon falling. He gets up, no longer laughing. He grabs Juvenal by the arms and twists them. Juvenal laughs but immediately begins to try to free himself, becoming rather serious. He seems to realize that the other boy is no longer 'playing' but is now angry.

Source: Whiting and Edwards, cited in Maccoby, 1999, pp. 34–5.

Activity 1

Allow about
10 minutes

Fighting or playing?

This activity will provide you with experience of analysing observational material.

Read through the observational field notes shown in Box 2 involving Juvenal and his friends. Try to identify aspects of their interaction that might indicate when their fighting is playful and note these down.

Comment

Smith and colleagues highlight that play fighting can *look* like real fighting and that a crucial indication that the children are playing is the presence of laughter. Children need to be able to both use laughter in this way and interpret the meaning when others use it if it is to successfully function as this form of social signal.

> Play fighting and chasing, or 'rough-and-tumble play', is a typical form of behaviour in children, taking up some 10 per cent of playground time in middle childhood ... It looks in many respects like real fighting but is clearly distinguishable in a number of respects by children and by trained adult observers ... It is often indexed by laughter or smiling. Play fighting and chasing normally show self-handicapping and restraint; participants do not fight or chase at full strength. This forbearance allows friendly play to continue, even between unequally matched partners. It often is characterized by reversal of roles, as first one child is on top, then the other.

> (Smith *et al.,* 1999, p. 122)

At the start of the observation in Box 2 the observer has noted that Juvenal and his partner are laughing as they wrestle, which is a strong signal that they are having fun. Another indicator is what Smith terms 'self-handicapping and restraint'. This is hinted at although not fully explored in the researchers' fieldnotes, when they record that when the boys are showing strength: 'it is easy to see that they are not trying to harm each other'. The playful mood seems to continue even though the wrestling partner changes. However, when Juvenal throws his partner to the ground and the boy lands heavily, the mood changes. In a brief moment the playful encounter is changed and the remainder of the sequence shows that the boys are now on the edge of aggression.

Figure 2 Fighting or playfighting?

The conventions of self-handicap and restraint are normally recognized in play fights. Some researchers have noted, however, that there can be ambiguity in respect of play fighting and that 'cheating' may also occur. Cheating might occur when 'play conventions' are used in such a way as to harm another when they have readily assumed or 'consented' to adopt an inferior position in a play context. In such cases it has been suggested (Smith *et al.*, 1999) that public humiliation of a play partner may be used to display dominance and, perhaps, to increase the status or reputation of the 'cheat' within their peer group.

More recently, Pelligrini (2003) has studied adolescents' 'rough and tumble play' (R&T) and play fighting, both by observing their play episodes and through interviewing some of the young people themselves. He also highlights the issue of dominance and aggression and raises two key points. The first is that when considering the developmental significance of children's playful interactions with other children, we need to recognize that within a particular group, the functions of such interactions may change with age:

> Contrary to findings with juveniles, where R&T is not related to aggression or dominance, theory and research (Fagen, 1981; Humphreys & Smith, 1987; Pellegrini, 1985, 1998) suggest that R&T for adolescent males is related to physical aggression and may be used as a way to establish peer status in the form of dominance.
>
> (Pellegrini, 2003, p. 1522)

Second, even when at an equivalent age, the functions of playful interactions may be different for different groups of children – for example boys and girls:

> boys engage in R&T with other boys in the service of dominance and [it] is related to aggression. Girls, on the other hand see it as playful. Girls seem to engage in R&T with boys as an early and relatively low-risk form of heterosexual interaction.
>
> (Pellegrini, 2003, p. 1531)

We will return to the issue of gender later in this section. For the moment, however, it is sufficient to note that some researchers (Smith *et al.*, 1999) have suggested that even the negative aspects of children's experiences, such as dealing with aggression, can be a useful preparation for adult life.

3.3 The importance of children's playground experiences

Up to this point we have been discussing the nature and significance of children's playful interactions with others largely through considering what can be *observed* when children play together. Some researchers argue that when investigating the *significance* of children's playful encounters and playground experiences it is important to use self-report data and to actually ask children what they feel about play and playtime. An example of research adopting this approach was undertaken by Blatchford and colleagues (1990) from the London University Institute of Education. As part of a longitudinal study of children's educational progress, they investigated how children's perspectives on the playground change as they move through junior school and into secondary school. A summary of this work is given in Research summary 1.

RESEARCH SUMMARY 1

Children's playground experiences

More than 300 children in 33 inner London primary schools were questioned in the Institute of Education study. In the initial phase both 7 and 11 year olds were interviewed about their schools; school work; break-time; teasing and fighting. All children were interviewed individually and the interviewers used structured interview schedules that contained a mix of closed and open questions.

For example, children were asked to give three reasons why they liked and did not like break-time. They were also asked to describe three activities or games they played at break-time, and were asked to judge how much they enjoyed playtime according to a five-point scale. Children from the first phase of the study were interviewed again once they reached the age of 16 (Blatchford *et al.*, 1990; Blatchford, 1994).

The study showed that, on the whole, most children reported that they enjoy going out to play games and socialize with their friends at break-time. Quite a sizeable minority, mostly girls, however, reported that they did not like being made to go out in bad weather, and that they did not like the bullying, fighting, and teasing that took place. The most popular games among the younger children were soccer, chasing games and other ball games. With the exception of soccer, the 16 year olds did not play games at break-time, preferring instead to spend the time talking to their friends. Blatchford comments that 'During the course of their secondary school years (11–16 years) children seem to have forgotten the games and lost the incentive to play ... By 16 years the culture is more obviously a youth culture, with social life and friendships more independent of particular activities (Blatchford, 1994, p. 10).

Blatchford came to the conclusion that for children of all ages there is a separate, child-governed break-time culture in the playground from which adults are for the most part excluded. This culture is not always a benign one; racist and sexist teasing and fighting can occur (e.g. Kelly, 1994; Short, 1999). It is nevertheless extremely important to children, as it allows them freedom from adults. Without adult intervention children have to learn how to regulate playground games and space, and also how to manage teasing and bullying. In doing so, Blatchford argues, they are beginning to develop a sophisticated set of social understandings.

Sources: Blatchford et al. 1990; Blatchford, 1994.

What is striking about the study in Research summary 1 and other similar ones is that there seems to be a reasonably clear consensus that playground experiences help children develop important social skills. Even so, other studies have shown that the incidence of bullying and aggression in the playground is sufficiently widespread to cause serious concern (e.g. Whitney and Smith, 1993). In Britain this has led to a number of initiatives to try and improve the quality of playground life. This has been achieved either by changing the physical environment to make it more attractive, or by explicitly teaching children social skills and strategies for dealing with aggression and conflict (see for example Blatchford and Sharp, 1994; Blatchford, 1999).

As both observational and interview studies confirm that children create their own culture in the playground, an important message for programmes designed to improve the playground climate is that interventions are unlikely to be successful unless they take children's views and knowledge of this culture into account (Cowie, 1999).

Figure 3   Children at play in the school playground.

3.4 Children's cultures

One of the key issues in looking at children's conflicts and disputes is to identify satisfactory criteria to distinguish *negative* interactions among pupils, especially bullying, from other kinds of dispute. Conflicts and disputes per se are not necessarily a negative experience in children's development. Recognizing the existence of conflicts of interest, and learning how to negotiate those conflicts and how to respect each other's points of view are inevitable and desirable childhood experiences in the context of liberal, democratic societies. Much 'conflict' takes place in the context of children's play, games and verbal repartee. In these circumstances conflict is understood by those in the children's peer culture. This shared meaning system sets the emotional tone of the exchange, the boundaries on what is acceptable, and the rules that regulate infringement of what is 'fair'. Smith and colleagues (1999) address this distinction directly, arguing that play fighting and play chasing are not only normal among primary school age children but are positively enjoyed among friends as an expression of intimacy within their relationship. However, that said, Smith *et al.* acknowledge that there is *not* a sharp dividing line between play fighting and real fighting, play teasing and nasty teasing. An important implication is that criteria for distinguishing 'positive' from 'negative' conflict cannot be listed in a simple observational checklist of unambiguous behaviours. The analytic criteria and associated interpretations are highly dependent on the 'cultural mores' (customs and beliefs) of the peer group in question, the contexts in which the dispute is taking place (e.g. classroom, playground or street) and the standards set by the adults responsible for regulating children's behaviour within a framework of cultural norms. Most crucially, whether a conflict is 'positive' or 'negative' also depends on the subjective experience of those involved. Friendship pairs and wider peer groups employ subtle 'ground rules' to distinguish the playful from the non-playful – the boundaries of what is seen as acceptable sparring among children who are relative equals. This is especially relevant to teasing. At worst, a simple word, action or gesture can acquire highly provocative symbolic power, to which only one targeted individual may be sensitive. Thus the perceived playfulness of children's behaviour is only one of the criteria set out by Smith *et al.* They also list the following criteria to distinguish bullying behaviour (including 'nasty teasing') from other conflict incidents: to 'count' as bullying, behaviour should be *intentional, unprovoked, repeated* and *dominant.* It is also important to recognize that peer groups are not homogenous, and that within any group, competing sub-cultures may adhere to different values, attitudes to authority and expectations for behaviour, including conflict. A study of 8- to 12-year-olds' perspectives on school life by Pollard (1987) provides a good example of such differences in sub-group values and orientations. Pollard identified three distinct clusters of friendships: the 'goodies', the 'jokers' and 'the gangs':

> There were clear differences between the children in such groups. Children in groups that other children termed 'good groups' regarded groups which they called 'gangs' very negatively for their 'roughness' and 'destroying' behaviour. Groups which I termed 'joker' groups puzzled at the quietness of Good groups, regarded each other as 'good fun' and 'sensible' but were also clear about the 'bigheaded', 'thick' 'roughness' of gangs. Gang groups condemned Good groups as 'soft' and 'goodie-goodies' and Joker groups as 'show-offs' and 'big heads'. Whilst their own gang was regarded as 'great' other gangs were usually labelled as 'soft', 'rubbish' or 'cocky', thus reflecting the extent of inter-gang rivalry.
>
> (Pollard, 1987, pp. 165–6)

Activity 2

Allow about 10 minutes

Goodies, jokers and gangs

This activity will help you interpret extracts of dialogue.

The descriptions below are taken from Pollard's longitudinal study of children's perspectives on school life. Working in one school over a 2-year period, Pollard identified three 'types' of friendship group: the Goodies, Jokers and Gangs. Each type had a well-defined sense of identity that determined how its members behaved, and how they felt about themselves in relation to their peers and teachers.

Read the extracts carefully and then identify (a) which group each girl appears to belong to and (b) what the three groups' standpoints are.

Extract 1

Gill: We like playing with a ball and skipping and playing out in the playground. We like to talk and have a good laugh. Sometimes we play chasing with the boys or watching them playing football.

Extract 2

Tina: I have a good group of friends when I don't fall out with them. Katherine is always falling out with me and going off with Carly. If that happens, like, she has pinched my friend, then Carly's a fat cow. When I'm friends with Susan, just because I'm small for my age, she always pushes me around and blames me for things, but Lucy, if we are friends and we play hitting one another it's good fun. But if I hit her too hard she will not play at all. She can be a baby sometimes.

Extract 3

Linda: We call our club the Lion Club and it's very successful. We are all friends in it. We are honest and fair. We all have nicknames for being in the club, mine is 'Rory', Caroline's is 'Little Boots', Mandy's is 'Shelly' and Kirsty's is 'Thackey'. Ours is a friendly group, we never fall out, or if we do it's only because of silly things.

(Pollard, 1987, pp. 170, 173, 168)

Comment

In his description of the characteristics of the Goodies, Jokers and Gangs, Pollard notes that the 'good' groups, of which Linda's group is an example (Extract 3), had a positive attitude towards themselves and to their teachers. They conformed to the school rules, and were quiet and studious. The Lion Club (Linda's group) identify themselves as a group with high moral standards, and everybody in it has a nickname. The 'Jokers' (Gill's group, Extract 1) also have a positive attitude towards school and each other, but also like to have a laugh and play around. Tina (Extract 2) belongs to a 'gang'. Relations within her gang do not seem to be based on a coherent sense of group identity, but more on changing patterns of like and dislike. It is interesting that while both Linda and Gill refer to themselves as 'we', which reflects their identification with their respective groups, Tina refers to herself as 'I'.

▲

Pollard's work, like that of Pelligrini discussed earlier, highlights the complexity of interactions between children and it is through such work that an understanding of the diversity of children's lived experiences is gained, which enables them to move beyond stereotypes and simple assumptions about their interactions with other children.

3.5 The role of gender in conflicts and disputes

As an example of how research can challenge commonly held assumptions and beliefs, consider briefly the gendered dynamics of conflict and dispute. Many researchers, for example Maccoby (1999), have noted that boys' play more frequently places them on the edge of aggression. This accords with the commonly held assumption that boys' interactions are conflictual, whilst those of girls are co-operative. However, as Maccoby (1999) points out there is clear evidence that girls do have conflicts and disputes, but that the characteristics of their talk (discourse) in such conflicts are different from the style of boys' talk when they are disagreeing or arguing.

Activity 3   *Understanding girls' and boys' talk when disagreeing*

Allow about
15 minutes

This activity will develop your understanding of how researchers analyse discourse.

Box 3 contains two extracts of children's talk, both taken from Sheldon's (1992) work. In the first extract Tony and Charlie (both aged 4 years) are in a playroom, playing with a touch-tone telephone. In the second, Arlene and Elaine, also both aged 4 years, are playing with a doctor's kit. Read through each of these extracts in turn and for each of them make notes concerning how the children manage the conflict between them. Then read the comment below.

Comment

Extract 1 is an example of what Sheldon calls 'single-voiced discourse', found more commonly in interactions among boys than among girls. In this kind of discourse the children do not negotiate or make attempts at persuasion. Moreover, they do not attempt to adapt their perspective in light of their partner's wishes or point of view. Each child pursues their own objectives and thus the conflict between them develops. Extract 2 is an example of what Sheldon calls 'double voiced discourse', which she found girls used more often than boys. Here, each child is clearly pursuing their own objective; there is evidence of negotiation with their partner and the other person's wishes are taken into account.

BOX 3

Discourses of conflict

Extract 1: Tony and Charlie

1   Tony: I pushed two squares (giggles), two squares like this.

2   Charlie: (comes closer, puts his fist up to his ear and talks into an imaginary
3   phone): Hello!

4   Tony: (puts his fist up to his ear and talks back): Hello

5   Charlie: (picks up the receiver that is on Tony's couch) No, that's my phone!

6   Tony: (grabs the telephone cord and tries to pull the receiver away from
7   Charlie) No, tha-ah, it's on *my* couch. It's on *my* couch, Charlie, it's on *my*
8   couch.

9   Charlie: (ignoring Tony, holding onto the receiver and talking into it.) Hi.

10 Tony: (gets off couch, sets phone base on floor). I'll rock the couch like this.
11   (turns the chair over on top of the base and leans on it as Charlie tries to
12   reach for it under the chair) Don't! That's my phone!

13 Charlie: (pushes the chair off the phone and pulls it closer to himself). I needa
14   use it.

15 Tony: (sits back on his heels and watches Charlie playing with the phone)

Extract 2: Arlene and Elaine

1   Arlene: Can I have that – that thing? (referring to the blood-pressure gauge
2   in Elaine's lap). I'm going to take my baby's temperature.

3   Elaine: (who is talking on the toy telephone) You can use it – you can use my
4   temperature. Just make sure you can't use anything else unless you can ask.
5   (turns back to telephone)

6   Arlene: (picks up thermometer from table and takes her baby's temperature)
7   Eighty-three! She isn't sick. Yahoo! May I? (She asks Elaine, who is still on the
8   phone, if she can use the hypodermic syringe)

9   Elaine: No, I'm gonna need the shot in a couple of minutes.

10 Arlene: But I – I need this though.

11 Elaine: (firmly) Okay, just use it once.

Although it appears that Elaine is dominating a compliant partner, later in this considerably extended discourse Arlene demands and gets some reciprocal compliance:

> Arlene has given her doll a shot [i.e. injection], and picks up the earscope to
> check her ears.

1   Elaine: (picks up the syringe) now I'll give her – I'll have to give her – a shot.

2   Arlene: There can only be one thing that you – that – no, she only needs one
3   shot

4   Elaine: Well, let's pretend that it's another day, that we have to look in her
5   ears together.

Source: Maccoby, 1999, pp. 47–48.

3.6 Negotiation and the joint development of ideas

The importance of being able to negotiate and manage differences of perspective and competing aims and ideas is not just significant in play contexts. In situations where children are working together in pairs or groups on tasks in the school classroom there is evidence that the resolution of conflicting perspectives and the negotiation and joint development of ideas is important for learning and intellectual development (Littleton *et al.*, 2004). We will, however, consider this issue here, briefly, by looking at what is happening in the joint story writing episode reproduced in Box 4.

BOX 4

Fluffy the wonderful hamster

This extract of dialogue concerns the negotiation between two 8 year olds of a story theme. They have been asked to write a story in class, about either 'bullying' or 'loss/death'. Their instructions were to make a bullet-point list describing: the theme they had chosen; the characters; and a summary of the beginning, the middle and the end of their story. In this extract two girls are formulating ideas regarding the theme of their story. They have chosen to write about a pet hamster, 'Fluffy', drawing in part on personal experiences.

1 Julie: ((reading the whiteboard)) "What's the story about?" Fluffy the dead
2 hamster.

3 Lisa: No, no.

4 Julie: Yeah, you have to do it when he is dead. So you go like, say Fluffy was
5 very ill-

6 Lisa: ((is trying to interrupt Julie)) No, no, you have to start it when Fluffy is
7 (still) alive.

8 Julie: Yeah, So one day Fluffy was very ill, when he, and he suddenly died early
9 on.

10 Lisa: It's a girl.

11 Julie: I know. And she only died in the story. Then we do number 2. So Fluffy
12 the dead hamster.

13 Lisa: No, don't say-, put Fluffy the dead hamster. That's not nice, isn't it?

14 Julie: Yeah, but it's got to have something about death. Not unless he gets
15 bullied by another hamster.

16 Lisa: ( )

17 Julie: Then we've got to do about death, don't we.

18 Lisa: ( )

19 Julie: Ok, the story is-

20 Lisa: ((interrupting)) Fluffy, the wonderful hamster.

21 Julie: It's not the title, it's what the story is about. What it is about. A
22 hamster. So it's about a ((pause))

23 Lisa: We are doing a story plan!!!

24 Julie: Yeah, I know, but it has, it says, "What is your story about?" ((points at
25 the whiteboard)) The story is about your ham-, ermm, Fluffy the hamster.

26 Lisa: Fluffy the wonderful hamster. ((Pause. Julie is writing))

27 Julie: Who dies. There you go! Yeah? Who dies. In the end.

In her analytic commentary Vass notes:

> at the start of the extract Julie formulates her ideas about the theme for the story ("Fluffy the dead hamster" – line 1). This is immediately challenged by Lisa and this leads to reflection on Julie's side ("Yeah, you have to do it when he is dead" – line 4), which is followed by an extension of her own proposition ("So you go like, say Fluffy was very ill-" ... lines 4–5). This suggestion prompts a challenge from Lisa (lines 6–7), initiating the reflective processes of evaluation, contemplation and modification. This pattern is characteristic of the whole episode, with each proposition for the story plan being immediately reflected upon, evaluated and challenged. There are some clear differences of opinion and orientation to be resolved ... For example, when formulating ideas for the theme, Julie concentrates on the outcome of the story (focusing on the death of the main character) whereas Lisa sees the formulation of the theme in terms of a more general aspect of the story, seeing the description of the main character before her death – *Fluffy the wonderful hamster* – as an integral part of it.

Source: Vass, 2004, pp. 169–70.

It is thus through such processes of negotiation and evaluation that progress emerges and knowledge and understanding are created jointly. Crucially, for these processes to be effective in helping children learn, it is important that children are able to distinguish between conflict and criticism of ideas, which are constructive in this context, and personal criticism and interpersonal conflict which are not (Littleton *et al.*, 2004).

3.7 Emotion and sensitivity in sibling relationships

One of the things that you may have noticed throughout the research presented in this section is the sensitivity with which children assess and react to interactions with others and how many of the interactions between children are emotionally laden. Children's interactions with their siblings can be particularly intense as they are characterized by (in varying degrees) 'pleasure, affection, hostility, aggression, jealousy, rivalry, and frustration' (Dunn and Kendrick, 1982, pp. 210–11). It is the emotional quality of the sibling relationship that is one of the facets said by Dunn to have significance for the development of children's social understanding. Interactions between siblings are not emotionally neutral. They are encounters where personal interests are at stake and where the child pays attention, reacts and responds to, as well as learns about others.

> It may be that the special nature of children's relationships with father, mother, siblings, grandparents, and close friends ... elicits the development of their ability to understand other people's feelings, intentions, and relationships – and their ability to grasp the nature of authority relations, principles of justice, and so on. What drives children to read and understand their mothers' moods or their siblings' intentions ...? It may be the very quality of those relationships that motivates the child to

understand the family world – the emotional power of attachment and rivalry, of dominance, envy, competition and affection.

(Dunn, 1988, p. 73)

When asked about their interactions with their siblings many children stress their dislike of aggression and comment on the frequency of fights between them:

I don't like her; she's horrible, she is, 'cause uhm hits, disgusting; she shouts at me, kicks me, hits me [Does she do it much?] She doesn't do anything else.

I just don't like him, I don't know why. He fights me and I don't like it.

(Pointing at bite she received from her younger brother). He does that a lot, quite a lot of pinching me, he does that all over my face. I pull most of the scabs off.

(Adapted from Dunn and Kendrick, 1982, p. 207)

However, while they may fight and squabble, siblings can also be highly protective of their brother or sister, for example protecting them at school from problems in the playground or bullying. This is readily apparent in a study by Stalker and Connors (2004) who interviewed children in families with a disabled child about their perceptions of each other and family life. The children commented on how their disabled sibling was seen by others and talked about the ways in which they protected them from negative reactions from other people:

Sometimes folk just stand and stare at him as if he has got horns or something coming out of his ears or his head or ten million arms or something ... I just go like that and put my hands on my hips and they will turn their back or something.

(Stalker and Connors, 2004, p. 223)

This notion of care and protection leads us to consider the positive aspects of children's interactions with other children and these are discussed further in Section 4.

Summary of Section 3

- Interactions and play between peers and siblings are powerful sites for the development of key social skills: of communication; regulation of emotion and behaviour; and the understanding of another person's point of view. These are all skills that are important not only during childhood but also for successful adult social life.
- While it is important for children to learn how to manage difficult interpersonal situations without constant adult intervention, some care is needed from adults to structure the context (e.g. playground) appropriately and to teach children how to handle conflict constructively in order to avoid bullying and serious problems.

- There is a fine line between 'play fighting' and real aggression and the line is defined by the individuals involved, their sub-cultural groups and the wider culture in which the behaviour takes place (including adult views of what is appropriate).

4 Co-operation, collaboration and participation

In the previous section the focus was predominantly on conflict and disputes in children's interactions. Yet children also engage in co-operative and harmonious interactions with one another and the nature and significance of these are considered in this section.

Dunn has conducted a number of studies observing children in their everyday home settings with their siblings and parents, as well as with their friends and acquaintances (Dunn, 2004). In one of her early studies (Dunn, 1988) she and her colleague, Munn, observed siblings in their homes intensively during their second and third year of life. They paid particular attention to aspects of interactions that they felt indicated the children's growing social understanding and awareness of their social world – for example their jokes, arguments, fantasy play, teasing and co-operative behaviours. Research summary 2 outlines the work she undertook to investigate these aspects of children's interactions.

RESEARCH SUMMARY 2

Joint pretend play in siblings

Forty-three families took part in Dunn and Munn's Cambridge Sibling Study (Dunn, 1988). Detailed observations of sibling interactions were carried out when the second-born child in each family was aged 18, 24, and 36 months. Among other things, the observers noted the number of times the children engaged in joint pretend play which had a clear element of fantasy or make-believe in it. Dunn describes such play as 'The ability to share a pretend framework with another person, to carry out pretend actions in co-ordination with that other; [and] enacting the part of another person or thing, with the incorporation of another person into a reciprocal role' (Dunn, 1988, p. 117).

Older siblings directed their younger brothers and sisters in joint pretend play episodes and gave them instructions about what to say and how to behave when they were in their pretend roles. At 18 months, 15 per cent of the younger siblings in the study were playing in this way with their brothers and sisters. By the time they were aged 24 months, 80 per cent of younger siblings were observed in joint pretend play and over a third of these younger children clearly understood that they were taking on a different identity during the play episode.

Dunn's observations from this study (and substantiated by other studies she has conducted since) have revealed the extent to which, from a very young age, children are able to co-operate with each other, thereby demonstrating their appreciation of another's mood and goals. Initially the children she observed were seen 'to respond to the playful moods of their siblings, to laugh and frequently to join them by imitating their action ... such sensitivity to mood was observed in the secondborn baby siblings as early as 8 months old' (Dunn, 1988, p. 110).

During the second year of life, however, the children's interactions became more sophisticated and they began to participate in and contribute to their sibling's play in ways that reflected an understanding of their partner's goals. The extracts of interaction reproduced below illustrate this increasing sophistication. Note how at 8 months the young child can recognize and share the mood and action of their sibling, at 14 months the child can also recognize and co-operate in another's goals.

Recognizing and sharing mood and action

Child 8 months

Sibling puts hand on highchair where C is sitting and wiggles fingers on tray. Child watches. Sibling wiggles fingers; both wiggle their fingers together, with mutual gaze and laughter. Three minutes later C wiggles fingers on tray, looks at sibling, and vocalizes (adapted from Dunn, 1988, p. 110).

Recognizing and co-operating in the other's goals

Child 14 months

Sibling begins to sing. Child goes to toybox, searches, brings two toys to sibling, a music pipe and bells. Child holds out pipe to sibling and makes 'blow' gesture with lips (adapted from Dunn, 1988, p. 113.)

With age, children also become capable of co-operating in joint pretend play and Dunn's work has been crucial in furthering understanding of the nature and significance of joint pretend play between children. The findings of the Cambridge Sibling Study demonstrate that under some circumstances children begin to develop the capacity for engaging in joint pretend play at a very early age. Importantly, the study has also highlighted the significance of the complementary and reciprocal features of the sibling relationship (see Section 2), providing key insights into some of the processes underlying the development of social competence in young children. For example, Dunn has shown that older siblings give specific role-playing instructions and directions to younger siblings and this helps them make appropriate and relevant contributions to the play. Instruction seems to be welcomed in the context of joint pretend play but young children are much less tolerant of this kind of help in other contexts. (Indeed if you look back to the example in Box 1 of the play between Peter and Michael as

Dracula and the Monster-vanishing Hero you will see how they talked about how to 'do' the game and happily gave and took instructions in this context.) Dunn also found that during their third year children's ability to contest and negotiate the course of pretend play with their older siblings increased rapidly – we saw evidence of similar processes of contestation and negotiation in interactions between peers in Section 3. Joint pretend play and co-operative behaviour between siblings were most frequently observed in families where there was a friendly affectionate relationship between siblings. It was much less frequent in families where interactions between siblings were less harmonious. This implies that learning from siblings is not the only process contributing to the development of young children's role-playing ability. Other factors in the child's environment must also contribute to the development of social perspective taking, such as participation in discussions concerning other people's motives and intentions, otherwise how would first-born and only children acquire this ability? Note too that social competence should not be conceived of as a static set of abilities (Kantor *et al.*, 1999, p. 152).

Dunn's work has highlighted the significance of the association between co-operative joint pretend play between siblings and the development of social competence and understanding. Although the use of the terms is somewhat inconsistent, many psychologists distinguish between different kinds of joint pretend play, identifying what they call socio-dramatic play and thematic fantasy play (e.g. Smilansky, 1968). Socio-dramatic play involves pretend activities, which are based on domestic scenes, such as putting baby to bed, going to tea at a friend's house, shopping, cooking and the like. This type of play may also reflect real life experiences outside the home, such as going to the doctor, visiting the zoo, or attending a wedding. Thematic fantasy play, by contrast, is based on fictional narratives and imaginary events, and can be observed whenever children create imaginary worlds for themselves and their toys, or when they act out the plots of stories in books, films and television programmes.

4.1 Fantasy and socio-dramatic play

William Corsaro (1986) has shown that the language and discourse used by children in socio-dramatic play is distinctly different from the language they use in fantasy theme play. When children are acting out socio-dramatic scripts the dialogues they create tend to be based on routine exchanges that echo the content and style of real-life significant exchanges between adults engaged in similar activities. These routine exchanges are essentially identical each time children decide to play out a particular script. Such play is seen as important in helping children develop their understanding of everyday social events with their accompanying routines and rituals. Thus, some researchers such as Stone (1981) suggest that socio-dramatic play functions as an 'anticipatory socialization' device. By this he means that through socio-dramatic play children prepare themselves for the types of roles they may be called upon to adopt as adults. Reviewing some of the many studies of gender differences in children's play, Stone claims that available evidence suggests that in Westernized societies socio-dramatic play involving domestic themes is more characteristic of girls than it is of boys, and that boys are more likely than girls to act out thematic fantasies. He suggests that 'the dramatic play of children in our [i.e. Western] society may function more to prepare little girls for adulthood than little boys' (Stone, 1981, p. 263). Descriptions of children's play in other societies, however, indicate that *both* boys and girls engage in types of play which appear to function as anticipatory socialization devices. The following description of children's play in Malawi is an example of this and illustrates how children's understanding of social and cultural knowledge is constructed through play.

> A perennial amusement among Ngoni boys of five to seven was playing at law courts. They sat around in traditional style with a 'chief' and his elders facing the court, the plaintiffs and defendants presenting their case, and the counsellors conducting proceedings and cross-examining witnesses. In their high, squeaky voices the little boys imitated their fathers whom they had seen in the courts, and they gave judgements, imposing heavy penalties, and keeping order in the court with ferocious severity.

(Read, cited in Leacock, 1976, p. 468)

In contrast to the dialogues involved in socio-dramatic play, the dialogues children create for their fantasy theme play are much more creative and flexible and are likely to change from one occasion to the next, even though the theme of the play might be the same. One play episode based on the theme of monsters and heroes may be completely different from the next, even though it is the same children who are developing the theme. According to Corsaro, fantasy theme play between children has two very important functions. First, it facilitates the development of interpersonal skills and a sense of trust and mutual support between children. Second, it allows children to gain control over their fears and anxieties by sharing them with other children and developing mutual coping strategies. Corsaro suggests that:

> in spontaneous fantasy play the children cooperatively construct fantasy events in which they communally share the tensions associated with such fears as being lost, encountering danger, and thinking about death and dying. In these same play events the children also share the relief of these tensions in the enactment and resolution of the fantasy episodes. In this way the children gain *control* over their fears and uncertainties and at the same time *communally share* this sense of control and the resolution of the tension generated in the spontaneous fantasy play.

(Corsaro, 1986, pp. 93–4, original emphases)

Corsaro argues that this communal sharing of fears and anxieties makes a key contribution to the development of the kinds of interpersonal skills and coping strategies that children will need later in life. Corsaro (1986) also suggests that analyses of thematic fantasy play can reveal some of the wider, extra-familial sources of tension in children's emotional lives. From his observations of nursery school children he was able to show that three major themes recurred time and again in their spontaneous fantasy play. These themes were: lost–found, danger–rescue, and death–rebirth. Wickes (1927/1978), who was a Jungian psychotherapist, would argue that these are basic human, or archetypal themes, which unconsciously preoccupy all people in all cultures throughout their lives.

4.2 Peer collaboration and learning

It is not just in their playful interactions that children co-operate and collaborate with one another. They can also work effectively to solve problems together from a very young age. Brownell and Carriger (1999), for example, have shown that toddler peers aged under 3 years can collaborate to solve simple problems and in doing so are able to establish joint goals and flexibly adapt their behaviour in light of these goals. Their research suggests that 30 month olds possess mutual awareness of each other's behaviour in relation to the outcome and their activity was 'in part conditioned on the recognition of one another's relationship to the goal' (Brownell and Carriger, 1998, p. 208). From their observations of 18, 24 and 30 month olds they also suggest that as they get older, children become better able to comprehend and affect the behaviour and intentions of another. Work with older children, young people and adults suggests that such opportunities for joint working on a problem can have considerable benefits for learning (Miell and Littleton 2004; Littleton *et al.*, 2004).

Having seen that children can co-operate and collaborate in play and work, it is also important to consider the distinction between playful and work-related interactions, which is often blurred. For example, playful, jokey and humorous interactions are also evident when children work together in classroom settings. This can be seen in Box 5 where two 8-year-old friends are working together on planning a story.

BOX 5

Choosing a story character

1   Zak: Choose the characters.

2   Robbie: Robbie Williams ((giggle))

3   Zak: No, come on!

4   Robbie: Billie Piper. ((giggle))

5   Zak: Nooooo! Choose different characters, dude. Any characters. Animals.

6   Robbie: Yeah. ((Zak starts to write)) Monkeys. Hyenas. David Beckham.

7   Zak: Well, David Beckham is a bit of an animal, ain't he? (Both boys laugh)

Source: Vass, 2004, p. 161.

Vass argues that the prevalence of giggles, joking and playfulness means that at first glance one could easily dismiss this episode as two boys messing about when they should be working. However, Vass suggests that the boys simply combine working on the task with playful banter and: 'actually use verbal humour to make sense of the school task together (for example, what it means to choose characters or what should the central criterion be)' (p. 161). She also notes that later in their session of joint work the boys come to make creative use of the ideas that were originally presented as a joke. Thus, humorous interactions between children can sometimes have a positive role to play in helping children generate ideas in creative writing tasks, the seemingly off-task jokes feeding into on-task content generation and dissipating potential conflict arising from differences of perspective.

Summary of Section 4

- Joint interaction and play requires mutual understanding and social awareness in order to co-ordinate moods and actions successfully.
- Pretend play can broadly be divided into two types: socio-dramatic play and thematic fantasy play. Socio-dramatic play is typically based around familiar themes or 'scripts' and adult roles (e.g. parents and babies, doctors and patients), whereas thematic fantasy play is more varied and creative and allows children to work out their feelings about major life events such as threat and loss.
- Even very young children can be observed to participate in pretend play when they are in the familiar context of playing with their siblings where there is motivation to engage with each other and relatively deep mutual understanding.
- Co-operation and collaboration are seen not only in pretend play but also in formal work settings, for example at school and in problem solving situations.
- Successful work-based collaboration is characterized by a good understanding of the aim of the activity and of each other, and can combine work and play/humour to achieve the necessary ends.

5   The limitations of psychologists' accounts of peer and sibling interactions

Looking back over the research discussed in this chapter, we are now going to consider some of the limitations of the work. You may have noticed that the research reviewed here has tended to place considerable emphasis on understanding children's face-to-face interactions. In recent years, however, there have been rapid technological developments that mean that many children and young people, particularly those in affluent societies, regularly communicate with each other using technologies such as mobile phones and the internet. Not only are such technologies used in the process of getting to know others, they are also used to maintain and develop existing relations and facilitate young people's contact with each other. From the young people's perspective, use of such technologies can offer a greater degree of privacy and independence in their communication with others. Use of a mobile phone, for example, has provided young people with 'a new flexibility, privacy and independence in personal communication and social arrangements. They could contact each other directly without having to go through a parental intermediary, at any time of the day or night' (Maybin, 2003, p. 110).

Figure 4   Mobile phones: changing young people's relationships?

A further limitation that you may also have noted is that the account of peer and sibling interactions presented in this chapter is based largely on research conducted in Western industrialized settings. We are thus unable to address how the nature and extent of sibling and peer interactions are influenced by the specific society and cultural contexts within which a child is developing. This is a significant limitation, as there is evidence to suggest that the time spent in the company of, for example, parents, siblings, peers, grandparents and friends varies from culture to culture (Schaffer, 1996). Moreover, in many cultures older siblings have significant child-rearing responsibilities and interactions with peers may occur in work-settings. It is because of limitations such as these that it is important that psychologists do not over-generalize from patterns of relationship observed in a particular society at a particular historical moment in time. Care must be taken not to turn descriptions of particular relationship patterns into prescriptions for healthy development. Psychologists therefore need to develop an understanding of the processes of development that respects the plurality of pathways from infancy to maturity.

Throughout the chapter you have seen how psychologists have attempted to understand children's interactions with other children and how researchers have tried to study the experiences of children and young people – highlighting in many cases what they themselves have to say about their social world. This reflects an important shift in social research, one which views children's own accounts as central and valuable. As children and young people are the central 'stakeholders' in the developmental process it is vital that their voices and experiences are heard. However, is it enough for adult researchers to set the research agenda in this field? Some (e.g. Kellet *et al.*, 2004) believe that it is important to empower children and young people to undertake, not just participate in, research of significance and importance to them. Research chosen, designed, carried out, analysed and reported entirely from the perspective of the children and young people themselves has the potential to make a distinctive contribution to our understanding of social development and children's experiences and understanding of their interactions with siblings and peers.

6 Conclusion

The material presented in this chapter suggests that interactions between children constitute a powerful site for the development of their social skills and social understanding. We have also introduced you to some of the methods used by psychologists to explore the nature and significance of peer and sibling interaction. While the emphasis in this chapter has been on the development of social skills and social understanding, it is clear that children's interactions with other children are also significant for identity development. This is because identity is a socially constructed feature of life, affected fundamentally by the ways in which we think that others perceive us and our view of how we see and present ourselves to others in interactions. The issue of identity development is considered in Chapter 4.

References

Bateson, G. (1955) 'A theory of play and fantasy', *Psychiatric Research Reports*, vol. 2, pp. 39–51.

Blatchford, P. (1994) 'Pupil perceptions of breaktime and implications for breaktime improvements: evidence from England', paper presented to the Annual Meeting of the American Research Association, New Orleans, April 1994.

Blatchford, P. (1999) 'The state of play in schools', in Woodhead, M., Faulkner, D. and Littleton, K. *Making Sense of Social Development*, London, Routledge.

Blatchford, P. and Sharp, S. (eds) (1994) *Breaktime and the School: understanding and changing playground behaviour*, London, Routledge.

Blatchford, P., Creeser, R. and Mooney, A. (1990) 'Playground games and play time: the children's view', *Educational Research*, vol. 32, pp. 163–74.

Brownell, C. A. and Carriger, M. S. (1999) 'Collaborations among toddler peers: Individual contributions to social contexts', in Woodhead, M., Faulkner, D. and Littleton, K. (eds) *Cultural Worlds of Early Childhood*, London, Routledge.

Corsaro, W. (1986) 'Discourse processes within peer culture: from a constructivist to an interpretative approach to childhood socialization', *Sociological Studies of Child Development*, vol. 1, pp. 81–101.

Cowie, H. (1999) 'Children in need: the role of peer support', in Woodhead, M., Faulkner, D. and Littleton, K. (eds) *Making Sense of Social Development*, London, Routledge.

Dunn, J. (1988) *The Beginnings of Social Understanding*, Oxford, Blackwell.

Dunn, J. (2004) *Children's Friendships: the beginnings of intimacy*, Oxford, Blackwell Publishing.

Dunn, J. and Kendrick, C. (1982) *Siblings: love, envy and understanding*, London, Grant McIntyre Ltd.

Fein, G. G. (1984) 'The self-building potential of pretend play or "I got a fish, all by myself" ', in Yawkey, T. D. and Pellegrini, A. D. (eds) *Child's Play: developmental and applied*, Hillsdale, NJ, Lawrence Erlbaum Associates.

Göncü, A. (1998) 'Development of intersubjectivity in social pretend play', in Woodhead, M., Faulkner, D. and Littleton, K. (eds) *Cultural Worlds of Early Childhood*, London, Routledge.

Harris, J. R. (1998) *The Nurture Assumption: why children turn out the way they do*, New York, Free Press.

Kantor, R., Elgas, P. M. and Fernie, D. E. (1999) 'Cultural knowledge and social competence within a preschool peer-culture group', in Woodhead, M., Faulkner, D. and Littleton, K. (eds) *Cultural Worlds of Early Childhood*, London, Routledge.

Kellet, M., Forrest, R., Dent, N. and Ward, S. (2004) 'Just teach us the skills, we'll do the rest: empowering ten-year-olds as active researchers', *Children and Society*, vol. 18, pp. 329–43.

Kelly, E. (1994) 'Racism and sexism in the playground', in Blatchford, P. and Sharp, S. (eds) *Break-time and the School*, London, Routledge.

Leacock, E. (1976) 'At play in African villages', in Bruner, J. S., Jolly, A. and Sylva, K. (eds) *Play: its role in development and evolution,* Harmondsworth, Penguin.

Littleton, K., Miell, D. and Faulkner, D. (2004) *Learning to Collaborate, Collaborating to Learn*, New York, NY, Nova Science.

Maccoby, E. (1999) *The Two Sexes: growing up apart, coming together,* Cambridge, MA, Harvard University Press.

Maybin, J. (2003) 'Language relationships and identities', in Kehily, M. J. and Swann, J. (eds) *Children's Cultural Worlds*, Chichester, Wiley/in association with The Open University.

Miell, D. and Littleton, K. (2004) *Collaborative Creativity*, London, Free Association Books.

Ochs, E. (1979) 'Transcription as theory', in Ochs, E. and Schieffelin, B. B. (eds) *Developmental Pragmatics*, London, Academic Press.

Pellegrini, A. D. (2003) 'Perceptions and functions of play and real fighting in early adolescence', *Child Development*, vol. 74, pp. 1522–33.

Pinker, S. (2002) *The Blank Slate: the modern denial of human nature*, London, Allen Lane.

Pollard, A. (1987) 'Goodies, jokers and gangs', in Pollard, A. (ed.) *Children and Their Primary Schools*, Lewes, Falmer.

Schaffer, H. R. (1996) *Social Development*, Oxford, Blackwell Publishing.

Schaffer, H. R. (2003) *Introducing Child Psychology*, Oxford, Blackwell Publishing.

Sheldon, A. (1992) 'Preschool girls' discourse competence: managing conflict and negotiating power', in Bucholtz, M., Hall, K. and Moonwomon, B. (eds) *Locating Power*, Volume 2 of the Proceedings of the 1992 Berkeley Women and Language Conference, pp. 528–39, Berkeley, CA, Berkeley Linguistic Society.

Short, G. (1999) 'Children's grasp of controversial issues', in Woodhead, M., Faulkner, D. and Littleton, K. (eds) *Making Sense of Social Development*, London, Routledge.

Smilansky, S. (1968) *The Effects of Sociodramatic play on Disadvantaged Pre-school Children*, New York, Wiley.

Smith, P. K., Bowers, L., Binney, V. and Cowie, H. (1999) 'Relationships of children involved in bully/victim problems at school', in Woodhead, M., Faulkner, D. and Littleton, K. (eds) *Cultural Worlds of Early Childhood*, London, Routledge.

Stalker, K. and Connors, C. (2004) 'Children's perceptions of their disabled siblings: "'She's different but it's normal for us'"', *Children and Society*, vol. 18, pp. 218–30.

Stone, G. P. (1981) 'The play of little children', in Stone, G. P. and Faberman, H. A. (eds) *Social Psychology Through Symbolic Interaction*, New York, NY, Wiley.

Vass, E. (2004, unpublished) 'Understanding collaborative creativity: an observational study of the effects of the social and educational context on the processes of young children's joint creative writing', PhD thesis, The Open University, Milton Keynes.

Whitney, I. and Smith, P. K. (1993) 'A survey of the nature and extent of bullying in junior/middle and secondary schools', *Educational Research*, vol. 35, pp. 3–25.

Wickes, F. G. (1927/1978) *The Inner World of Childhood: a study in analytical psychology*, Boston, Sigo Press, pp. 156–8.

Chapter 4
The early development of identity

Dorothy Miell and Sharon Ding

Contents

Learning outcomes

After you have studied this chapter you should be able to:

1 discuss the relationship between the individual and social factors which contribute to the early understanding of identity;

2 describe the distinction between the existential and categorical self and give an account of the infant's early development in these two areas.

1 Introduction

What is meant by identity, and how can its development be studied? These are important questions for developmental psychologists but they are not easy ones to answer. The term 'identity' is used in different ways, and so it is important to explain what psychologists mean when they use it. Important parts of identity are the individual character traits people have, and the ways in which they usually behave. For many people these constitute personality – you may describe yourself as being a generally happy person, for example, who is very keen to meet new people. In addition, though, an identity also includes some active engagement with others in the environment. People take up an identity and share it with some groups and not with others. In this way identity is fundamentally about how people see themselves in relation to others and how others see them. Identities are complex, and it is perhaps not surprising that children's sense of identity develops and changes over the whole span of childhood.

This chapter will introduce you to some of the key concepts associated with the development of identity in young children, and the classic studies that have investigated them. It focuses on the first few years of a child's life, and discusses research that has investigated how infants come to an understanding that they exist as individuals. The chapter ends by looking forwards to the next three chapters in the book, each of which focuses on a different aspect of later identity development. Again, a key component of identity formation involves children and young people drawing distinctions between themselves and others. They identify with other people by seeing themselves as being the same as some groups, and different from others.

1.1 How children and young people talk about their identities

Activity

Allow about
20 minutes

Defining features of self-descriptions

This activity will set you thinking about how children and young people of various ages describe themselves and how they talk about their identities.

Look at the self-descriptions below. They were obtained when a group of children and young people were asked to answer the question 'Who are you?'

First of all, look at the ways in which the children and young people are describing themselves. Are they describing physical characteristics or activities, or are they describing more psychological aspects of who they are – such as feelings, thoughts or hopes? Do any of the self-descriptions include references to other people (either explicitly or implicitly)? Then decide whether all of the children and young people describe themselves in similar ways. Do they all use mainly physical characteristics, for example? Can you identify any developmental trends in the way in which the children and young people describe themselves?

Self-descriptions

Emily, aged 4 years 9 months

[*Dictated description*] Emily is a sister and I am big. I got toes and a belly button (are you allowed to say that?). I've got a head, eyes, mouth, elbow, finger, ear. I draw. I write, 'cause I do write, don't I? I do gluing at school, I do. I go to see my teachers. I go outside to play with all the toys and the bikes and when it's time to go in, we all walk into nursery. I eat a lot. I walk. I go to PE [physical education] and I go on the climbing frame – it's not like Linda's. And I go to the 'sembly [assembly], but I always eat my lunch up. I always go outside to play in our garden. I sit on chairs. I play with my toys. Can I knit or can I do sewing? ... I sew. I can talk numbers [count]. And we always have a wash. I brush my teeth. I always hoover up. Just very one more ... I wash my face and I sit down to listen to books.

Malini, aged 7 years

I am a girl. I am seven years old. I am Indian and Malaysian. I like playing football with Matthew. I like doing work because it is nice to learn things. I like reading and making models of cartoon characters. My hobby is badges. I get a lot of things that I need. I love playing schools, it is my favourite game because I can teach children how to do things.

Luke, aged 10 years

Hello I'm Luke. I live in the countryside so I often like going on adventures. I love insects and I love my family and friends. Often I can be a bit mean. I like reading but my handwriting's scruffy and I'm not very good at grama [*sic*].

James, aged 13 years

I am a 13-year-old boy called James. I enjoy playing sport, in particular cricket, tennis and hockey. I also quite like to walk and cycle and I like to relax with a good fantasy or sci-fi book or listen to some music. I occasionally listen to something quiet and classical, but I prefer rock or grunge. I follow a football team heavily and I listen to any match or buy any books on the subject. I tend to take life as it comes rather than plan ahead which makes me a bit disorganized – as my teachers keep telling me! I like to learn Spanish and French and I like to do my best at *most* subjects at school. I am quite committed at things when I want to be and I am really enjoying my Duke of Edinburgh award. Overall I tend to be happy, but at times I can get frustrated with my teachers and parents, and get depressed. I have one very close best friend and a few other good friends. I would like to become a journalist, or perhaps a cricketer.

Anna, aged 16 years

Over the last few years my personality has changed drastically, mostly due to pressures from my peers to conform, although I am happier with my new 'image' than I was before. However I now feel the need to find my true personality, if this is possible, and to define myself. It is difficult not to do this by fitting into a stereotype, as I see many people doing, where the way they dress, their way of talking and even their values are defined by something as immaterial as their taste in music. I think quite deeply about my personality. From talking to my friends I think I am fairly unusual in this. Most people seem to take the way they are for granted whereas I see myself as having to work at myself to find a state in which I am happy. I worry a lot about what people think of me so it is important to me to be complimented.

Comment

You will probably have noticed that as a general rule the younger children's descriptions focused more heavily on things that other people are able to observe – that is, their external characteristics. For example, Emily has focused on her physical appearance and on the everyday activities that make up her daily routine, such as walking to nursery or eating a lot. The older children and young people have focused more on internal characteristics such as their emotions and their relationships with others. Luke mentions his love for his family and friends, and James indicates that his view of himself as disorganized has been confirmed (and possibly instigated) by his teachers. He also talks about becoming frustrated and depressed. Harter (1983) reviewed several studies in which children of various ages were interviewed about themselves. She outlined a developmental sequence in which young children described behaviour and objective facts which could potentially be described by others. As the children became older the focus moved to 'qualities of character' (happy, cheerful etc.) and then to intrapersonal traits (shy, friendly etc.). The oldest participants in this activity included descriptions of themselves in terms of their emotions and attitudes. Of course, there may well be a difference between how children and young people describe themselves to another person, and how they actually think about themselves. Descriptions of emotions and feelings can often involve quite complex language and are not usually a typical topic of conversation for young children. Later sections in this chapter will discuss how psychologists have found out about children's identity by using methods other than self-descriptions.

You may also have noticed a difference in the level of complexity between the self-descriptions given by the oldest and youngest participants. Developing an identity is often seen in Western cultures as the long process of becoming a self-aware individual – becoming aware, for example, of what you look like, your gender, what makes you happy and sad, what roles you play (all themes raised in the self-descriptions above). This is a long and complex process. As the psychologist Eleanor Maccoby (1980) has pointed out, developing a sense of self is not accomplished quickly. Instead, this self-awareness develops incrementally and is produced by understandings which become more and more complex. Because of this, many researchers argue for a view of identity as developing over a lifetime, rather than just throughout childhood.

1.2 Cultural differences in the importance of individuality

Up until now, this chapter has implied that everyone experiences the gradual development of a sense of an autonomous, unique and reflexive self, of a private inner world distinct from that of other people. This may ring true to many people. However, this 'primacy of the individual' may not be a universal experience – other cultures may have a different view of the relationship between the individual and society at large. Anthropologists such as Geertz (1984) have argued that this emphasis on the uniqueness of the individual is a Western cultural view.

Tobin *et al.* (1998), as part of a study which reports a comparison between pre-school settings in Japan, China and the United States, compare the views of pre-school teachers on the videotaped behaviour of one of the children who attended the Japanese pre-school. The American teacher described the child as being 'intellectually gifted and easily bored', whereas the Japanese teachers, in contrast to this, were concerned with the child's social behaviour, and focused on his lack of social skills and his inability to be dependent. Tobin and colleagues asked the Japanese teachers what traits they were trying to encourage in their pupils, and found that empathy, gentleness and co-operativeness, obedience and enthusiasm were among the characteristics that were highly valued. In addition, they encouraged the children to see themselves as like others. One of the main roles of early education was seen as trying to cancel out differences between children, by highlighting group similarities. According to Tobin and his colleagues, this was because the teachers believed strongly that children benefit from the security of belonging to a large, homogeneous group, and that the emphasis on 'groupism' makes possible 'the experience of camaraderie, of fusion, of unity with something larger than the self' (Tobin *et al.*, 1998, p. 274). This focus on group membership, harmony and obedience contrasts with typical Western values concerning the primacy of independence and creativity in the development of identity.

Group membership is of course an important part of the Western definition of the self (consider, for example, the number of references to this in the Activity), but it is seen only as a *part* of a more global self. While many theorists have incorporated social roles into their accounts of how the self is formed, the private inner world is often seen as the more basic, more central part of the self than the face Westerners show to the outer social world. In talking about the self, Westerners are more concerned to distinguish themselves from others and stress what makes them unique, rather than emphasizing what they share with society in general. You saw examples of this in the Activity, where the children tended to focus on individual characteristics. For example, James talked about his musical preferences and Malini described her hobbies and favourite games.

The important thing to take away from this brief discussion is that ideas about individuality are not universal, but instead are culturally bound. From the viewpoint of the Western world, concepts such as autonomy, self-control and uniqueness are natural. They just characterize the way that people are. It is difficult to think that what are viewed as fundamental truths about how the self is understood are not in fact universal. Instead, they are a set of understandings or beliefs that are so integral to Western culture that, to people in the West, it seems as if there is no other way to think about identity. To consider, even briefly, the ways in which different cultures view the self helps individuals to put their taken-for-granted views into perspective – to see them as theories, as assumptions. While the rest of this chapter discusses the Western view of the self, it is worth bearing in mind the *constructed* nature of this concept, rather than assuming that it is a natural and universal way of conceptualizing the nature of the individual.

Summary of Section 1

- Western ideas of identity are fundamentally concerned with establishing features which mark the person out from others and emphasize the role of a private inner life.
- Some other cultures are more concerned to emphasize those aspects that make a person part of society, such as roles and relationships to other people.
- Views of what constitutes a self are assumptions or theories which are culturally developed and not universal experiences.

2   An emerging sense of identity

Maccoby pointed out that a sense of self develops by degrees. This process can usefully be thought of in terms of the gradual emergence and elaboration of two somewhat separate features: the *self as a subject* of experience and the *self as an object* of knowledge. This distinction is quite a difficult one to grasp, and has continued to be a focus of discussion among psychologists for many years. William James, in 1892, introduced the topic and contemporaries of his, such as Charles Cooley (1902), added to the developing debate. George Mead, working in the first part of the twentieth century, continued researching in the area, and psychologists today continue to build on the theories which the early researchers introduced. This chapter will now explore the theoretical background to these two aspects of the self and consider their implications for the developing child's understanding of him- or herself and, indeed, for the identities of other people.

2.1 First steps: establishing that I exist

A child's first step on the road to self-understanding and the establishment of a personal identity can be seen as the recognition that he or she exists. In his studies, James labelled this self the 'I', or the 'self-as-subject', now often referred to as the 'existential self' (Lewis, 1990). James gave it four elements:

(1) an awareness of one's own agency (i.e. one's power to act) in life events;
(2) an awareness of the uniqueness of one's own experience, of one's distinctiveness from other people;
(3) an awareness of the continuity of one's identity;
(4) an awareness of one's own awareness, the element of reflexiveness.

These features gradually emerge as infants explore their world and interact with caregivers. Particularly striking is their development of an understanding of themselves as having power, of being an *agent* in the environment; that is, of being able to cause things to happen and control objects. Cooley was a sociologist concerned with personal development and he also discussed this aspect of the self, suggesting that a sense of self was primarily concerned with being able to exercise power. He suggested that the earliest examples of this are an infant's attempts to control physical objects, such as toys or his or her own limbs. This is followed by attempts to affect the behaviour of other people, thus extending a young child's feeling of power (Cooley, 1902). Infants learn that when they close their eyes the world goes dark; when they let go of something it drops; when they touch a toy it moves; when they cry or smile someone responds to them. In this way a sense of agency emerges and is consolidated.

Many parents spend a lot of time, particularly in the early months, imitating the infant's behaviour, vocalizations and expressions. This is another powerful source of information for infants, not only about their particular relationship with their parents, but also about the effects they can have on the world around them generally. The young child's liking for imitation can be seen in a study described in the Research summary.

RESEARCH SUMMARY

Liking for imitation

In Meltzoff's (1990) study, 14-month-old children were individually seated at a table opposite two adults. The child and the two adults each had an identical toy, and whenever the child moved or manipulated it one of the adults copied the child's actions exactly while the other adult did something different with it. The infants smiled and looked more and for longer at the adult who imitated them, thereby indicating that they preferred the imitative activity.

The same amusement with and liking for imitation is also apparent in a study by Dunn and Kendrick, who observed the behaviour of young siblings in their home environment.

> Joyce (8 months) vocalizes while playing. Warren looks at her, she looks at him; mutual gaze. Warren 'imitates' her vocalization. Joyce repeats her vocalization. Both laugh.
>
> *Source: Dunn and Kendrick, 1982, p. 141*

Since young children appear very interested in and attracted to imitation and similar behaviours, perhaps this is why they enjoy looking in mirrors, where they detect not just similar but *identical* behaviour to their own, through the movements they can see there which are dependent (contingent) upon their own movements. Such contingency has important lessons for infants, learned from the fact that what they *do* in front of the mirror and what they *see* in it are the same. Lewis and Brooks-Gunn (1979) suggest that this contingency of movement is a powerful cue for the infant's emerging sense of the self as an independent agent – that it is the self that is 'making things happen'.

This is not to say that infants *recognize* the reflection as their own image (a later development). However, Lewis and Brooks-Gunn suggest that infants' developing understanding that the movements they see in the mirror are identical to and contingent on their own, contributes to their growing knowledge that they are distinct from other people. This is because they, and only they, can cause the reflection in the mirror to move.

These achievements represent the first two aspects of James's definition of the self-as-subject which was given earlier. Children's understanding of themselves as active agents continues to develop in their attempts to co-operate with others in play. They use their knowledge of their own power to act on their world, and therefore change their environment, when they offer to share a toy or join in pretend play with a friend. Dunn (1988) points out that it is in such day-to-day relationships and interactions that the child's understanding of his- or herself emerges.

Empirical investigations of the self-as-subject in young children are, however, rather scarce. This could in part be due to the fact that it is difficult to think about or articulate the different aspects of the 'I', and so even more difficult to study them empirically – indeed James himself 'despaired of ever studying the "I" in an empirical and nonspeculative way' (Damon and Hart, 1988, p. viii). Even if young infants *can* reflect on these experiences, they certainly cannot articulate this aspect of the self directly.

2.2 Later developments: social categories

A second step in the development of a full sense of self can be seen as the acquisition and elaboration of what James (1961, first published 1892) called the 'me', or the 'self-as-object', and which is now often referred to as the 'categorical self' (Lewis, 1990). This aspect of the self concerns the qualities or characteristics that define a person, such as gender, name, size, and relationship to others. Once children have gained a certain level of self-awareness (of the existential self), they begin to place themselves – and to be placed by others – in a whole series of categories which go on to play such an important role in defining them uniquely as 'themselves'. Chapters 5, 6 and 7 in this book each focus on one of these important characteristics.

Since James put forward this distinction between the 'I' and the 'me', others have developed and elaborated it, and particularly the understanding of the 'me' – the categorical self. This has been seen by many to be the aspect of the self which is most influenced by social factors, since it is made up of social roles (such as student, brother, colleague) and of characteristics which derive their meaning from comparison or interaction with other people (such as trustworthiness, shyness, sporting ability). As a result, emphasizing the importance of the social context in self-development has been an important feature of the work of many theorists in this area.

The looking-glass self

Among other researchers, Cooley and Mead developed the suggestion of the close connection between a person's own understanding of their identity and other people's understanding of it. Cooley believed that people build up their sense of identity from the reactions of others to them and from the view they believe others have of them. Cooley called this the 'looking-glass self', since it is as if others provide a 'social mirror', and people come to see themselves as they are reflected in others. Mead was one of the founders of the 'symbolic interactionist' school of thought which emphasized the importance of language and interaction. He saw the self and the social world as inextricably bound together:

> The self is essentially a social structure, and it arises in social experience ...
> it is impossible to conceive of a self arising outside of social experience.

(Mead, 1934, p. 135)

He believed that through their use of language, their games and their play, young children begin to adopt the perspectives that other people have of them, and, in so doing, become capable of reflecting on themselves. So, for Cooley and Mead, the child cannot develop a sense of self without the chance to interact with others, in order to begin to understand how these others view the world, including how they view the child.

Such analyses by theorists lead us to conclude that without being part of a community a child could not develop a sense of self, as understood in the West. Most explicitly in Mead's work, children are seen to develop concepts of themselves as they learn to communicate and interact with those around them.

He suggests that people gain from others a perspective on themselves and on the world around them that they cannot obtain alone. The importance of this interplay of social experience with personal and emotional development can be illustrated by briefly examining the rare cases of children who have suffered extreme social deprivation early in life, and by looking at the effects of this deprivation on the development of their sense of self, their emotions and their ability to interact with others. These children are called feral or wild children, since some were found abandoned in the wild, having had to fend for themselves for several years. Other cases report children who have been kept isolated from all but minimal human contact, for example in attics or cellars. (Rymer (1993) presents a fascinating discussion of the case of Genie, who was kept locked in an attic for several years.) Perhaps the most famous case of a feral child was Victor, the 'wild boy of Aveyron', found living in a wood in France in 1800. It emerged that he was about 12 years old, but no details of his earlier years were ever fully established.

It is clear from contemporary accounts that Victor had a very limited understanding of the world about him when he was first found. He was obviously skilled at survival in the wild, being able to gather and store food and keep away from danger, but he had no real ability to reason, to engage in human interaction, or to think about himself in an abstract way. Even after intensive training, some of these abilities never developed fully. At the time it was suggested that these problems were largely the result of his lack of social experience during his formative years. Itard, the doctor who adopted and studied Victor, said:

> The mind of a man deprived of the commerce of others is so little exercised, so little cultivated, that he thinks only in the measure that he is obliged to by exterior objects. *The greatest source of ideas among men is their human interactions.*

(quoted in Lane, 1977, p. 38; author's emphasis)

Victor lacked the social experience that Mead saw as all-important. He had managed to establish many of the features of the existential self (except the capacity for reflexiveness) but had very few, if any, of the elements of the categorical self. He could not recognize himself in a mirror, and apparently had no sense of his psychological characteristics or of social roles. He had not been able to develop the capacity to reflect on himself, because he did not have others around him whose behaviour he could observe, or who could give him feedback about his own behaviour and characteristics. Some caution is necessary in drawing conclusions from this account, particularly since so little is known about Victor before he lived in the wild; he may have been abandoned for the very reason that he was unresponsive socially or a slow developer. However, the case does suggest that his isolation from other people affected his ability to develop a complete sense of self.

Around their second birthday, many children display visual self-recognition (an aspect of knowledge of the self-as-object or categorical self) when they see themselves in a mirror or in a photograph. As Lewis and Brooks-Gunn (1979) have shown, some form of self-recognition can be observed from about the age of 15 months. In a series of studies, these researchers observed how often young children touched their noses during a control period playing in front of a mirror. Then they dabbed some rouge on the children's noses (during a 'routine nose wipe' by the mother) and counted how often the children touched their noses when they again played in front of a mirror. Lewis and Brooks-Gunn reasoned that if the children knew what they usually looked like, they would be surprised by the unusual red mark on their noses and would explore it by touching their own nose. However, this early self-recognition is not stable, since Lewis and Brooks-Gunn showed that children of 15 to 18 months are generally not able to recognize themselves if other cues (such as movements corresponding to their own) are absent. Lewis and Brooks-Gunn investigated this by showing infants a still photograph of themselves and video images of themselves filmed on a previous occasion. In each case the researchers looked for signs of recognition from the child, and they found that the video images elicited more signs than the still images. Lewis and Brooks-Gunn argued that an important developmental milestone is reached when children become able to recognize themselves without the support of seeing contingent movement. A full appreciation of what the self looks like develops fairly gradually from this age, until children have an awareness of what their own features look like, even when their image is no longer contingent on their current movements or expressions.

2.3 Disagreement as an expression of self-awareness

Perhaps the most graphic expressions of self-awareness in the young child can be seen in the displays of rage and aggression which are most common, certainly in Western societies, from 18 months to 3 years of age, when the infant is already displaying an increasing awareness of the self through the use of the words 'me' and, particularly in this context, 'mine'. Cooley, in his early writings on development of the self (Cooley, 1902), stressed the importance of struggles with rivals. In a longitudinal study of groups of three or four children over the course of their second year Bronson (1975) found that the intensity of the frustration and anger in their disagreements increased sharply between the ages of 1 and 2 years. Often, the children's disagreements involved a struggle over a toy that none of them played with before or after the tug-of-war was over: the children seemed to be disputing possession itself rather than wanting to play with the toy. The link between the sense of 'self' and of 'ownership' may be less marked in other cultures where sole possession of objects is less emphasized, but such struggles are a notable feature of childhood in Western societies.

Summary of Section 2

- The self can be divided into two aspects, the existential and the categorical.
- The existential self (also referred to as the 'I' or the self-as-subject) involves an awareness of being distinct from others, of having the power to act on the world, and of continuity – and the ability to reflect on this awareness.
- The categorical self (also referred to as the 'me' or the self-as-object) involves a recognition of the physical characteristics of the self, as well as an understanding of various other characteristics, such as gender, name and a growing range of social roles.
- Major developments in these two areas occur during the second and third years of life, in the context of social interactions and relationships. The developments may be dependent on these factors.

3   Taking stock and looking forwards

Section 2 has explained in some detail the classic work that has been undertaken with infants and young children in the first 2 to 3 years of life. These studies have emphasized the importance of the social context in the development of identity, particularly those aspects that are incorporated into the categorical self. As children become older their identity becomes even more dependent on meanings which have been formed through comparison or interaction with others. Recent research in the area of identity development has investigated these more complex meanings by focusing on certain aspects of identity, and the next three chapters of this book will introduce three of these aspects: gender, national identity and consumerism. As well as differing in topic, each of these chapters is distinct from the others in that it focuses on a different phase of development, and on different theoretical perspectives. However, each of the perspectives emphasizes the role of social context in the development of a sense of identity.

At the beginning of this chapter we emphasized that the development of identity is lengthy and complex. It is perhaps not surprising then that different aspects of identity come into focus at different times in the life of a child or young person. The chapter went on to explain how young children develop a good understanding of their basic characteristics and their experiences and actions. Later development consists of acquiring more complex understandings of identity. These are inextricably linked to social factors – how individuals see themselves in relation to other people, how other people see them, and how they actively engage with those people with whom they share an aspect of their identity. Of course, it is not the case that children acquire these understandings in a strictly linear fashion. There is a large amount of overlap, because children do not focus exclusively on one aspect of identity. Nonetheless, it does seem that some aspects feature more heavily in identity formation at different phases in a child's life, and so Chapters 5, 6 and 7 each focus on different age groups. Of the three topics that feature in this group of chapters, gender is the one which receives the most attention relatively early on in childhood (Chapter 5). This aspect of identity is one which is key to children at an early age, but continues to be built on as children and young people negotiate more complex understandings. Aspects of national identity (Chapter 6) feature relatively prominently during middle childhood. The importance of a national identity varies according to features such as geographical location, but there is no doubt that for many children and young people, the significance of, for example, describing themselves in terms of where they or their parents were born, is high. However, when you read the chapter on young consumers (Chapter 7), you will see that this is situated largely within the experience of adolescents. The author argues that it is at this stage that young people are most likely to construct their identities, at least partly, on the basis of their consumption of goods such as clothes or leisure activities. These products and lifestyles are symbolic – they represent and display particular values and kinds of style. Of course, it is important to remember that young children are also consumers – the advertisement breaks in children's television programmes are ample witness to this.

4 Conclusion

Children become more sophisticated in their understanding of themselves as they acquire more complex understandings of how other people think and also as they begin to take more account of how they themselves are perceived and evaluated by others. As we reach the end of this chapter, it is appropriate to return to the self-descriptions in the Activity and to the distinction between the 'I' and the 'me'. Many of the concepts and processes we have been examining are linked together. As well as this, they are linked in turn to the subject matter of the first three chapters in this book, that of relationships. The ways in which children construct a view of themselves are inextricably bound up with their developing understanding of other people around them and of the web of relationships in which they live. This complex environment has a fundamental impact on a child's sense of identity, and in turn the environment is shaped by the individuals existing within it. While the focus of this chapter has been on what seems to be an entirely personal feature (the development of an identity or a sense of self) it should be clear that it is essential to study this within a social context which takes full account of the transactional relationship between children and their environment. The chapters which follow on from this one provide further illustrations of this important relationship.

References

Bronson, W.C. (1975) 'Developments in behaviour with age mates during the second year of life' in Lewis, M. and Rosenblum, L.A. (eds) *The Origins of Behaviour: friendship and peer relations*, New York, NY, Wiley.

Cooley, C.H. (1902) *Human Nature and the Social Order*, New York, Scribner.

Damon, W. and Hart, D. (1988) *Self Understanding in Childhood and Adolescence*, Cambridge, Cambridge University Press.

Dunn, J. (1988) *The Beginnings of Social Understanding*, Oxford, Blackwell.

Dunn, J. and Kendrick, C. (1982) *Siblings: love, envy and understanding*, Cambridge, MA, Harvard University Press.

Geertz, C. (1984) 'From the natives' point of view. On the nature of anthropological understanding' in Schweder, R. and Levine, R.A. (eds) *Culture Theory: essays on mind, self, emotion*, Cambridge, Cambridge University Press.

Harter, S. (1983) 'Developmental perspectives on the self-system' in Mussen, P.H. (ed.) *Handbook of Child Psychology*, vol. 4, New York, NY, Wiley.

James, W. (1961) *Psychology: the briefer course*, New York, NY, Harper and Row (first published 1892).

Lane, H. (1977) *The Wild Boy of Aveyron*, Cambridge, MA, Harvard University Press.

Lewis, M. (1990) 'Social knowledge and social development', *Merrill-Palmer Quarterly*, vol. 36, pp. 93–116.

Lewis, M. and Brooks-Gunn, J. (1979) *Social Cognition and the Acquisition of Self*, New York, NY, Plenum Press.

Maccoby, E. (1980) *Social Development, Psychological Growth and the Parent–Child Relationship*, New York, NY, Harcourt Brace Jovanovich.

Mead, G.H. (1934) *Mind, Self and Society*, Chicago, IL, University of Chicago Press.

Meltzoff, A. N. (1990) 'Towards a developmental cognitive science: the implications of cross-modal matching and imitation for the development of representation and memory in infants', *Annals of New York Academy of Sciences*, vol. 608 (December).

Rymer, R. (1993) *Genie*, Harmondsworth, Penguin Books.

Tobin, J.J., Wu, D.Y.H. and Davidson, D.H. (1998) 'Komatsudai: a Japanese preschool' in Woodhead, M., Faulkner, D. and Littleton, K (eds) *Cultural Worlds of Early Childhood*, London, Routledge.

Chapter 5
Gender identity and the development of gender roles

Robin Banerjee

Contents

Learning outcomes

After you have studied this chapter you should be able to:

1 identify and understand basic concepts in gender development;
2 identify and understand contemporary uses of terms relating to gender development;
3 describe and evaluate dominant theoretical frameworks, identifying commonalities as well as distinguishing characteristics;
4 report critically on methods used in empirical research on gender-related processes in childhood and beyond;
5 understand how children's gender development involves an interaction between cognitive and social contextual factors;
6 identify ways in which the development of gender identity and gender roles is associated with other aspects of social development, as well as with other areas of psychology and related disciplines;
7 recognize multiple possible interpretations of 'sex differences' discussed in both academic and non-academic sources;
8 discuss the role of gender in children's behaviour, emotion, and motivation in specific social contexts.

1 Introduction

Think for a moment about someone you know. How would you describe that person? You might refer to their relationship to you, their psychological traits, their physical appearance, their occupation, and a multitude of other characteristics. But perhaps the most fundamental part of your description is whether that person is a man or a woman, a boy or a girl. Even if you do not state this explicitly, it would be evident every time you refer to the person using 'he', 'she', 'him', or 'her'. Indeed, if someone was describing a person to you and failed to clarify this detail, it would probably be missed more than any other single piece of information. For children also, it seems that gender is one of the most salient dimensions in their concepts of themselves and of other people.

This chapter addresses the ways in which psychologists have tackled three critical questions:

- How do children come to have a sense of being a boy or a girl?
- How do children come to have a sense of what being a boy or being a girl means, to them personally and to society in general?
- How does this development relate to the way children think, feel and act in everyday life?

Throughout history, there have been innumerable characterizations of the differences between men and women, in both popular and academic discourses.

What is particularly striking is that, in the Western world at least, these broad stereotypical characterizations have remained fairly constant over lengthy historical periods. Indeed, despite the many social changes over the last century, the psychological profile commonly labelled as masculine still centres on assertiveness, dominance, competence and competitiveness, while the corresponding feminine profile continues to focus on nurturance, compassion, warmth, and sensitivity. Williams and Best (1990) further report that similar distinctions are made across a range of different cultures. Thus, someone whose beliefs about gender might today be regarded as 'stereotyped' follows a tradition of thought reaching as far back as Ancient Greece (see Box 1).

BOX 1

Men and women: views through history

Hence woman is more compassionate than man, more easily moved to tears, at the same time is more jealous, more querulous, more apt to scold and to strike. She is, furthermore, more prone to despondency and less hopeful than the man ... the male is more courageous than the female.
Aristotle, *History of Animals* (350 BCE) (trans. D'Arcy Wentworth Thompson)

For contemplation he and valour form'd,
For softness she and sweet attractive grace;
John Milton, *Paradise Lost* (1667)

Man for the field and woman for the hearth:
Man for the sword and for the needle she:
Man with the head and woman with the heart:
Man to command and woman to obey;
All else confusion.
Alfred, Lord Tennyson, *The Princess* (1850)

Now their separate characters are briefly these. The man's power is active, progressive, defensive. He is eminently the doer, the creator, the discoverer, the defender. His intellect is for speculation and invention; his energy for adventure, for war, and for conquest, wherever war is just, wherever conquest necessary. But the woman's power is for rule, not for battle, – and her intellect is not for invention or creation, but for sweet ordering, arrangement and decision ... . The man, in his rough work in open world, must encounter all peril and trial ... But he guards the woman from all this.
John Ruskin, *Of Queens' Gardens* (1865)

There is, of course, a lot more to gender than simply identifying people's stereotypical notions about masculine and feminine characteristics. One body of work, which largely lies beyond the scope of this chapter, concerns the vast research literature on actual similarities and differences between the sexes on physical and psychological characteristics. This work centres on studies which are designed to test the extent to which males and females differ on given variables such as aggression and cognitive abilities, and on the biological explanations that have been put forward for such differences, such as contrasts in brain structure, the influence of hormones and the consequences of evolutionary change. Such work is of great value but it is important to note that there is a larger number of myths about gender differences than there are differences that have been consistently found in scientific research. For example, in the 1970s, two psychologists carried out a comprehensive review of the large amount of research conducted on the development of gender differences (Maccoby and Jacklin, 1974). They found that not only were consistent differences rather thin on the ground, but the few differences that were identifiable were usually of a small to moderate magnitude. There was greater variability *within* each sex than *between* the sexes. More recently there have been disagreements about whether certain gender-related differences in physical, cognitive, and social functioning are small enough to dismiss or big enough to be seen as meaningful (for example, Hyde and Plant, 1995; Eagly, 1996). However, it is very clear that stereotypical notions of masculinity and femininity are much more than simple reflections of actual differences between the sexes.

In this chapter, you will explore how children come to have a sense of maleness or femaleness, and how they come to form beliefs about masculine and feminine characteristics. You will tackle fundamentally different approaches to developmental psychology – some that focus on social influences as being the primary driving force in children's development, and others that assign a more central role to cognitive processes – and you will examine ways in which contemporary accounts have tried to integrate these different approaches. However, before turning to some of the research on this topic it is important to clarify some of the key concepts and methods used in the area. These will be covered in Section 2.

Summary of Section 1

- For both children and adults, gender is one of the most important parts of their concepts of themselves and others.
- Notions of masculinity and femininity have shown considerable stability over lengthy historical periods.
- There is great controversy about the existence and origins of gender differences.
- Some approaches to children's gender development focus primarily on social influences, while others emphasize cognitive processes.

2 Key concepts in gender development research

The first question concerns when to use the word 'sex' and when to use the word 'gender'. One common perspective would reserve 'sex' for references to biological aspects of males and females and 'gender' for references to social characteristics defined by cultural norms and beliefs. However, Eleanor Maccoby (1988) has argued, justifiably, that simply assuming biological causes for some characteristics and social causes for certain others is problematic: 'uncovering the biological and social connections to behavior is a major research objective, not something to be assumed at the outset through the choice of terminology' (p. 755). Indeed, it seems highly likely that biological and social factors may interact with each other. Many researchers therefore choose to use sex and gender interchangeably.

Activity I

Allow about
I hour

Sex and gender

This activity enables you to explore people's differing understandings of the nature and origins of differences between males and females.

Some authors identify the word 'sex' with the male/female (biological) distinction, and the word 'gender' with the masculine/feminine (social) distinction. But identification of a characteristic as biological or social in origin cannot be taken for granted.

Ask some people to come up with a list of characteristics they think represent biological or innate differences between men and women, and those they think are simply part of the social roles assigned to men and women. Do your respondents share a common understanding about differences between males and females? How sure are you about which differences are biological and which are social in origin?

Now ask some parents you know the same questions *with regard to children*. Do you get the same answers?

Comment

Although it is easy to agree on some anatomical differences between men and women, people will probably come up with a huge range of other characteristics, ranging from communication skills and map reading to intimacy and competitiveness. You are likely to find considerable disagreement about whether these characteristics are biological or social in origin, and views may differ depending on whether you are talking about adults or children. Research suggests that biological and social factors often interact with each other, and it is important to remember that there are far more myths about gender differences than there are robust, consistently found gender differences.

The authors of the research studies that inform this chapter employ a number of different terms which it is important to understand. *Gender identity* refers to an individual's sense of being male or female. In nearly all cases gender identity matches biological sex, but in some cases individuals may have a sense of

Figure 1
Boys will be boys?

maleness despite being physically female or a sense of femaleness despite being physically male. Such 'transsexuals' may choose to have surgical procedures for sex-reassignment in order to resolve this discrepancy between gender identity and biological sex. *Gender role* refers to the attributes, behaviours, and attitudes that are associated with being male or female. They reflect *gender stereotypes*, commonly held beliefs about the characteristics of males and females, including abilities and skills, psychological dispositions, physical appearance, and patterns of behaviour. Gender roles, and the individual stereotypes that they reflect, may vary from one cultural community to another. Although similarities exist across many cultures, substantial differences have also been noted: the anthropologist Margaret Mead (1935) noted that men and women in one New Guinea culture, the Arapesh, both displayed a 'personality that ... we would call maternal in its parental aspects, and feminine in its sexual aspects', while both the men and the women from another New Guinea culture, the Mundugumor, 'approximated to a personality type that we in our culture would find only in an undisciplined and very violent male' (pp. 190–1). Finally, the extent to which an individual adheres to his or her gender role reveals how *gender typed* that individual is.

Summary of Section 2

- The use of the terms 'sex' and 'gender' is controversial. Some authors have tried to reserve 'sex' for biological characteristics and 'gender' for social characteristics, but others find this distinction too simplistic and use the terms interchangeably.
- Gender identity refers to one's sense of being male or female.
- Gender roles consist of the characteristics associated with males and females in a given socio-cultural community. They are based on stereotypes of what is masculine and feminine. People are identifiable as gender typed if they adhere to these gender roles.

3   Key methods of gender development research

Psychologists have developed a number of different techniques for measuring stereotypical gender role beliefs and gender typing. For example, in early psychological research on gender typing (such as that conducted by Terman and Miles, 1936), masculine and feminine characteristics were thought to lie at the opposite ends of a single dimension. In the 1970s, new measurement tools (Bem, 1974; Spence and Helmreich, 1978) allowed assessment of masculinity independently of femininity, so that, for example, an individual could score high on both masculinity and femininity, a pattern that would result in a classification as 'androgynous'. More recent measurement tools (for example, Lippa and Connelly, 1990) have moved away from simple distinctions between masculine and feminine psychological traits, to take a more multidimensional approach that looks at different facets of the individual.

Measurement tools for children have evolved in similar ways, though the focus is usually on more concrete preferences for – or beliefs about – toys, games, and activities distinctively associated with boys and girls. The degree of gender typing in children has been identified through observation of their play behaviour, as well as through parental reports of activities, toys, and characteristics (Golombok and Rust, 1993). In addition to looking at children's own behaviour, psychologists have also been interested in when and how they come to form stereotypical beliefs about masculine and feminine characteristics. Early measures of such *gender role knowledge* required children to assign given attributes either to males or to females in order to determine their perceptions of masculine and feminine characteristics. However, the Sex Role Learning Index (SERLI) made the substantial advance of allowing children to assign attributes to both males and females, thus making it possible to determine when they believe that a given characteristic is not limited to males or to females (Edelbrock and Sugawara, 1978).

Research in the area of gender development has involved a wide range of measures, and different investigations often require very different forms of assessment, some of which are described in Box 2. For example, just as self-ratings of abstract psychological characteristics may be appropriate for adults but not children, the same set of toy or activity preference items is unlikely to be suitable for measuring gender typing in both pre-school children and pre-adolescents. Similarly, one short period of naturalistic observation of children's play in a nursery environment may yield a rich source of data, but will not necessarily provide a reliable index of the children's usual toy and activity preferences. As two experienced researchers have noted, 'it is always important to consider what aspects of gender are being measured, and whether the measures employed are reliable and valid for that purpose' (Golombok and Fivush, 1994, p. 12).

BOX 2

Measures used in research on gender development

Measurement of gender typing in adults usually involves ratings of how well certain psychological characteristics describe the individual. In using Bem's Sex Role Inventory (1974), those who rate themselves highly on both masculine and feminine characteristics (see below) are classified as 'androgynous'.

Table 1   **Masculine and feminine characteristics from the Bem Sex Role Inventory**

Masculine characteristics	Feminine characteristics
Acts as a leader	Affectionate
Ambitious	Gentle
Assertive	Compassionate
Competitive	Warm
Athletic	Tender
Dominant	Sensitive to the needs of others

Source: adapted from Bem, 1974.

In order to assess gender typing in young children, rather more concrete characteristics are typically used. Parents, carers, or the children themselves, rate toy and activity preferences or behavioural characteristics. Table 2 lists some items from the Pre-School Activities Inventory (Golombok and Rust, 1993).

Table 2   **Sample items from the Pre-School Activities Inventory**

Toys	Activities	Characteristics
Guns (or used objects as guns)	Playing house (e.g. cleaning, cooking)	Enjoys rough and tumble play
Dolls	Fighting	Avoids getting dirty
Tool set	Sports and ball games	Likes pretty things
Tea set	Playing at taking care of babies	Shows interest in snakes, spiders, or insects

Source: adapted from Golombok and Rust, 1993.

Measures of gender typing do not assess children's *beliefs* about gender role stereotypes. Such beliefs may be identified by providing children with pictures of common objects, behaviours, or occupations, some of which are traditionally masculine and some of which are traditionally feminine. The children are asked to sort the pictures into three categories: for boys/men only, for girls/women only, or for both sexes. Children with more stereotyped beliefs will allocate traditionally masculine items to 'for boys only' and traditionally feminine items to 'for girls only', while children with more flexible attitudes will assign more items to the 'both' category.

As will become evident later in this chapter, other measurement tools are used to assess children's understanding of the permanence of gender, how they handle information which runs counter to stereotypes, and the extent to which gender stereotypes influence their own preferences.

The next section introduces dominant theoretical perspectives on how children come to form a gender identity, how they develop a sense of gender roles (and the stereotypes that make them up), and how they may come to be gender typed themselves. As you read about these you should bear in mind that different perspectives often focus on distinct issues, so even approaches that seem very different are not necessarily mutually exclusive. Indeed, by the end of the chapter you should have a sense of how the different accounts of gender development may be synthesized.

Summary of Section 3

- Researchers have moved from viewing masculinity and femininity as the opposite ends of a continuum, and have instead recognized that individuals can score high on both masculine and feminine characteristics.
- The extent to which children are gender typed is usually measured by eliciting preferences for toys or activities, either from the children themselves or from their parents or carers.
- Children's knowledge of gender role stereotypes is assessed by asking them to attribute behaviours, occupations, and other characteristics to boys only, girls only, or to both sexes.

4   Approaches to gender development

In this section, five different theoretical approaches to gender development will be explored. Following a brief overview of *psychoanalytic perspectives*, which first highlighted for psychologists the importance of childhood processes in gender development, the spotlight turns to a dominant debate in this field: Is the acquisition of gender roles driven from the outset by the behaviour of parents, peers, and the media – what are labelled *social* processes – or do aspects of children's thinking – their *cognitive* processes – encourage them to seek out and adopt these roles? The *social learning* approach focuses on the role of the social environment in children's gender development: it argues that children come to identify and endorse stereotypes because they are rewarded for gender-typed behaviour and/or because they observe such behaviour in the world around them. *Social cognitive theory,* a more recent adaptation of social learning theory, includes an examination of cognitive factors involved in observational learning but still largely focuses on environmental influence. By contrast, *cognitive-developmental theory* assigns a far more important role to cognitive processes: rather than assuming that parents, peers and the media simply impose gender stereotypes on children, children are regarded as actively seeking out information about gender roles for themselves, once they have a notion of gender as permanent and unchanging. Finally, *gender schema theory* places a similar emphasis on cognitive processes as driving gender development, but suggests that this happens earlier on in childhood, as soon as children can identify their own sex.

4.1 Psychoanalytic perspectives

The first psychological theory of gender development derived from the experience of the psychoanalysts. Sigmund Freud's classic account (1962, first published in 1905) of psychosexual development centred on the Oedipus complex. He claimed that in early childhood boys develop a sexual attraction towards their mother and, in the process, fear punishment by their father. In an effort to resolve this conflict they come to identify with their father. Distinct but related processes were thought to account for female sexual identity. Aside from Freud's own contribution, there have been a number of more recent psychoanalytic interpretations. Chodorow's (1978) feminist standpoint – which has influenced the views of many other contemporary theorists – has emphasized the process of identification with the mother as a basis for gender development. Early in life, both male and female infants are said to identify with their mothers as the provider of comfort, nurturance, and care. However, in developing a sense of self, daughters can draw on their identification with their mothers (since they are of the same sex), while sons must separate from their mothers in order to develop a masculine identity. The retained identification with the mother gives developing girls a strong sense of interpersonal relatedness, while for boys their separation from the mother leads to a rejection of femininity and a sense of independence.

These kinds of arguments have had a wider impact on other aspects of psychological investigation as well. For example, Gilligan (1982) has suggested that the different processes of identification in males and females lead to different moral orientations: the focus on interpersonal relationships in girls was said to lead to distinctive ways of reasoning about moral dilemmas, centred on concerns about the needs and desires of others. It is important to note that, across all of these writings, there seems to be a shared assumption that gender roles arise naturally out of children's early family experiences.

Although the psychoanalytic perspectives are provocative they will not be afforded further space in this chapter. The Freudian approach to gender development has been attacked by many because the basic ideas about early sexual conflicts within the family are based on little empirical evidence – indeed, there are few testable hypotheses to generate such evidence. Similarly, while the interpretations of contemporary psychoanalytic theorists do have some intuitive appeal as explanations of gender roles in modern culture, there is inadequate specific evidence regarding the roles played by the different processes of identification. This lack of direct empirical research has contributed to a fall from favour of the psychoanalytic approach in mainstream psychological investigations of gender development. Nonetheless, it is important to acknowledge the substantial contribution of this approach in highlighting the significance of early childhood in the development of a sense of gender identity. The theoretical perspectives that follow all address processes in childhood, even though the particular processes they emphasize are very different.

4.2 Social learning processes

Are gender stereotypes simply transmitted to children by other people and institutions, such as schools and the media? This is an intuitively appealing idea and one that has been explored in some detail. In 1966 the American psychologist Walter Mischel presented the social learning perspective on gender development. According to this perspective, gender-typed behaviours are those that typically lead to different consequences for one sex than for the other. How children acquire and demonstrate gender-typed behaviours is thus dependent upon the same principles of learning that apply to other aspects of their behaviour (Mischel, 1966). This is consistent with the behaviourist approach which had been dominant in Western psychology since the early twentieth century: learning takes place through conditioning, rewards and punishment, and observation of the behaviour of others. A major step forward in behaviourist thinking here is the addition of that last point – observation of others – as a critical element in the learning process. It is not necessary for you yourself to be rewarded or punished in order to learn to do or not to do something: you can learn simply by watching other people in real life, on television and films, or in books, and this may well be the first step in the development of gender-typed behaviour.

There is undoubtedly an enormous amount of information available about what is masculine and what is feminine. Just after being born, boys and girls are often described differently – boys as 'strong' and girls as 'delicate', for example (Rubin *et al.*, 1974). Fathers engage in distinctive playful interactions, especially with their sons (for example, Lamb, 1987). Boys' and girls' environments and experiences may be shaped by their parents and carers in distinct ways, ranging from the colours of the clothes they are dressed in to the toys and activities provided for them. Intuitively it makes sense to assume that the growing child, exposed to all of this information, will be influenced by their social experience. But does the research evidence support this idea as an explanation of children's gender development?

Do children become masculine or feminine simply because they are rewarded for behaviour that is consistent with their gender role and punished for role-inconsistent behaviour? Most summaries of research suggest that the evidence for such processes is limited. Maccoby and Jacklin's analysis of the available research found that boys and girls had very similar experiences: they were treated with equal affection, they were allowed and encouraged to be independent in equal measure, and both sexes were discouraged from dependent behaviour. There was even no evidence that parental reactions to aggressive behaviour differed between boys and girls (Maccoby and Jacklin, 1974). A more recent study which scrutinized a large body of research into gender differences concluded that the only significant effect from among a long list of possible ones examined was the encouragement of gender-typed activities, and this was evident more in fathers' behaviour than in mothers' (Lytton and Romney, 1991).

Despite the evidence that the differential reinforcement of gender roles for boys and girls is not widespread, the one effect that is often found – the encouragement of gender-typed activities – may be more important than is often recognized. Gender-typed activities themselves would seem to encourage different psychological orientations: the games that are played with dolls typically involve nurturance and caring, in contrast to the mastery and competitiveness that a rough-and-tumble masculine game might generate. Furthermore, where differential reinforcement does occur, it might be of substantial importance to the child. Research summary 1 provides details of a study that showed that while mothers often responded tolerantly or even positively to boys playing with girls' toys, fathers and peers tended to respond negatively, often with clear ridicule. Such ridicule cannot be dismissed easily, either by the children concerned or indeed by psychologists. Experimental studies have also demonstrated that the encouragement that adults give to gender-typed activities is not simply a reflection of boys' and girls' inherent tendencies. Adults respond differently to infants, in stereotype-consistent ways, when the information they are given about the infants' sex is false. For example, they may start playing with dolls when interacting with boys who they have been told are girls (Seavey *et al.*,1975; Smith and Lloyd, 1978).

RESEARCH SUMMARY 1

Fathers at play

The idea that parents reward gender-appropriate behaviour and punish gender-inappropriate behaviour is intuitively appealing, but there is surprisingly little consistent evidence of differential reinforcement of boys' and girls' behaviour. Much of the research that Maccoby and Jacklin (1974) reviewed had been based on mothers' behaviour and there had been little investigation into fathers' responses to children's behaviour. In this context, Langlois and Downs (1980) looked at how mothers, fathers and peers responded to young children's gender-appropriate and gender-inappropriate play behaviour. One of their studies focused on fathers' responses.

Forty-eight children aged 3 and 5 years were observed for two 15-minute sessions playing with their fathers in an unoccupied but familiar room in their nursery schools. Sets of 'masculine' toys were available for one of the sessions and 'feminine' toys for the other. The response of the fathers to the children's play with masculine and feminine toys was classified into several categories of reward (for example, attending to the child, smiling, showing affection, giving praise) and punishment (for example, ridiculing, interfering with the child's behaviour, ignoring). The researchers calculated the proportion of 10-second observation intervals in which each response occurred (out of the total number of 10-second observation intervals when the child was playing).

The data in Table 3 illustrate how fathers responded differently to their children's gender-appropriate and gender-inappropriate behaviour, rewarding the former and punishing the latter. Moreover, the tendency to reward gender-appropriate behaviour more than gender-inappropriate behaviour was much more in evidence with boys than with girls.

Table 3   **Mean percentage of observation intervals when each response type occurred**

	Same-gender toy	Cross-gender toy
Behavioural help	8.90	5.71
Smile	6.58	3.38
Praise	3.77	1.94
Positive talk	55.79	41.33
Behavioural interference	0.10	0.83
Behavioural ridicule	0.46	5.81
Verbal ridicule	0.04	2.71
Negative talk	1.73	4.54

Source: adapted from Langlois and Downs, 1980.

Langlois and Downs summarized the results of their research programme as follows: 'When boys exhibited masculine-typed play they encountered only modest approval from mothers, they were generally ignored by other boys, but they received clear approval from fathers. When playing with feminine-typed toys, however, they received reward from mothers and active punishment from peers and fathers' (p. 1246).

This kind of evidence illustrates how the social influences on children's gender development are likely to be complex; generalizations about whether children are or are not rewarded for gender-typed behaviour do not paint a complete picture.

As noted earlier, direct reinforcement or punishment is not the only mechanism of social influence within social learning theory. Emphasis is also placed on the role of observational learning. Albert Bandura had shown in a series of experiments in the 1960s that aggressive behaviour could be elicited in pre-school children by first showing them video recordings of models acting in aggressive ways (Bandura, 1965). Furthermore, imitation was more likely if they had seen the model being rewarded following the aggressive activity than if they had seen the model being punished. Perry and Bussey (1979) went on to show that observation of *multiple* same-sex models, most or all of whom were displaying the same behaviour, is particularly likely to lead to imitation. There is certainly no shortage of models in the child's day-to-day environment who illustrate stereotyped gender roles. Parents, teachers, peers, books, television and films, all may provide ample opportunity for what is referred to as *vicarious learning* about gender.

Vicarious learning
Learning through observation of the behaviour and experiences of others.

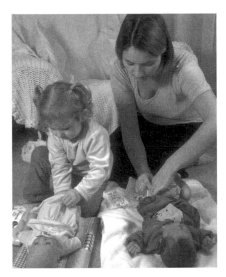

Figure 2 The social influences on children's gender development are likely to be complex.

However, estimating precisely how important any one model or set of models is for gender typing is extremely difficult. Experimental set-ups like Bandura's, where children's behaviour is measured following exposure to specific models, are often far removed from children's experiences in everyday life. On the other hand, simple correlations of children's gender typing with variables such as television viewing or parental activities and occupations (for example, Durkin, 1985; Turner and Gervai, 1995) do not allow the conclusion that the exposure to stereotypical models *causes* the gender typing.

Activity 2   *Observational learning of gender roles*

Allow about
1 hour

This activity encourages you to identify information about gender roles that is available to children.

When you next have the opportunity, carry out some informal research to explore how much information about gender roles is readily available in children's social environments. The following suggestions may help you with this task.

- Talk to some parents about their daily activities (such as work patterns, household chores, leisure activities), and try to identify the extent to which mothers and fathers engage in gender-typed behaviour.

- Look at a selection of books for children and compare the number of male and female characters and their activities/characteristics.

- Watch some television programmes for children, and record the behaviours and psychological profiles of male and female characters.

- Look at advertisements on television and in magazines which relate to children's toys and games. What are the roles of adults and children in these and how do they relate to the nature and features of the activity?

What conclusions can you draw about the presence of gender-role information in the child's social environment?

Comment

People are often surprised to discover just how prevalent gender-typed information is. Despite all the social changes in the last fifty years or so, women still contribute far more to housework and childcare than men. Even among egalitarian couples, the birth of the first child often leads to a more traditional division of labour. Similarly, books and television programmes often show males and females in traditional roles. However, be careful not to make assumptions about the influence of such social information on children's gender development. If gender-typed children are found to watch more gender-typed television, that does not necessarily mean that the programmes caused them to be more gender-typed; the children may have chosen to watch such programmes precisely because they were already gender-typed.

There seems no doubt that the social environment contains a great deal of information about what it means to be a boy or a girl. However, social learning approaches to gender development have been criticized because they have not sufficiently addressed the mechanisms involved in development. In particular, these approaches do not explain satisfactorily why children's gender-related beliefs and behaviours often change as they get older – why many young children's beliefs about masculinity and femininity are often much more rigid than those of their parents. Most contemporary theorists argue that cognitive processes need to be taken into account in order to explain *how* the social environment makes its mark on the child's gender development and how the child plays an important role in directing his or her own gender development.

4.3 Cognitive processes

The theories covered in this section all relate to aspects of children's thinking that are central to their gender development. They focus on the ways in which children attend to and then process and organize information in their environment, and have in common a justifiable emphasis on the *active* role of children in shaping their own development; children are not simply passive respondents to stereotyped information that is imposed upon them. This notion of the child as active helps psychologists understand why consistent effects of the social environment are so difficult to find – the effects themselves are, in one way or another, dependent on the child.

Social cognitive theory

Early social learning theories, where the main focus was on the simple, one-way effect of environment on behaviour, were criticized because they provided too simplistic a picture of human development. Bandura's social cognitive theory (SCT) builds on the earlier social learning approaches by addressing the fact that human development involves a complex interplay of many factors. SCT is usually presented (Bandura, 1986) in terms of a 'model of causation' that links three sets of variables, all of which influence each other: *behaviour* (such as activity patterns), *person* (such as expectations, intentions and goals), and *environment* (such as modelling and reinforcement). The emphasis is still very much on how children's social experiences influence their behaviour, but SCT highlights the active role of children in their observational learning. They can attend selectively to particular events or people in the environment, then mentally organize, combine, and rehearse the observed behaviours, decide when to enact the behaviour, and finally monitor the outcomes of that behaviour.

What are the implications of SCT for an understanding of gender development? Just as in early social learning approaches, Bussey and Bandura (1999) point to evidence of negative parental and peer responses to children's behaviour that runs counter to gender stereotypes as confirmation of the idea that gender development is heavily based on external sanctions early in the child's experience. Children's socialization history, it is argued, provides distinctive information about masculinity and femininity from birth – for example, clothes, nursery decor and the toys and activities provided. Moreover, there is undoubtedly widespread modelling of gender stereotypes in the family as well as in wider culture. When a child's behaviour is inconsistent with their gender role and is met with open ridicule by adults and peers, there is a clear motivation for the child to behave in a gender-stereotyped manner. However, there is also evidence of choice and flexibility in children's behaviour, and this is where cognitive processes come into play. Once children have begun to internalize the standards of behaviour appropriate for males and females, based on the social experiences described above, their own behaviour is no longer dependent on external rewards or punishments. Rather, they become capable of directing their own behaviour in such a way as to satisfy their internalized standards. Furthermore, they monitor their behaviour against those standards, so that they can feel pride on performing gender role-consistent behaviour, even if there is no explicit external praise.

In a study which supported this view of gender development (Bussey and Bandura, 1992), nursery children aged between 3 and 4 years were asked to evaluate gender-typed behaviour by peers (as presented on videotape) and to rate how they would feel about themselves if they were playing with masculine and feminine toys. Even the younger children disapproved of gender role-inconsistent behaviour by peers (such as boys playing with dolls), but when they rated their own feelings they were the same for both masculine and feminine toys. In contrast, the 4 year olds not only disapproved of others' role-inconsistent behaviours, but were also self-critical when judging how they would feel if they were playing with role-inconsistent toys. Furthermore, these self-evaluations predicted how the children actually went on to play with masculine and feminine toys. This was taken as evidence that while social sanctions for gender-typed behaviour are clearly present in the younger children, self-regulation becomes more important with age.

Cognitive-developmental theory

Despite the focus on cognition and internal self-regulation in Bandura's more recent work, many theorists argue that there are more fundamental cognitive processes that need to be taken into account when analysing children's gender development. In particular, researchers have suggested that children's concepts of themselves as male or female play a critical role in encouraging children to identify and endorse gender roles. This notion was first set out at the same time as the early social learning approaches to gender development. The book that contained Mischel's (1966) account of the social learning approach to gender development also included Lawrence Kohlberg's (1966) equally significant report on his cognitive-developmental theory. While recognizing the importance of observational learning, Kohlberg presents a very different account of how children come to understand and enact gender roles: in his own words, his theory 'assumes that basic sexual attitudes are not patterned directly by either biological instincts or arbitrary cultural norms, but by the child's cognitive organization of his social world along sex-role dimensions' (p. 82). In Kohlberg's view, boys think 'I am a boy, therefore I want to do boy things, therefore the opportunity to do boy things (and to gain approval for doing them) is rewarding' (p. 89). His emphasis, then, is on gender role development as being 'self-socialized'; certainly, there is plenty of information about gender roles in the social environment, but it is the child who actively seeks out, organizes, and then behaves in accordance with that information. This contrasts markedly with the view of the child as behaving in a gender-typed way simply because he or she is rewarded – or sees someone else being rewarded – for it.

A major implication of this perspective is that children's appreciation of – and adherence to – gender roles is dependent on their gender identity, their sense of being male or female. Kohlberg and other proponents of this approach argue that children develop a sense of gender identity in a sequence of distinct stages, an idea that owes a great deal to Jean Piaget's influential work on cognitive development. Piaget had argued that children's logical thought could be seen to develop through a sequence of discrete stages, each qualitatively different from the others. Kohlberg connected this development with growth in children's sense of gender identity. The Kohlbergian sequence of gender identity development involves three stages, as shown in Box 3.

Figure 3
Football practice or
self-socialization in
practice?

Kohlberg's stages of gender development

Stage 1: Gender labelling

Children can identify themselves and other people as girls or boys (mummies or daddies). However, gender is not seen as stable over time or across changes in superficial physical characteristics (such as length of hair, clothes).

Stage 2: Gender stability

Children recognize that gender is stable over time: boys will grow up to be daddies, and girls will grow up to be mummies. However, the unchanging nature of gender – that it remains the same regardless of changes in superficial appearance or activity choice – is not yet appreciated.

Stage 3: Gender consistency

Children have a full appreciation of the permanence of gender over time and across situations.

By the age of around 3 years, in the *gender labelling* stage, children become able to label themselves and others accurately as boys or girls. It is not for another couple of years, however, that children are thought to enter the *gender stability* stage and appreciate that this classification will remain stable over time (a boy will grow up to be a daddy, and a girl will grow up to be a mummy). But only in the final *gender consistency* stage, at around the age of 6 or 7 years, are children judged to have an insight into the constancy of sex regardless of the passage of time, changes in context, or transformations of physical features. This understanding is thought to develop in parallel with classic Piagetian changes in children's appreciation of conservation (for example, understanding that the volume of water in a beaker will remain the same after the water is poured into a beaker of different dimensions). Most importantly, Kohlberg argues that the 'child's gender identity can provide a stable organizer of the child's psychosexual attitudes only when he is categorically certain of its unchangeability' (1966, p. 95). Thus, the mature understanding of gender constancy is considered critically important for the gender-typing process.

The research literature provides some support for the notion that more advanced gender concepts are associated with selective attention to same-sex models. The classic study of Slaby and Frey (1975) assessed children's understanding of gender as a fixed, unchanging attribute using a structured gender concept interview. Children's responses to the questions seemed to support Kohlberg's sequence of gender identity development. Furthermore, when shown a videotape that depicted both male and female models, the children who demonstrated an appreciation of gender stability were more likely than children with a less mature gender concept to pay greater attention to the model of their own gender (see Research summary 2). On the whole, however, the research evidence for a link between the appreciation of gender constancy and gender typing is not strong (see reviews by Huston (1983) and Ruble and Martin (1998)). In fact, most of the evidence suggests that it is the most immature form of the gender concept – the accurate labelling of oneself as a boy or girl – that is often associated with gender-typed conduct and stereotyped beliefs. Bussey and Bandura (1999) note that 'long before children have attained gender constancy, they prefer to play with toys traditionally associated with their gender, [...] to model their behavior after same-sex models, [...] and to reward peers for gender-appropriate behavior' (p. 678).

RESEARCH SUMMARY 2

Which model to watch?

Social learning approaches indicated that children's gender development was largely based on observation of same-sex models. However, Kohlberg's (1966) cognitive-developmental theory suggested that children's understanding of gender as a permanent, unchanging attribute was of critical importance. Slaby and Frey (1975) set out to determine whether children's attention to same-sex models was influenced by their level of gender constancy.

The level of gender constancy in 55 children aged between 2 and 5 years was assessed by using a series of fourteen questions and counter-questions. Several questions tapped gender labelling. For instance:

'Is this a girl or a boy?' (showing boy/girl doll)

'Are you a girl or a boy?'

Further questions tapped gender stability. For instance:

'When you were a little baby were you a little girl or a little boy?'

'When you grow up, will you be a mummy or a daddy?'

'Could you ever be a [opposite of previous response]?'

A final set of questions tapped gender consistency. For instance:

'If you wore [opposite of child's sex] clothes, would you be a girl or a boy?'

'Could you be a [opposite of child's sex] if you wanted to be?'

Children were classified as low on gender constancy if they answered incorrectly on the gender labelling or gender stability items, and otherwise were identified as high on gender constancy. Several weeks after this interview the children watched a short film showing a man and a woman engaging in simple parallel activities on different sides of the screen. The amount of time that children's eyes were fixed on each side of the screen was measured.

Slaby and Frey found support for their hypothesis that children with higher levels of gender constancy would show more selective attention to models of their own sex. The data in Table 4 show that high-constancy boys watched the male model rather than the female model more than did low-constancy boys, while the reverse was true for the girls. Interestingly, the selective attention to the same-sex model was much stronger among the high-constancy boys than among the high-constancy girls. In fact, both boys and girls spent more total time watching the male model than the female model. Overall, the results indicate the influence of both cognitive and social factors in gender development.

Table 4   Mean percentage of time spent watching the male rather than the female model (standard deviations in brackets)

Sex of participant	Low gender constancy	High gender constancy
Boy	47.9 (8.5)	61.4 (9.6)
Girl	57.8 (9.9)	50.8 (11.7)

Source: adapted from Slayby and Frey, 1975.

Gender schema theory

Despite the limited research evidence for the role of gender constancy in the development of gender-typed behaviour, many contemporary researchers have built on Kohlberg's basic point that cognitive processes play a key role in driving gender development. In fact, the question now is not *whether* cognition is important – everyone agrees that it is – but *which* particular cognitions should be emphasized. Where Kohlberg highlighted the relatively late-developing full understanding of gender constancy, the gender schema theorists argue that it is the *early* cognitive processes underlying children's ability to label themselves as boys or girls that play the key role in gender development (Martin *et al.*, 2002).

In 1981, Martin and Halverson presented a new account of gender typing that drew on the ideas of earlier cognitive developmental accounts but included considerably more detail about the exact cognitive processes involved in gender development. They proposed that the emergence of stereotypes in childhood was not purely a function of environmental input, but rather was the perfectly normal consequence of children's information processing. Stereotypes, in this view, are simply an efficient way of handling and predicting large amounts of information. If people do not categorize information and make generalizations (for example, about what boys like and what girls like) on that basis, they simply would not be able to manage their lives effectively. For children exposed to an endless stream of new information and novel input, such processes of simplification are necessary in order to make sense of the complex world around them.

Activity 3   *What's in your gender schema?*

Allow about
20 minutes

This activity will help you to explore your own use of gender schemas.

Do you make any automatic assumptions about people based on whether they are male or female to help you manage your everyday interactions?

Imagine you are at a party and you meet a person for the first time. You really want to have fun and make a good impression. Would the person's gender influence how you approach the situation: how you behave, what you talk about, what you ask questions about, what you joke about, and so on?

Now imagine that you had to look after an 8-year-old child for the first time. You really want the child to have fun. Would the child's gender influence how you approach the situation: what activities you prepare, what you talk about, what you ask questions about, and so on?

Think about other everyday situations, such as going for a job interview, talking to the checkout clerk at a supermarket, or meeting a new work colleague. Try to list some of the inferences you make about people simply from knowing their gender.

Comment

The theoretical framework presented by Martin and Halverson is a reminder that stereotypes are not necessarily an abnormal or irrational way of thinking; rather, they often play a key role in simplifying a very complex world. People often use gender stereotypes as rules of thumb to guide them in their social interactions. Care is needed, however, to avoid an over-reliance on gender stereotypes – there may be a need to revise beliefs, expectations, and behaviour when presented with counter-stereotypical information (such as a girl with 'masculine' toy preferences). Research suggests that children become increasingly flexible in their reasoning about gender as they grow older.

At the core of the theory is the notion of 'schema', a mental structure that guides the processing of information and experiences. According to the initial model proposed by Martin and Halverson (1981), two key schemas are involved. The first, the 'in-group–out-group' schema, includes a broad categorization of attributes, activities and objects as being either for boys or for girls. In other words, boys and girls are said to have a mental representation of what is suitable for their in-group (boys for a boy, girls for a girl) and what is appropriate for their out-group (girls for a boy, boys for a girl). A second schema, the 'own sex' schema, involves more detailed information about those behaviours, traits, and objects that are considered to be characteristic of the child's in-group. As soon as children are able to label themselves as boys or girls, they will start to form these schemas in order to make sense of the world around them.

In many ways, the basic proposition of Kohlberg (1966) still applies: 'I am a boy, therefore I want to do boy things'. The difference is that the notion 'I am a boy' need only reflect basic gender labelling, as opposed to a full appreciation of gender constancy. Once this understanding is present and the environment provides information about certain toys or activities as masculine or feminine (which is organized in the in-group–out-group schema), children will be driven to find out more about the in-group set of toys or activities. In this way, the in-group–out-group schema determines what information goes into the more detailed and elaborate own-sex schema: if a boy views an object or activity as masculine he will approach it, interact with it, and find out more about it. Thus, unlike the SCT view that internal standards for behaviour are formed through the internalization of social rules taught through rewards and punishment (or learned through observing the outcomes of others' behaviour), children are seen here as having internal, self-regulating standards as soon as they label themselves as boys or girls.

A major advantage of the gender schema approach is that stability and change in children's gender-linked cognition and behaviour can be understood by tracking the development of children's schemas. For example, this approach offers a good insight into why children seem to cling so tightly to gender stereotypes, sometimes despite the best efforts of parents who are attempting to reduce or eliminate stereotyping. Schemas govern what people pay attention to, what they try to find out more about, what they interact with, and what (and how) they remember. For example, Bradbard *et al.* (1986) gave some unfamiliar objects to 56 children aged between 4 and 9 years, for them to explore for 6 minutes. The children explored new objects more when they were labelled as being for their own sex than for the other sex. One week later they remembered more detail about the toys for their own sex than about those for the other sex. In a similar vein, Liben and Signorella (1993) showed 106 primary school children 60 drawings of male and female characters engaged in masculine, feminine, and neutral activities and occupations (for example, firefighter, washing dishes), and then asked them to recall as many of the pictures as possible. Children recalled more pictures of men performing masculine behaviours than of men performing feminine behaviours. The influence of gender schemas can be so strong that counter-stereotypical information may be distorted to make it fit in with the schemas. Martin and Halverson (1983) showed pictures of males or females engaged in activities that were consistent or inconsistent with gender roles to 48 children aged between 5 and 6 years of age. A week later the children showed distorted memories of role-inconsistent pictures: for example, a picture of a girl sawing wood was remembered as a picture of a boy sawing wood.

The gender schema approach also helps explain why younger children often seem to adhere to stereotypes more rigidly than older children. When children were asked to predict how much the characters in a story would like masculine and feminine toys, the younger children relied only on the gender of the character to make their judgements (Martin, 1989). They predicted that a boy character would like to play with trucks regardless of the information given about that character's interests. By contrast, the older children took into account both the gender of the character and the 'individuating' information about that particular character. So they would predict that a girl who was described as having counter-stereotypical attributes (for example, 'likes playing with airplanes') would be less likely to want to play with a doll than a stereotypical girl. This kind of flexibility is likely to be the result of changes in children's cognition, such as an increased understanding of masculinity as distinct from maleness and femininity as distinct from femaleness, and an increased ability to draw on several sources of information (such as both a person's gender and his or her idiosyncratic interests) simultaneously. Younger children, with a more simplistic gender schema that links certain activities with boys and certain other activities with girls, seemed to rely only on the character's gender when inferring his or her toy preferences.

Summary of Section 4

- The psychoanalytic perspective highlights the importance of early childhood experience in gender development, but the emphasis on psychosexual dynamics within the family has not received empirical support.
- A dominant debate in current research on gender development concerns the relative importance of social and cognitive factors.
- Mischel's social learning approach suggests that children's gender development is a product of their social experiences. This theoretical approach focuses on reinforcement of gender-typed behaviour by parents and peers, and on children's observation of gender stereotypes in the world around them.
- Bandura's social cognitive theory is a more recent version of social learning approaches that highlights the active role of children in their observational learning.
- Kohlberg's cognitive-developmental theory proposes a developmental sequence of stages in children's conception of gender. Children's appreciation of the unchanging permanence or 'constancy' of gender is thought to underlie their tendency to seek out and adhere to gender role information.

- The gender schema approach proposed by Martin and Halverson suggests that children form cognitive schemas about gender as soon as they discover their own sex. These schemas drive gender development, guiding children's attention and memory in such a way that they focus on and remember gender-typed information much more than counter-stereotypical information.

5 Gender development: an integration

Leaving aside the temptation to try to select one of the above perspectives on gender development as the 'right' or 'best' approach, careful examination of the theories and research findings suggests that each of the viewpoints has made important contributions to the understanding of gender development. This section considers ways of integrating these contributions.

The biggest source of tension among gender development researchers concerns the question of whether the primary focus of attention should be on the plentiful supply of gender-related information in the environment or on the child's cognitions about gender. Proponents of social learning theory, and of its more recent incarnation as social cognitive theory, favour the former, while cognitive-developmental theory and gender schema theory favour the latter. This tension, however, should not be insurmountable. All contemporary approaches to gender development recognize that important roles are played by both social *and* cognitive factors. There is no doubt that family, peers, school, media and various other social agents provide a great deal of information about gender roles. Equally, there is agreement that any model of gender development must take into account children's cognition. In fact, the existence of different theoretical perspectives in this area has been of great advantage because each one has highlighted – and thereby enabled a better understanding of – different social and cognitive aspects of gender development.

The social learning theory described above has revealed important new information concerning the processes by which the social environment can have an impact on the child. Most importantly, research within this framework has contributed to an understanding of how modelling and observational learning, as well as direct reinforcement, play a critical role in children's acquisition of knowledge from their social experiences. Cognitive theories build on these ideas by demonstrating that children's behaviour is a product not just of social experiences, but also of internal cognitive and motivational factors. Bandura's social cognitive theory highlights the fact that children come to regulate their own behaviour according to internal standards. Kohlberg's cognitive-developmental theory focuses on developmental processes in how children come to understand gender as a permanent attribute of a person, unchanging over time and across situations. Finally, the gender schema theory described by Martin and Halverson

Figure 4
Learning more than
how the wheels go
round.

places an emphasis on children's early ability to label themselves and others as
male or female as a guiding force in gender development, with schemas
influencing children's attention, judgements and memory.

It makes sense to assume that there is a reciprocal relationship between social
experiences and gender conceptions. That is, features of the social environment,
such as the behaviour of others, influence children's construction of gender
schemas, but these gender schemas in turn guide children's behaviour in that
social environment and influence their cognitive processing of their social
experiences. This kind of interplay can help to explain differences between boys
and girls in their gender development: one of the most striking findings in this
area is that girls seem to have a much more flexible attitude towards gender roles
than boys. For example, in a study by Banerjee and Lintern (2000), where
children aged between 4 and 9 years had to predict toy preferences for story
characters, girls were in general much better than boys at recognizing that
counter-stereotypical characters would have different preferences from those of
stereotypical characters. The younger boys, on the other hand, showed a
particularly rigid adherence to stereotypes about toy preferences, and in a
separate part of the experiment also were especially likely to present themselves
as more masculine when they were asked to express their own toy preferences in
front of other boys (see Research summary 3). These differences between the
sexes in cognition about gender – and in the motivation to appear gender typed –
tie in with observations from social learning theorists that social sanctions for

behaviour inconsistent with gender role are more severe for boys than for girls: it is worse to be a sissy than it is to be a tomboy, and boys are especially ridiculed by their peers for engaging in feminine activities (Bussey and Bandura, 1999). However, Banerjee and Lintern also demonstrated that there was a significant age group effect, just as was observed by Martin (1989). As might be expected from gender schema theory, younger children were more rigid in their adherence to gender stereotypes than older children. Moreover, this age effect was no different for boys than for girls. This indicates therefore that while gender schemas are likely to develop in similar ways for boys and girls, the degree of importance or salience of simple gender role stereotypes ('a boy will always prefer to play with a truck than a doll') may be greater among boys because of their social experience.

RESEARCH SUMMARY 3

Counter to expectations ...

The way that children handle counter-stereotypical information offers some insight into their gender schemas. In turn, those gender schemas should have an impact on how children present themselves in social contexts: children with more rigid beliefs about gender would be expected to be more motivated to portray themselves as gender typed in front of same-sex peers. Banerjee and Lintern (2000) tested this hypothesis with a sample of 64 children aged between 4 and 9 years.

In the first part of the study, the children were asked to make judgements about the toy preferences of stereotypical and counter-stereotypical characters. Figure 5 is an example of a counter-stereotypical boy and girl, of the kind shown to the children.

This is a boy called Peter. His best friend is a girl, and he likes playing with toy prams.	This is a girl called Julie. Her best friend is a boy, and she likes playing with toy aeroplanes.

Figure 5 Counter-stereotypical characters.

The children were asked to respond to the following questions.

Do you think Peter/Julie would like to:

* Play with dolls?   No/Sometimes/A lot
* Play football?   No/Sometimes/A lot
* Do skipping?   No/Sometimes/A lot
* Play with toy guns?   No/Sometimes/A lot

They received a score which reflected how differently they judged the toy preferences of the stereotypical and counter-stereotypical characters: the lower the score, the more rigidly they adhered to traditional stereotypes. The 8 and 9 year olds were much more flexible in handling counter-stereotypical information than the younger children, and the boys were in general far less flexible than the girls (see Figure 6).

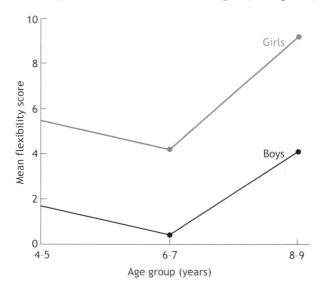

Figure 6   Mean stereotype flexibility score of children, by age and gender.

On the day after completing this task, children completed a self-description task involving ratings of how much they played with masculine, feminine, and gender-neutral toys/activities. No other children were present when they made their responses. Then on the third day they completed the same self-description task publicly, in a group of three to five same-sex peers. Children received a score for how gender typed they were in the 'alone' and in the 'group' condition, which allowed a calculation to be made of changes in their gender-typed score between the two conditions.

Results showed that the younger boys were especially likely to describe themselves as more gender typed in the group condition compared to the alone condition. In confirmation of the hypothesis, there was a significant correlation between scores on the two tasks: the more rigid their beliefs about gender, the more the children increased their gender-typed score in the 'group' condition.

In a similar way, it is necessary to look at the interaction of social and cognitive factors in order to explain why there are *individual* differences in gender development: some children are far more focused on gender role notions than others. Levy and Carter (1989) measured this in an innovative way. Children aged between 2 and 5 years were shown pairs of pictures depicting toys. Some of the pairs showed two masculine toys, some showed two feminine toys, some showed one masculine toy and one feminine toy, and others showed gender role-neutral toys. For each pair, children were asked to choose as quickly as possible which toy was their favourite. Crucially, some children responded much more quickly than usual when shown masculine–feminine pairs, and/or took much longer than usual on masculine–masculine or feminine–feminine pairs. These children were viewed, justifiably, as being highly gender schematized: they used their gender schemas to guide their preferences, quickly picking out a toy that matched their own gender when it was paired with an other-gender toy, and/or finding it harder than usual to choose between two masculine toys or between two feminine toys. If, on the other hand, gender schemas were not especially important for a particular child, he or she might be expected to spend about the same amount of time on any pair of toys, regardless of their gender appropriateness. The critical question is why some children appear to be so much more guided by gender roles in their thoughts and behaviours than other children. It seems reasonable to suppose that this is where social experience comes into play. No two children have identical socialization experiences, and it is reasonable to expect that each child's distinctive experiences (for example, of parental modelling and peer reinforcement) are likely to have an impact on how salient gender schemas will be for him or her. In other words, while all children are likely to develop schemas about masculinity and femininity, those schemas will be more influential for some children than for others, depending on their social experiences.

Summary of Section 5

- Social and cognitive approaches to gender development are not mutually exclusive. Contemporary researchers recognize that both social and cognitive processes play important roles in children's gender development.
- Although older children tend to have a more flexible view of gender stereotypes than younger children, girls' gender beliefs in general are more flexible than those of boys. Attention to both cognitive and social factors helps to explain these differences.
- There are significant individual differences in children's gender development: some children are far more focused on gender role stereotypes than others. These differences are likely to reflect the unique socialization experiences of each child.

6 Gender in context

One main conclusion to be drawn from an overview of this area of research is that children's gender development must be examined in context. Whatever the approach to gender typing, the role played by social context cannot be ignored: children do not simply develop ideas about gender and gender roles in a vacuum. The content of children's beliefs about gender has to come, in large part, from the social context in which they grow up. This section illustrates some of the ways in which researchers have explained features of gender development by looking closely at the experiences of boys and girls in the contexts of peer interaction and school.

6.1 Play interaction and friendship

So far in this chapter many of the examples have concerned children's preferences for toys and activities, and that mirrors the emphasis in much of the research on this topic. But what about the psychological dispositions that are typically associated with women and men in society (for example, nurturant and intimate versus competitive and ambitious)? What are the developmental precursors of these gender role attributes? One argument is that these aspects of children's gender development – which relate to certain gender-typed styles of social interaction – must be viewed at the level of the group rather than the individual. That is, children develop particular ways of interacting with each other through being part of a same-sex peer group. Maccoby, for example, argues persuasively that sex-segregated peer groups are of critical importance: 'I would place most of the emphasis on the peer group as the setting in which children first discover the compatibility of same-sex others, in which boys first discover the requirements of maintaining one's status in the male hierarchy, and in which the gender of one's partners becomes supremely important.' (Maccoby, 1990, p. 519),

To take a specific example, Benenson *et al.* (1997) observed 26 same-sex groups of 4-year-old and 6-year-old children playing on a carpet with the same set of non-gender-typed toys. Interestingly, although boys and girls spent equal amounts of time in two-child (dyadic) interactions, the boys had a large number of separate dyadic episodes of short duration, while the girls had a smaller number of separate dyadic episodes of longer duration. At the same time, co-ordinated group activity was significantly more frequent among the 6-year-old boys than among any other group. The more extended dyadic interaction style found among girls seems to fall neatly in line with the characterization of the feminine gender role as one emphasizing intimacy and interpersonal communication. In addition, the larger-group activity that developed among the boys would seem to provide a perfect context for the emergence of competitive motives. In fact, in a subsequent study where children were required to play a game in which they could choose between competitive and non-competitive moves (Benenson *et al.*, 2001), only the boys were significantly more competitive when playing in groups of four than in pairs. Moreover, there was less smiling in those foursomes. Given evidence from numerous studies that boys generally play in larger groups than girls (Belle, 1989), these striking findings provide support for the notion that the context of play may have a significant impact on the development of gender-typed social interaction styles.

More direct links between childhood play and the psychological characteristics associated with masculinity and femininity can be found when studying the content of what boys and girls are actually doing when they play. Ethnographic studies of children's play regularly show more rough-and-tumble play and physical fighting (both real and pretend) among boys than among girls. As Thorne notes in her insightful report on playground observations, 'boys more often grabbed one another from behind, pinned down one another's arms, pushed and shoved, wrestled one another to the ground, and continually pressed the ambiguous line between "play" and "real" fighting' (Thorne, 1993, p. 92). Moreover, Thorne demonstrates how boys' talk seems to involve competitive discussions about strength and physical ability, turning almost any activity into a contest. This is mirrored in their increased participation in rule-based sporting contests such as football. In their highly detailed report on primary school playground activities, Blatchford *et al.* (2003) observe that boys were more likely than girls to be involved in ball games and fantasy play, with girls engaged more than boys in conversation, sedentary play (such as drawing and reading), skipping, and verbal games. Furthermore, boys' games did indeed involve a much larger network of children than girls' games. Overall, boys' play is more likely than girls' play to involve a focus on mastery of the physical world and on competitive comparisons of competence; these concerns clearly relate to the psychological traits customarily associated with masculinity: leadership, ambitiousness, assertiveness, competitiveness, athleticism, dominance, and so on.

Studies of children's friendships have also revealed gender differences that seem to mirror gender roles in society at large. A common finding is that girls' friendships are characterized by more intimacy and self-disclosure than those of boys, consistent with the evidence described above that girls' play groups are often smaller in size and that girls engage in more conversation in the playground. For example, Parker and Asher (1993), in their questionnaire-based study of friendship quality in middle childhood, found that boys reported 'less intimate exchange, more difficulty resolving conflict, less validation and caring, and less help and guidance in their friendships than did girls' (Parker and Asher, 1993, p. 617). This is confirmed when children are asked about specific incidents. One study by Buhrmester and Carbery (reported in Buhrmester, 1996) involved interviewing children aged between 12 and 15 years by telephone each evening over a 5-day period, asking them to list the social encounters that had taken place that day. The young adolescents were asked to rate the extent of self-disclosure and emotional support present in each interaction lasting 10 minutes or longer. Girls rated self-disclosure and emotional support when interacting with best friends higher than did boys. These self-report data are confirmed by independent observation. Lansford and Parker (1999) asked children to invite two of their friends to come to a laboratory session with them as their guests. The resultant triads of children completed a sequence of structured and unstructured activities, including a discussion task, a jigsaw puzzle, a potentially competitive game, and the preparation and consumption of a snack, and clean-up afterwards. Observations throughout revealed that the triads of girls, as well as showing less verbal and physical aggression, were more intimate (gossiping, talking about personal facts or experiences, sharing secrets, for example) and exchanged more information than the groups of boys. These kinds of patterns seem to foreshadow the association of femininity with a relating, caring, and sharing orientation.

As Thorne (1993) rightly points out, caution is needed with generalizations like 'boys emphasize status, and girls emphasize intimacy' (p. 108), since they usually refer to *average* differences between boys and girls – differences between some, but certainly not all, groups of boys and girls. An important direction for further research is to determine when and why particular boys and girls fall into and out of line with the gender 'norms' for peer interaction. Nonetheless, the message from the research findings presented here remains clear: broad differences in boys' and girls' peer interactions seem to tie in closely with the cultural construction of masculinity and femininity. This kind of evidence has led researchers to focus on the peer group as a powerful socializing force, in gender development and in social and personal development more generally (Harris, 1995). The implications for the theoretical approaches discussed earlier are as yet uncertain, however, since the reasons why boys' and girls' peer groups operate as they do in the first place are not fully understood: do the differences stem from adult reinforcement and modelling, can they be explained with reference to biological/evolutionary processes, and are they connected to children's gender concepts and/or gender schemas? Searching for the answers to these questions remains a major challenge for contemporary researchers.

Activity 4   Gender differences in peer groups

Allow about
1 hour
30 minutes

This activity will help you to explore some of the ways in which children's social activities are related to their gender.

If you have access to young children, keep a record over a few days of their favourite social activities – for example, games with other children. Alternatively, ask some parents you know to tell you about their children's favourite activities. Consider:

- the type of social activity (including the nature of any crazes/fads)

    Is it competitive?

    Does it focus on physical/athletic skills?

    Is there much opportunity for self-disclosure and intimacy?

- the size of the social group involved in the activity.

Do boys and girls play differently? If so, do these differences tie in with psychological traits customarily associated with masculinity and femininity?

Comment

Research suggests that boys' games are more physical/rough-and-tumble and competitive in nature, and usually involve larger groups of children than girls' games. It seems probable that these different play patterns are associated with the psychological patterns that are commonly identified as masculine and feminine. For example, boys' ball and superhero fantasy games often seem to favour leadership, dominance and competitiveness, while girls' role-play games often focus on nurturance and close interpersonal relationships. However, you should also consider whether these patterns change as children grow older, and whether social changes in the last fifty years are reflected in the nature of children's play.

6.2 Academic development

This chapter has already described how research into the social life of children in school contexts such as the playground can help to explain peer interaction patterns in boys and girls. Another major strand of work focuses specifically on the social dynamics that underlie gender differences in academic interests, behaviours, and achievements. Frequently, researchers have sought to provide neuropsychological explanations for apparent gender differences in certain intellectual abilities, such as spatial skills and verbal skills. However, a number of investigations have shown that the social context of schooling is itself of considerable importance. Some studies of mathematics in children are a case in point. In one series of investigations involving thousands of children in Taiwan, Japan, and the United States (Lummis and Stevenson, 1990), mothers tended to rate the achievement of young boys in mathematics as better than that of girls, even though the research did not in fact find gender differences in tests of children's general mathematical concepts and skills. Furthermore, mothers showed this pattern especially in the case of their kindergarten children – children who had yet to experience any formal mathematics instruction!

These discrepant parental expectations for boys and girls seem to be mirrored in children's own cognitions about academic performance. In one study, several hundred children, most of them aged between 8 and 14 years, were given questionnaires before and after a school mathematics test, in order to assess their expectations, evaluations, and feelings about their test performance. Although the average marks received were not different for boys and girls overall, there were striking differences in how boys and girls responded to the questionnaires.

> Girls rated their ability lower, expected to do less well, were less likely than boys to attribute success to high ability and failure to luck, and were more likely to attribute failure to low ability. Girls also reported less pride in their success and a stronger desire to hide their [test] paper after failure and were less likely to believe that success could be achieved through effort.
>
> (Stipek and Gralinski, 1991)

Other evidence suggests that teachers may be one important source of such differences. For example, negative teacher feedback about boys' work often refers to misbehaviour or lack of motivation; in contrast, negative feedback given to girls is more often directed at intellectual inadequacies (Dweck *et al.*, 1978). In this way, teachers' differential feedback to boys and girls can contribute to entirely different patterns of achievement-related beliefs, emotions, and motivation.

Gender differences in the academic interests and achievements of children and adolescents are of interest to psychologists, educators, and the wider public. The choices that boys and girls make regarding advanced courses in secondary school – for example, whether or not to take mathematics and science courses – may have significant long-term consequences in terms of later career development. There is no doubt that some mathematics and science courses still have great difficulty in recruiting female students, and this is likely to reflect attitudes and expectations that are closely associated with gender roles. As demonstrated by Stipek and Gralinski (1991), girls have more negative beliefs and expectations about their performance in mathematics classes. Similarly, Weinburgh's (1995) review of eighteen studies involving more than 6,000 students concluded that boys have more positive attitudes towards science than girls. Also, Colley and Comber (2003) report that despite the more widespread use of ICT skills in the mainstream academic curriculum in the United Kingdom, boys still have more positive attitudes towards computers than girls. Importantly, several studies have indicated that adolescents' academic and career pursuits are connected to broader aspects of gender development. In one investigation of 409 girls in the final year of an all-female high school (O'Brien and Fassinger, 1993), students with more liberal attitudes regarding gender roles in general were more likely to value their career pursuits, and students who selected non-traditional and prestigious careers rated themselves as high on traditionally masculine traits such as independence and assertiveness – so called 'agentic' characteristics.

To summarize, research studies have consistently shown important gender differences in the academic and career interests, beliefs, motivations, achievements and pursuits of boys and girls. These are linked to the beliefs and behaviours of parents and teachers, as well as to the broader gender development of the children themselves. At the same time, many programmes in various countries (for example, the Women Into Science and Engineering (WISE) programme in the United Kingdom) seek to enhance the recruitment of women into careers involving science and mathematics. It seems clear that psychological research regarding the social and cognitive factors that promote traditional versus non-traditional career paths can play a valuable role in informing the construction of effective intervention strategies within such programmes.

Summary of Section 6

- Gender-typed behaviours often emerge in the context of children's peer group interactions. Boys have been observed to play together in more physical, rough-and-tumble, and competitive ways than girls.
- Research suggests that girls' friendships are more intimate and involve more self-disclosure than those of boys.
- Gender differences have also been observed in the academic context, where researchers have studied boys' and girls' achievements, beliefs, expectations, and motivation in subjects such as science and mathematics. Such gender differences are closely linked to the behaviour and attitudes of parents and teachers, and research in this area has implications for social and educational policy.

7 Conclusion

Gender development is complicated! It involves many aspects of children – their social life, their cognitions, their motivations, their emotions – and working out how all of these elements fit together is a challenging task. This chapter has illustrated how researchers have used different methods and different theoretical frameworks to try to make sense of gender development. Indeed, the developmental research examined here is linked with cognitive psychology and social psychology, as well as with other disciplines such as sociology, cultural anthropology, and education. But the ideas and findings of different researchers may not necessarily be mutually exclusive. Most importantly, approaches focusing on the social environment can actually complement perspectives that emphasize children's cognitions about gender. Section 5 focused on this interaction of social and cognitive factors in order to try to explain why there are age differences, sex differences, and individual differences in gender typing. And the chapter concluded with an examination of gender differences as emerging within specific contexts (such as peer interaction and the school environment), with a recognition that gender development cannot be fully understood unless it is investigated in the contexts in which it naturally occurs. Ultimately, however, there remains the sense that there is plenty of work yet to be done, and plenty of big questions yet to be answered: What makes gender so important in the social environment to begin with? What are the origins of the different peer group interaction styles of boys and girls? Precisely where do individual differences in gender schematization come from? And ultimately: How does all of this relate to actual biological differences between males and females? Research over the last fifty years has provided some valuable clues about where to look for the answers to these questions. The challenge for the future is to work out how the clues all fit together.

References

Aristotle (1910, written 350 BCE), tr. D'Arcy Wentworth Thompson, 'Historia Animalium' in Smith, J.A. and Ross, W.D. (eds) *The Works of Aristotle*, London, Oxford University Press.

Bandura, A. (1965) 'Influence of models' reinforcement contingencies on the acquisition of imitative responses', *Journal of Personality and Social Psychology*, vol. 1, pp. 589–95.

Bandura, A. (1986) *Social Foundations of Thought and Action: a social cognitive theory*, Englewood Cliffs, NJ, Prentice Hall.

Banerjee, R. and Lintern, V. (2000) 'Boys will be boys: the effect of social evaluation concerns on gender-typing', *Social Development*, vol. 9, pp. 397–408.

Belle, D. (1989) 'Gender differences in children's social networks and supports', in Belle, D. (ed.) *Children's Social Networks and Social Supports*, Oxford, John Wiley and Sons.

Bem, S. L. (1974) 'The measurement of psychological androgyny', *Journal of Consulting and Clinical Psychology*, vol. 42, pp. 155–62.

Benenson, J. F., Apostoleris, N. H. and Parnass, J. (1997) 'Age and sex differences in dyadic and group interaction', *Developmental Psychology*, vol. 33, pp. 538–43.

Benenson, J. F., Nicholson, C., Waite, A., Roy, R. and Simpson, A. (2001) 'The influence of group size on children's competitive behavior', *Child Development*, vol. 72, pp. 921–8.

Blatchford, P., Baines, E. and Pellegrini, A. (2003) 'The social context of school playground games: sex and ethnic differences, and changes over time after entry to junior school', *British Journal of Developmental Psychology*, vol. 21, pp. 481–505.

Bradbard, M. R., Martin, C. L., Endsley, R. C. and Halverson, C. F. (1986) 'Influence of sex stereotypes on children's exploration and memory: a competence versus performance distinction', *Developmental Psychology*, vol. 22, pp. 481–6.

Buhrmester, D. (1996) 'Need fulfilment, interpersonal competence, and the developmental contexts of early adolescent friendship', in Bukowski, W. M., Newcomb, A. F. and Hartup, W.W. (eds) *The Company They Keep: friendship in childhood and adolescence,* Cambridge, Cambridge University Press.

Bussey, K. and Bandura, A. (1992) 'Self-regulatory mechanisms governing gender development', *Child Development*, vol. 63, pp. 1236–50.

Bussey, K. and Bandura, A. (1999) 'Social cognitive theory of gender development and differentiation', *Psychological Review*, vol. 106, pp. 676–713.

Chodorow, N. J. (1978) *The Reproduction of Mothering: psychoanalysis and the socialization of gender,* Berkeley, CA, University of California Press.

Colley, A. and Comber, C. (2003) 'Age and gender differences in computer use and attitudes among secondary school students: what has changed?', *Educational Research*, vol. 45, pp. 155–65.

Durkin, K. (1985) 'Television and sex-role acquisition: II. Effects', *British Journal of Social Psychology*, vol. 24, pp. 191–210.

Dweck, C. S., Davidson, W., Nelson, S. and Enna, B. (1978) 'Sex differences in learned helplessness: II. The contingencies of evaluative feedback in the classroom and III. An experimental analysis', *Developmental Psychology*, vol. 14, pp. 268–76.

Eagly, A. H. (1996) 'Differences between women and men: their magnitude, practical importance, and political meaning', *American Psychologist*, vol. 51, pp. 158–9.

Edelbrock, C. S. and Sugawara, A. I. (1978) 'Acquisition of sex-typed preferences in preschool-aged children', *Developmental Psychology*, vol. 14, pp. 614–23.

Freud, S. (1962, first published in 1905) *Three Essays on the Theory of Sexuality*, New York, NY, Avon.

Gilligan, C. (1982) *In a Different Voice: psychological theory and women's development*, Cambridge, MA, Harvard University Press.

Golombok, S. and Fivush, R. (1994) *Gender Development*, Cambridge, Cambridge University Press.

Golombok, S. and Rust, J. (1993) 'The Pre-School Activities Inventory: a standardized assessment of gender role in children', *Psychological Assessment*, vol. 5, pp. 131–6.

Harris, J. R. (1995) 'Where is the child's environment? A group socialization theory of development', *Psychological Review*, vol. 102, pp. 458–89.

Huston, A. C. (1983) 'Sex-typing', in Hetherington, E. M. (ed.) *Handbook of Child Psychology: socialization, personality, and social development*, vol. 4, New York, NY, Wiley.

Hyde, J. S. and Plant, E. A. (1995) 'Magnitude of psychological gender differences: another side to the story', *American Psychologist*, vol. 50, pp. 159–61.

Kohlberg, L. (1966) 'A cognitive-developmental analysis of children's sex-role concepts and attitudes', in Maccoby, E. E. (ed.) *The Development of Sex Differences*, London, Tavistock.

Lamb, M. E. (ed.) (1987) *The Father's Role: cross-cultural perspectives*, Hillsdale, NJ, Erlbaum.

Langlois, J. H. and Downs, A. C. (1980) 'Mothers, fathers, and peers as socialization agents of sex-typed play behaviors in young children', *Child Development*, vol. 51, pp. 1237–47.

Lansford, J. E. and Parker, J. G. (1999) 'Children's interactions in triads: behavioral profiles and effects of gender and patterns of friendships among members', *Developmental Psychology*, vol. 35, pp. 80–93.

Levy, G. D. and Carter, D. B. (1989) 'Gender schema, gender constancy, and gender-role knowledge: the roles of cognitive factors in preschoolers' gender-role stereotype attributions', *Developmental Psychology*, vol. 25, pp. 444–9.

Liben, L. S. and Signorella, M. L. (1993) 'Gender-schematic processing in children: the role of initial interpretations of stimuli', *Developmental Psychology*, vol. 29, pp. 141–9.

Lippa, R. and Connelly, S. (1990) 'Gender diagnosticity: a new Bayesian approach to gender-related individual differences', *Journal of Personality and Social Psychology*, vol. 59, pp. 1051–65.

Lummis, M. and Stevenson, H. W. (1990) 'Gender differences in beliefs and achievement: a cross-cultural study', *Developmental Psychology*, vol. 26, pp. 254–63.

Lytton, H. and Romney, D. M. (1991) 'Parents' differential socialization of boys and girls: a meta-analysis', *Psychological Bulletin*, vol. 109, pp. 267–96.

Maccoby, E. E. (1988) 'Gender as a social category', *Developmental Psychology*, vol. 24, pp. 755–65.

Maccoby, E. E. (1990) 'Gender and relationships: a developmental account', *American Psychologist*, vol. 45, pp. 513–20.

Maccoby, E. E. and Jacklin, C. N. (1974) *The Psychology of Sex Differences*, Stanford, CA, Stanford University Press.

Martin, C. L. (1989) 'Children's use of gender-related information in making social judgments', *Developmental Psychology*, vol. 25, pp. 80–8.

Martin, C. L. and Halverson, C. F. (1981) 'A schematic processing model of sex typing and stereotyping in children', *Child Development*, vol. 52, pp. 1119–34.

Martin, C. L. and Halverson, C. F. (1983) 'The effects of sex-typing schemas on young children's memory', *Child Development*, vol. 54, pp. 563–74.

Martin, C. L., Ruble, D. N. and Szkrybalo, J. (2002) 'Cognitive theories of early gender development', *Psychological Bulletin*, vol. 128, pp. 903–33.

Mead, M. (1935) *Sex and Temperament in Three Primitive Societies*, Oxford, William Morrow.

Milton, J. (1961, first published in 1667) 'Paradise Lost' in Darbishire, H. (ed.) *The Poems of John Milton*, London, Oxford University Press.

Mischel, W. (1966) 'A social-learning view of sex differences in behavior', in Maccoby, E. E. (ed.) *The Development of Sex Differences*, London, Tavistock.

O'Brien, K. M. and Fassinger, R. E. (1993) 'A causal model of the career orientation and career choice of adolescent women', *Journal of Counseling Psychology*, vol. 40, pp. 456–69.

Parker, J. G. and Asher, S. R. (1993) 'Friendship and friendship quality in middle childhood: links with peer group acceptance and feelings of loneliness and social dissatisfaction', *Developmental Psychology*, vol. 29, pp. 611–21.

Perry, D. G. and Bussey, K. (1979) 'The social learning theory of sex differences: imitation is alive and well', *Journal of Personality and Social Psychology*, vol. 37, pp. 1699–712.

Rubin, J. Z., Provenzano, F. J. and Luria, Z. (1974) 'The eye of the beholder: parents' views on sex of newborns', *American Journal of Orthopsychiatry*, vol. 44, pp. 512–9.

Ruble, D.N. and Martin, C. (1998) 'Gender development' in Eisenberg, N. (ed.) *Handbook of Child Psychology: Social, emotional and personality development*, vol. 3, New York, NY Wiley.

Ruskin, J. (1970, first published in 1865) 'Of Queens' Gardens' in Ruskin, J. *Sesame and Lilies*, London, Dent.

Seavey, A. A., Katz, P. A. and Zalk, S. R. (1975) 'Baby X: the effect of gender labels on adult responses to infants', *Sex Roles*, vol. 1, pp. 103–9.

Slaby, R. G. and Frey, K. S. (1975) 'Development of gender constancy and selective attention to same-sex models', *Child Development*, vol. 46, pp. 849–56.

Smith, C. and Lloyd, B. (1978) 'Maternal behavior and perceived sex of infant: revisited', *Child Development*, vol. 49, pp. 1263–5.

Spence, J. T. and Helmreich, R. L. (1978) *Masculinity and Femininity: their psychological dimensions, correlates and antecedents*, Austin, TX, University of Texas Press.

Stipek, D. J. and Gralinski, J. H. (1991) 'Gender differences in children's achievement-related beliefs and emotional responses to success and failure in mathematics', *Journal of Educational Psychology*, vol. 83, pp. 361–71.

Tennyson, Lord Alfred (1897) *The Princess: a medley*, London, Macmillan.

Terman, L. M. and Miles, C. C. (1936) *Sex and Personality: studies in masculinity and femininity*, New York, NY, McGraw-Hill.

Thorne, B. (1993) *Gender Play: girls and boys in school*, Buckingham, Open University Press.

Turner, P. J. and Gervai, J. (1995) 'A multidimensional study of gender typing in preschool children and their parents: personality, attitudes, preferences, behavior, and cultural differences', *Developmental Psychology*, vol. 31, pp. 759–79.

Weinburgh, M. (1995) 'Gender differences in student attitudes toward science: a meta-analysis of the literature from 1970 to 1991', *Journal of Research in Science Teaching*, vol. 32, pp. 387–98.

Williams, J. E. and Best, D. L. (1990) *Measuring Sex Stereotypes: a multination study*, Thousand Oaks, CA, Sage.

Chapter 6
National identities in children and young people

Martyn Barrett

Contents

Learning outcomes

After you have studied this chapter you should be able to:

1 describe the various affective and cognitive aspects of the subjective sense of national identity;

2 outline the research methods that have been used to investigate how a sense of national identity develops during childhood and adolescence;

3 describe the principal empirical findings concerning the development of affective and cognitive aspects of the sense of national identity;

4 explain how the developmental patterns which children and adolescents display vary across and within countries;

5 list the principal theoretical frameworks that have been used to explain the development of national identity in childhood and early adolescence;

6 evaluate these theoretical frameworks against the available evidence;

7 identify the type of theory that is required to explain the development of national identity.

1 Introduction

1.1 Listening to what children have to say

Sangita is a 9-year-old girl from an Asian family background, who was born in Britain and attends a multiethnic school in London. Here is a conversation between Sangita and a researcher interested in children's sense of their own national identity.

INTERVIEWER: Are you British or something else?

SANGITA: I'm quarter Ugandan, quarter Kenyan and half British.

INTERVIEWER: Why do you say 'Uganda'?

SANGITA: My Dad comes from Uganda.

INTERVIEWER: And where does Mum come from?

SANGITA: Kenya.

INTERVIEWER: And where does the British come from?

SANGITA: Here, because I was born in Britain.

(Carrington and Short, 1995, pp. 224–6)

Ruth is an 11-year-old girl who was born in Scotland and attends an 'all-white' primary school in Edinburgh:

INTERVIEWER: Is being British important to you?

RUTH: I would say being Scottish is more important to me than being British.

INTERVIEWER: That's interesting because when I asked you the question 'Are you British or are you something else', you said 'British'. Do you regard yourself as British and Scottish?

RUTH: Yes.

INTERVIEWER: Can you explain ... why being Scottish is more important [to you] than being British?

RUTH: Well – I was born in Scotland and it's more like a home base.

[...]

INTERVIEWER: Are you one of these people who gets slightly angry when you are confused with being English?

RUTH: Yes – a wee bit.

INTERVIEWER: Can you tell me why?

RUTH: Well, when people say you're British, they seem to think you're *English* – not Scottish. ... A lot of people automatically assume that you're English and I don't really like that much, because *we're not English*.

(Carrington and Short, 1996, pp. 208–10)

These examples reveal a number of things about children's sense of national identity, including the following.

1   Both Sangita and Ruth are quite happy to classify themselves in terms of their own national group memberships – neither hesitates to engage in a process of national self-categorization, and the interviewer's questions about the national groups to which they belong are willingly and readily answered.

2   Sangita's and Ruth's replies indicate that they both believe that an individual can have multiple national group affiliations – the triple affiliation of Ugandan, Kenyan and British in the case of Sangita, and the hierarchically nested affiliations of Scottish and British in the case of Ruth.

3   Sangita and Ruth both emphasize a person's place of birth in their reasoning: Sangita regards herself as half-British because she was born in Britain, while Ruth regards her Scottishness as being more important to her because she was born in Scotland.

As these extracts reveal, national identities within the United Kingdom are rather complex and multifaceted. Some of the complexities which are specific to the context of the United Kingdom are outlined in Box 1.

BOX 1

National identities in the United Kingdom

National identities in the United Kingdom are complex for two main reasons:

1   There are a number of different national categories with which people can identify in the United Kingdom.

2   Each of these available categories can carry different connotations in different contexts and for different individuals.

As far as the national categories themselves are concerned, there is an initial distinction between the United Kingdom and Great Britain. Notice that these are two distinct entities and are not synonymous (as many people assume them to be). The United Kingdom consists of two geographical territories: Great Britain and Northern Ireland. Great Britain itself consists of three countries: Scotland, Wales and England. Consequently, Scottish, Welsh and English people together comprise the British national group. Because the concept of Britishness has strong Anglocentric connotations (which stem historically from England's political and economic domination of Britain), Scottish and Welsh people tend to draw a very clear distinction between their Welsh or Scottish identity and their British identity. By contrast, many English people are far less clear about the difference between their English and their British identity, and they often confuse the two (Condor, 1996). As far as Northern Ireland is concerned, some Northern Irish people regard themselves as British, some as Irish, some as Northern Irish, and some as Ulster; their choice is usually related to their religion, that is, whether they are Protestant or Catholic (Trew, 1996).

However, the situation in the United Kingdom is even more complex than this, because categories such as British, English, Scottish, Welsh, etc., can be interpreted in different contexts and by different individuals in varying ways, as either national, ethnic or racial identities. And Britishness itself can be interpreted not only as a national, ethnic or racial identity but also as a citizenship, juridical or State identity (Kumar, 2003). This makes the United Kingdom a particularly challenging context for the investigation of people's national identities. For example, in the case of Sangita, it is possible that she regards Englishness as an ethnic category. So, because she herself has an Asian family background, she may think that she is not included within the English category, and this could be the reason why she identifies herself as being British rather than English. However, Sangita's comments do not reveal whether she herself construes Britishness as a national or as a citizenship category. Similarly, it is unclear from Ruth's comments whether she views being British as her citizenship or as a superordinate national identity.

Some of these complexities will be explored later on in this chapter, when considering some of the empirical findings about the patterns of national identification which are shown by children and adolescents.

In the light of these complexities, Ruth's comments are very interesting, because they show that she has begun to master at least some aspects of the distinctions between being Scottish, English and British. Ruth's comments also reveal that children's national self-categorizations are not affectively neutral. Instead, they can generate feelings and emotions, and children can resent being mis-categorized by other people. In fact, when you talk to children, you soon discover that they sometimes hold very strong views about national groups. For example, children often describe their own national group (their 'ingroup') in very positive terms. And they occasionally express very negative feelings about particular national groups to which they do not belong (sometimes called 'outgroups'). For example, Carrington and Short (1996) report that the following exchange took place with a 10-year-old Scottish girl who attended the same school as Ruth in Edinburgh:

INTERVIEWER: What are the best things about being British?

HILARY: Well, sometimes, I think it's good to be British because they won the war. And it's quite good – we're quite important for that; we never lost. I wouldn't like to be German either.

INTERVIEWER: What's wrong with being German?

HILARY: Well, they're awfully cruel and they're not very nice and I wouldn't like to go and live out there now.

INTERVIEWER: Have you met any German people?

HILARY: No.

INTERVIEWER: So when you say that German people are cruel, what gives you that view?

HILARY: Well, we've just been doing a project on World War II and I've heard about them killing lots of people and torturing them and things like that.

INTERVIEWER: Are all German people cruel do you think?

HILARY: Well, I'd say most of them are – but maybe, some of them are – OK?

INTERVIEWER: What are the worst things about being British?

HILARY: Well there isn't anything really bad about being British. Our country hasn't done anything wrong.

(Carrington and Short, 1996, pp. 220–1)

Hilary's comments provide a dramatic illustration of two further phenomena which characterize children's attitudes to national groups: ingroup favouritism (that is, liking your own group more than other groups and/or describing your own group in more positive terms than other groups) and the denigration of national outgroups which are traditional historical enemies of your own country (even though, in this instance, hostilities ended 50 years previously: the interview with Hilary took place in the summer of 1995).

This chapter will explore some of the research that has been conducted into how children's sense of national identity, and their attitudes to national groups, develop. Research into these kinds of issues has been undertaken for several reasons, some concerned with investigating 'real-world' problems, and others more focused on answering academic questions. Box 2 lists some of these reasons.

BOX 2

Why have developmental psychologists examined children's national identities?

Developmental psychologists have studied children's national identities for a number of different reasons, including the following:

To test theories about identity

Theories such as Piaget's cognitive-developmental theory and Tajfel's social identity theory make a number of empirical predictions about children's patterns of identification and their attitudes to social groups. (These theories will be discussed in Section 5.) Children's national identifications and attitudes towards national groups provide a useful domain for empirically testing some of these predictions.

To explore the development of emotionally 'hot' cognition

Children's thinking about nations and national groups, unlike their thinking in many other cognitive domains, is often accompanied by, or associated with, strong emotions. Furthermore, these emotions are sometimes present prior to the child's acquisition of any factual knowledge. This raises the possibility that these emotions play a significant motivational role in knowledge acquisition. Children's thinking in this domain therefore provides a fascinating opportunity to examine the development of emotionally 'hot' cognition.

To address important social issues

The rise of globalized cultural industries, the internet, cheap international air travel, and mass migration all mean that children who live in affluent societies can now communicate and interact with people from other national groups on a regular basis. However, inter-nation prejudice, hostility and conflict remain. Achieving a clear understanding of how emotional attachment to one's own nation develops, of how children view each other across national divides, and of how national prejudices and hostilities develop, is not only of scientific interest but also of considerable social importance.

To address more local policy-related issues

In some countries, shifts towards greater ethnic and cultural diversity, towards devolution and regional autonomy, or towards European federation, have posed more specific challenges. In order to address these challenges, social policies, educational curricula and media campaigns may be used either to promote or to prevent social change. However, for these to be effective, they need to be grounded in appropriate evidence about how people can be influenced by these means. Psychologists are able to provide that evidence. For example, Carrington and Short (1995) originally mounted their research within Britain in order to address the claim, frequently made by the New Right since the 1980s, that multicultural and anti-racist initiatives in education are undermining the societal and cultural cohesion of Britain. Carrington and Short discovered that, contrary to this claim, British children still display a monolithic view of British culture. They use the evidence from their study to recommend that, for multicultural and anti-racist educational initiatives to be effective, children need to be taught much more about the cultural differences that are to be found within any given national group, but in a context which also emphasizes the values, beliefs and cultural practices common to all ethnic groups within the nation (because this is a notion with which children are already familiar).

Before examining how children's sense of national identity develops, it is useful to consider the different aspects which contribute to it.

1.2 Some aspects of the subjective sense of national identity

To begin by going back to fundamentals, in order for someone to have, at the psychological level, a sense of their own national identity, they must have some knowledge of the existence of the national group. That is, the individual must, at the very least, have some rudimentary awareness that there is a group of people who are categorized together and labelled 'English people', or 'French people', or whatever. Although this seems a fairly obvious point, from a developmental perspective it is nevertheless important, because in their early years children do not yet have any knowledge of this kind. However, for a child to have a sense of his or her own national identity, it is not sufficient for that child simply to be aware of the existence of the national group; it is also necessary to understand that he or she is a member of that group. It is quite possible that children first acquire a knowledge of the existence of the national group, and only later begin to include themselves within that group. As Sangita's responses showed, children are capable of engaging in quite complex judgements about national self-categorization by the time they are nine years old.

Once they have begun to categorize themselves as members of national groups, individuals can attribute different levels of importance to their membership of them. In the case of adults, for example, there are some individuals who are only minimally concerned with their national identity; these individuals attribute very little importance to this identity, and may instead regard some of their other identities, for example, their gender identity or their ethnic identity, as being far more important to their self-concept. However, there are also other individuals who view their membership of their national group as being extremely important for the way in which they construe themselves. Children, just like adults, vary in terms of the importance they attribute to national identity, some of them attributing much higher importance than others to their membership of their national group.

Another key aspect of the subjective sense of national identity is the extent to which an individual experiences a personal sense of belonging to the national group. One important factor here can be the criteria which people employ either implicitly or explicitly to make judgements about whether someone is or is not a member of a particular national group. Some people may construe themselves as meeting all the necessary criteria for being a full member of their own national group. However, others may regard themselves as not meeting all the necessary criteria, or indeed they might be regarded by other people as not meeting all the necessary criteria (for example, because of their ethnic origin, level of patriotism, and so on). As a consequence, those individuals may feel marginalized or excluded from membership of the group. In other words, individuals' personal sense of belonging to the national group may be linked to the criteria that are used to judge people's membership of that group. Children (and adults) make interesting judgements about the types of characteristics that people need to have in order to be construed as members of national groups – as with Sangita and Ruth, children often regard a person's place of birth as an important criterion for inclusion in a particular national group.

Activity I

Allow about 20 minutes

The criteria used to judge people's membership of a national group

This activity encourages you to think about your own national or State identity, and what factors you use to decide whether other people share that identity with you.

If you consider yourself to be British, ask yourself the question, 'Is everybody who lives in Britain and who has formal British citizenship "British" to the same degree, or are some people more British than other people?'. If you have another nationality, ask yourself the parallel question about your own national or State group. As you answer this question, consider the wide variety of people who actually live in Britain today, and make sure that you think particularly about the large range of ethnic and religious groups.

If you decide that people can vary in their degree of Britishness, try to identify the criteria you are using in order to judge their degree of Britishness.

In addition, try repeating the same exercise but with reference to other national or State groups (such as English, Scottish, American, German, etc.), to see whether you are using the same criteria for these groups.

Comment

The likelihood is that you will have used a number of criteria in making your judgements. People commonly apply numerous criteria when thinking about who belongs to a particular national group, including parentage or ancestry, place of birth, ethnicity, religion, use of language, other cultural practices (such as preferred foods, clothes, etc.), and loyalty to or affection for traditional national institutions (such as the British monarchy). The Conservative politician Norman Tebbit notoriously argued in 1990 that the most important criterion was whether or not a person spontaneously supports national sports teams in international sporting fixtures (the so-called 'cricket test'). These criteria can interact in interesting ways to drive people's judgements. For example, think about a white person who was born overseas to British parents, who is an Anglican Christian, who wears traditional British clothes, but who dislikes the Royal Family intensely and supports the football team of their country of birth; then think of a black person who was born in London, whose parents were also born in London, who is a staunch Royalist, always supports England in football, but is Muslim and likes wearing brightly coloured African clothing. Which one do you judge to be the more British? Section 3 of this chapter will describe research which has investigated how children make judgements about people's national group memberships.

A further aspect of the subjective sense of national identity concerns the feelings of the individual towards other people who belong to their own national group. Empirical studies conducted using a range of different research methods have found that ingroup favouritism, as illustrated by Hilary's remarks about the British, is a very common phenomenon among both children and adolescents, not only in Britain but also in many other countries. That is to say, many children and adolescents express greater levels of liking for people who belong to their own national group than for people who belong to other national groups.

Individuals also hold stereotypes about the typical characteristics and traits of people who belong either to their own national group or to other salient national groups. It is not only children but also adults who hold these stereotypes. For example, many adults have a stereotype that English people are white, speak English, and are more socially reserved and less emotionally expressive than people from southern European countries. Also, they have stereotypes of what typically English people look like, as opposed to, say, typical Germans or typical Americans. As Hilary's comments reveal, these stereotypes about national ingroups and outgroups are present by the age of 10 years and research has shown that they begin to be acquired from the age of 5. However, while individuals may be familiar with these stereotypes, they may not always believe in them. A further interesting question is whether national stereotypes misrepresent reality and merely reflect the prejudices of the individual who holds them, or whether there is some truth to these stereotypes, reflecting genuine variations in national characters.

In addition, there are the various institutions, symbols, historical figures and traditions that serve as significant emblems or representations of the nation and national group. For example, in the case of England, the Queen, William Shakespeare, the Battle of Hastings and cream teas may all function as important and significant emblems of England and Englishness for many English people. National geographies can also be a fertile source of national emblems for the members of a nation; for example, the landscapes painted by Constable in the early nineteenth century have become a quintessential representation of England and of Englishness. In other words, knowledge of the national emblems which symbolize the nation and national groups is a further important aspect of the subjective sense of national identity.

Activity 2   *National emblems*

Allow about
15 minutes

This activity helps you to identify the different types of emblems which represent your own nation and national group.

Think of as many national emblems for your own nation and national group as you can and make brief notes. Do not edit or restrict in any way the emblems which you generate at this stage. Just think very broadly about the name of your country and your national group, trying to come up with as many emblems as you can.

Having generated these national emblems, try to classify them into different types. For example, some emblems could be people, whereas others could be well-known locations.

Comment

People can usually generate a large number of national emblems. These commonly include things like the national flag, the national anthem and national costumes; customs and traditions;

foods and drinks; famous people, places and events associated with the nation's history and cultural heritage; the monarch, prime minister or president; sporting figures; landscapes and cityscapes; and monuments and buildings. Some people also think of the name of the currency as a national symbol (which may be one reason why, at the turn of the twenty-first century, the adoption of the Euro has been strongly resisted by some groups within the populations of certain European countries). In the context of the United Kingdom, it is worth bearing in mind that some of these emblems may be British (such as the national anthem) whereas others may be English, Scottish, Welsh, etc. (for example, the flags of St George, St Andrew and the Welsh Red Dragon).

Figure 1 Some national emblems are current representations of the nation's history.

Finally, there is a wide range of emotions which the individual can experience by virtue of his or her membership of the national group, such as national pride, national embarrassment and national shame. These emotions may be directly elicited by national emblems: for example, pride by hearing the national anthem or seeing the national flag; embarrassment by thinking about how terrible English food is in comparison to, say, French and Italian food. These social emotions are not only elicited by national emblems, however. They can also be triggered by specific events: for example, national pride when someone from your own nation wins an Olympic gold medal or the Eurovision Song Contest; national shame when English football hooligans rioting in the streets of a foreign city make an English person feel ashamed to be English.

1.3 The context-dependence of national identity

The subjective sense of national identity is a complex psychological structure. It involves a substantial system of knowledge and beliefs about the national group, and an extensive system of feelings and emotions concerning it. It is important to emphasize, however, that the subjective sense of national identity is not a static psychological structure. The significance of national identity varies substantially from one situation to another. It is a dynamic psychological structure which may or may not be mobilized according to situational and motivational contingencies. In other words, national identity, like most of our other identities, is highly context-dependent.

1.4 Behaviours associated with national identity

National identities are not defined solely in terms of their internal psychological cognitive and affective characteristics, even though these have been stressed in this section. National identities are intimately and pervasively connected to our everyday behaviour. Indeed, it is hard to overestimate the extent of the association between the two. Think, for example, about the day-to-day world of a child. Things which are associated with the child's national identity permeate many different aspects of that child's life, including the language the child learns to speak, the way of life adopted by the child's family, the content of programmes the child watches on television, the content of the child's school curriculum (particularly in the study of subjects such as history and geography), the national holidays and festivals celebrated by the child and his or her family, and so on.

However, despite the pervasiveness of national identity, it is also true to say that national identities are often invisible, to children and adults alike. People simply do not normally think about national identity as they go about their everyday business, although daily life is permeated by things that are unnoticeably associated with national identity (Billig, 1995).

Summary of Section 1

- The subjective sense of national identity involves:
  1 knowledge of the existence of the national group;
  2 categorization of self as a member of the national group;
  3 the degree of importance attributed to the national identity by the individual at a subjective level;
  4 a personal sense of belonging to the national group;

    5   beliefs about the criteria which make someone a member of the national group;

    6   feelings towards other people who belong to the national group;

    7   beliefs about the typical characteristics and traits of people who belong to the national ingroup and to salient national outgroups;

    8   knowledge of national emblems; and

    9   knowledge of emotions such as national pride and national shame.

- National identity is a dynamic psychological structure which is context dependent and may or may not be mobilized according to situational and motivational contingencies.

- National identity is not defined solely in terms of internal psychological cognitive and affective characteristics, but is also deeply embedded in our everyday behaviours.

2 Empirical findings on national self-categorization in childhood and adolescence

This section and Section 3 examine some of the empirical findings which have emerged from studies of children's and adolescents' sense of national identity. These studies have been conducted with participants from a large number of different national groups.

2.1 The development of national self-categorization

Section 1 of this chapter described the work of researchers such as Carrington and Short (1995, 1996) who used open-ended interviewing to investigate the development of children's national self-categorization. The same method was used by Piaget and Weil (1951) and Lambert and Klineberg (1967). Piaget and Weil interviewed Swiss children living in Geneva. They found that, before the age of 5 years, children knew that they lived in Geneva, what language was spoken there, and that it was a big city. However, they did not yet know what country they lived in, or what country Geneva was in. From about 5 or 6 years of age onwards, these children typically did know the name of their own country; however, at this early point in their development, some of them nevertheless denied that they themselves were Swiss. A similar finding was obtained by Lambert and Klineberg (1967) in their much larger study of 6, 10 and 14 year olds living in ten different countries. They too found that, in certain countries, there were some 6 year olds who, although they could name their own national group, sometimes referred to the members of that group using words such as 'they' and 'them' in ways which suggested that they did not yet fully include themselves among them (for example, 'they dress as we do', 'they are like us').

Although open-ended interviewing can be revealing, it is important to be aware that there are problems associated with this method when working with children. Firstly, the wording of a question can easily encourage particular types of answers from children. For example, one question in Carrington and Short's interview schedule was 'Are you British or are you something else?' They found that 94 per cent of English ethnic majority children and 75 per cent of Scottish children responded that they were 'British'. However, this question only cued the children with the word 'British', not with the word 'English' or 'Scottish'. This was almost certainly the reason why Ruth only said that she was British initially, even though her Scottishness was more important to her. A further problem is that in interviews children tend to produce responses which they think the interviewer wants to hear. In other words, children's responses in interviews are often biased by social desirability effects, and children may withhold answers which they think are unacceptable to adults (such as openly racist or xenophobic answers – and, indeed, Carrington and Short found that openly xenophobic comments such as Hilary's were rare in their interviews). The use of open-ended questions in verbal interviewing is also cognitively very demanding for children.

Activity 3   *The demands placed on a child by open-ended interviewing*

Allow about
10 minutes

This activity helps you to reflect on the level of complexity involved in responding to an open-ended question.

Draw up a list of the cognitive processes involved in answering an open-ended question. When you have done this, order it into the sequence of processes which are involved, from the initial comprehension of the question through to the final articulation of the response. What cognitive processes are required in order to produce the correct response to a question?

Comment

Answering an open-ended question is a very demanding task. The individual has to comprehend both the lexical items and the grammar of the question, make an inference about what the interviewer wants to know by asking that question, use that inference to access information in memory, retrieve that information from memory, and then encode that information in a verbal response, using the appropriate lexical items and grammar to do so. Errors can occur at any stage in this process. As a result, open-ended interviewing may underestimate the knowledge, beliefs and patterns of reasoning of children.

In order to avoid some of these problems, colleagues and I have developed an alternative method for examining children's national self-categorizations and identifications. This method involves giving each child a set of cards on which the names of various possible identities are written. These include a range of national and State terms (such as 'English', 'Scottish' and 'British'), supra-national terms (such as 'European'), city terms (such as 'Londoner' and 'Roman'), gender terms ('boy' and 'girl'), and ages (for example, '6 years old', '9 years old'), as well as various distracter terms. The child is asked to choose all of the cards which describe him or herself. Notice that this method does not require the child to recall his or her own self-categorizations. All the child needs to do is recognize them (recognition is cognitively less demanding than recall). We have now used this method with children aged between 6 and 15 years who live in many different countries, including England and Scotland within Britain; the Basque Country, Catalonia and Andalusia within Spain; Italy; Russia; Ukraine; Georgia; and Azerbaijan. In all of these places, we found that the majority of children did typically choose at least one of the correct national terms for themselves, irrespective of their age. So, by the age of 6 years, most children not only know the name of their own national group but also spontaneously choose it in order to describe themselves.

2.2 The importance attributed to national identity by children and adolescents

In these same studies, we also assessed how much importance the children attributed to their national identity. We did this by asking each child to rank order all of the cards which had been chosen in terms of their importance to him or herself. We discovered that the children showed one of two different developmental patterns on this rank ordering task, depending upon their own national group membership.

In the first developmental pattern, very high importance was attributed to the national identity term right from the outset, at the age of 6, and this high level of importance continued to be shown by these children up to 15 years of age. For example, we found this pattern in all of the regions of Spain where we tested children. We found that Basque-speaking children in the Basque Country ascribed high importance to their Basque identity at all ages (Reizábal *et al.*, 2004), Catalan-speaking children in Catalonia ascribed high importance to their Catalan identity at all ages (Vila *et al.*, 1998), and children in Andalusia ascribed high importance to their Spanish identity at all ages (Giménez *et al.*, 2003).

In the second developmental pattern, national identity was not ranked as being very important at the age of 6, but its importance subsequently grew between 6 and 12 years of age. Thus, although these groups of 6 year olds may have spontaneously chosen this identity in order to describe themselves, they did not yet ascribe much importance to it. These children instead placed much greater importance on their age, their gender and their city identities at this early age. However, by 12 years of age, these groups of children had typically begun to attribute much greater importance to their national identity. This second developmental pattern was exhibited by children living in Scotland (Barrett, 2000) and Ukraine (Pavlenko *et al.*, 2001), amongst other places.

As far as supranational terms such as 'European' were concerned, these were not often chosen by the 6- and 9-year-old children in order to describe themselves in any of the countries where we collected data. However, by 12 and 15 years of age, children in both southern Spain and northern Italy had not only begun to choose this term to describe themselves, but had also started to attribute relatively high importance to this identity. In a notable contrast, the children in England and

Scotland rarely placed much importance on their European identity, at any age. (Notice that low levels of European identification may be one possible reason why English and Scottish people are not the most enthusiastic members of the European Union.)

In addition to these variations in the importance which children ascribed to their national identities as a function of age and nation, our studies revealed that variations in the importance of national identity can also occur as a function of three further factors: children's geographical location within the nation, their ethnicity, and their use of language.

Geographical location and national identity

We have discovered that there are differences in the importance attributed to national identity between children who live in the capital city and those in other locations within the country. For example, in England, children living in London attribute greater importance to both their British and their English identities than children who are living elsewhere in the south-east of England (Barrett, 2002). Similarly, in Russia, children growing up in Moscow attribute greater importance to their Russian identity than do children growing up in the provincial city of Smolensk (Riazanova *et al.*, 2001).

Activity 4   *How does living in a capital city affect children's sense of national identity?*

Allow about
30 minutes

This activity encourages you to think about the experience of living in a capital city, and how that might contribute to a sense of national identity.

Think about why living in one of the world's capital cities might mean that you as a child might attribute greater importance to your national identity than if you were living elsewhere in the same country. Some of the research you have read about earlier in this chapter will help you with this.

Comment

There are several possible reasons why these differences occur. It may be that simply knowing that you live in the capital city of a country serves to enhance the importance of that country for you. Or it could be that living in the capital city means that a child has more immediate familiarity with the most important national emblems. Many important national emblems such as the Houses of Parliament, Big Ben and the Tower of London are located in London, just as Red Square and the Kremlin are located in Moscow. It may be that the presence of these national emblems in their home city enhances the prominence of the country for these children. Another possible explanation is that capital cities are more cosmopolitan, and tend to contain more foreign tourists, than other locations within the country. Thus, capital cities may afford greater opportunities for inter-group comparisons, which could serve to enhance the salience of the child's own national group at an earlier age in these cities. There are no doubt other possible explanations of this finding as well. However, the basic point here is that it cannot be assumed that patterns of development exhibited by children growing up in one geographical location within a country will necessarily be displayed by children who are growing up in other locations in the same country.

Figure 2 Important national emblems are often, but not always, located in capital cities.

Ethnicity and national identity

Another factor which is related to the importance attributed to national identity is the child's ethnicity. For example, in one study (Barrett, 2002) we compared white English adolescents aged between 11 and 16 years with second-generation, London-born Indian, Pakistani, Bangladeshi and black African adolescents in the same age range (these ethnic categories were self-ascribed by the young people themselves in response to a question in which they were asked about their ethnicity). In this case, because these were older children, in addition to the rank ordering task, we asked two direct questions: 'How important is it to you that you are British?' and 'How important is it to you that you are English?' The response options were 'very important', 'quite important', 'not very important', and 'not important at all'. The findings revealed a clear picture: the white English adolescents attributed significantly higher importance to both the British and English national identities than all four groups of ethnic minority adolescents.

As far as the English identity is concerned, this finding is not surprising. Numerous commentators (for example, Parekh, 2000; Phoenix, 1995) have observed that many people in England implicitly (and sometimes explicitly) define Englishness in racial or ethnic terms, assuming that, in order to be English, an individual must be white. So the fact that these minority adolescents identified to a lesser extent than the white adolescents with being English is not at all surprising. What some people may find rather more unexpected is that the minority adolescents also identified with the British category to a far lesser extent than the white adolescents. Britishness is often held to be a superordinate and inclusive category which subsumes all of the ethnic groups living within Britain. However, our data indicate that these minority adolescents found the British category problematic as well.

Figure 3   A case of national identification and pride, or of national irony?

There are several possible reasons for the patterns of identification shown by these minority individuals. Firstly, some authors (for example, Hall, 1999; Parekh, 2000) have argued that the concept of Britishness is embedded within a set of implicit beliefs and stories about the imperial and colonial past in which ethnic minority groups are relegated to a subordinate and minor role (along with the Scots, Welsh and Irish). If this is the case, then it may be that members of minority groups find it more difficult than white English individuals to identify with this historical image of Britain, precisely because it relegates their own group to a subordinate and minor position. A second possibility is that some of these individuals' responses were a consequence of their religious beliefs, which had much greater relevance and importance for them in their everyday lives. For example, a Muslim individual may ascribe far greater importance to their membership of the worldwide Muslim community (the *Ummah*) than to any local national affiliation. Hence, some of these minority individuals may have identified with being British, but simply did not ascribe much importance to this identification, because of their religious beliefs.

A third possibility is that the category 'British' is, just like the category 'English', also defined for many people, at least partially, in terms of race (see Phoenix, 1995; Modood *et al.*, 1997 and Parekh, 2000, for discussions of this idea). Shah has expressed the point in the following way:

> The word British – rather like Chinese – conjures up many images. And just as you or I would be unlikely to imagine a black or brown face when thinking of the word Chinese, so the images brought to mind with the word British are more likely to be of an Anglican church rather than a Sunni mosque, warm beer rather than a cold lassi, a white face rather than a black or brown one.

(Shah, 2000)

In other words, Shah is arguing that our mental representations of not only Englishness, but also Britishness, contain a racial dimension. This is not to say that Britishness is an inherently racist concept. Instead, the argument is that the concept of Britishness, in practice, seems to carry racial connotations for many British people. If this is the case, then it is perhaps not surprising that some members of visible ethnic minority groups find it harder to identify with being British than white people do. They too may well have a mental representation of British people which contains a racial dimension.

The use of language and national identity

A further factor which is related to the importance which children attribute to national identity is their use of language. That is to say, there are differences in the importance attributed to national identity by children who live in the same geographical location and who belong to the same ethnic group, but who differ in their use of language. For example, in Catalonia in Spain, the importance attributed to being Catalan and to being Spanish varies systematically as a function of whether the child speaks only Catalan or only Spanish at home with their parents: higher levels of Catalan identification are exhibited by children who speak only Catalan at home and higher levels of Spanish identification are exhibited by children who speak only Spanish at home (Vila *et al.*, 1998). Parallel findings have been obtained in the Basque country with respect to the use of the Basque and Spanish languages (Reizábal *et al.*, 2004). And in Georgia and Azerbaijan, similar differences have been found to occur as a function of children's language of schooling: children who attend Georgian- or Azeri-language schools in Tbilisi or Baku (the capital cities of Georgia and Azerbaijan) attribute higher importance to their Georgian or Azeri national identity, respectively, than children who attend Russian-language schools in the same cities (Karakozov and Kadirova, 2001; Kipiani, 2001).

It is unlikely that the mere fact of speaking a particular language itself is the causal factor that determines the importance that the child attributes to their national identity. Instead, it seems much more likely that the child's use of language is a consequence of the ideological choices and value systems of his or her parents. For example, within the Basque Country in Spain, adults use language (either Basque or Spanish) deliberately to mark and express their own sense of national identity. Consequently, parents' own national identifications and practices are likely to be the key factors that determine both the child's use of language and the importance which the child attributes to particular national identities. Similarly, in Georgia and Azerbaijan (where Russian is the former imperial language), parents choose to send their children to study in Russian-language schools precisely because they wish their children to obtain the socio-economic advantages that schooling in a politically and economically dominant language can give. Hence, in both Georgia and Azerbaijan, children's language of schooling is a consequence of parents' aspirations and choices for them. In other words, the causal factor here, in determining both the child's use of language and the importance that the child attributes to particular national identities, is likely to be the parents' ideological choices, values and practices.

2.3 The theoretical implications of variability in development

There is thus considerable variability in the development of national identification, as a function of five main factors: the child's age, nation, geographical location within the nation, ethnicity, and language use. The existence of such variability poses serious problems for any theoretical account (such as Piagetian cognitive-developmental theory) which proposes that all children develop in a similar way, irrespective of the specific national or cultural situation in which they live. This issue of the theoretical implications of variability in development forms part of Section 5 of this chapter.

Summary of Section 2

- Children usually categorize themselves as members of a national group from the age of 6 years.
- The importance that children attribute to national identity develops in one of two ways: it either increases significantly between 6 and 12 years of age; or it is already present at a high level by the age of 6 and remains so up until at least 15 years of age.
- Within nations, there are systematic differences in the importance that children attribute to national identity, as a function of the child's geographical location, ethnicity and use of language.

3 Children's views about other people's membership of national groups

Section 2 discussed research which has investigated children's views about their own national group membership. This section describes research into children's views of other people's membership of national groups.

3.1 Children's beliefs about the criteria that make someone a member of a national group

Section 1 illustrated that an individual's subjective sense of belonging to a national group may be related to the criteria that people use to make judgements about whether or not someone is a member of a national group. Sangita's and Ruth's comments illustrate that children often emphasize a person's place of birth in their judgements about national group memberships. Carrington and Short's interview studies (1995, 1996, 2000) are very revealing here. They asked children aged between 8 and 12 years living in Britain and America 'What makes a person British/American?' The responses are given in Table 1.

Table 1 **The percentages of British and American children who mentioned each criterion as a determinant of nationality**

Nationality of participant	Criterion referred to as a determinant of nationality				
	Birthplace	English as first language	Place of residence	Nationality of parents or grandparents	Having legal citizenship
British	65	32	18	17	minimal
American	64	minimal	31	11	16

Source: Carrington and Short, 2000.

Typical comments made by the British children were:

It's just the way they talk and where they were born.

(White Scottish 9 year old)

If they're born in Britain and they were brought up in Britain and they've got relations that are British.

(White English 10 year old)

(Carrington and Short, 1995, p. 228)

By comparison, very few of the American children referred to the language a person spoke, but there were more references to having formal legal citizenship (having 'papers' or a passport) than there were in Britain. In all national contexts, there were very few explicit references to either race or ethnicity.

Carrington and Short also asked the children the question 'Is it possible to stop being British/American and become something else?' When children said 'yes' in response to this question, the most frequently cited reason, both in Britain and in America, was because people can go and live in another country. For example, one child said:

> 'If you move to another country and live there for a long time, you become that [nationality].'
>
> (White American 11 year old)
>
> (Carrington and Short, 2000, p. 189)

However, there were two differences between the British and the American children in their responses to this second question. Firstly, the British children sometimes said that people can change the language they speak and so they can stop being British for this reason. By contrast, the American children hardly ever referred to people's use of language. Secondly, when children said 'no' in response to this question, references to birthplace as the reason why people could not change their nationality were far more frequent among the British children. For example, one British child said:

> [No,] you've always got the British in you – because you were born in Britain.
>
> (Asian British 11 year old)
>
> (Carrington and Short, 1995, p. 231)

Nearly one-third of the British children referred to birthplace in this way, whereas hardly any American children did so. So, once again, cross-national differences were apparent in children's understanding of national group memberships.

RESEARCH SUMMARY

A different method to assess children's beliefs about the criteria that make someone a member of a national group

Because of the potential problems which can occur with open-ended interviewing, Penny, Barrett and Lyons (2001) used a different method to examine children's judgements about the criteria which make someone a member of a national group. They drew up a set of eight statements for testing English and Scottish children (the words 'English' and 'England' were used in these statements for the English participants, and 'Scottish' and 'Scotland' for the Scottish participants):

1 this child was **born** in England/Scotland
2 this child **speaks** English/Scottish
3 this child has English/Scottish **parents**

4   this child **lives** in England/Scotland
5   this child is **Christian**
6   this child is **white**
7   this child is **8 years old**
8   this child **goes to school**

Each statement was written on a separate card, and these cards were then presented in pairs to children aged between 6 and 12 years old. There are 28 possible pairs which can be formed from the 8 statements, and all 28 were presented to each individual child. Each pair was read out in turn to the child, and each time the child was asked to choose which of the two described children was most likely to be English (in the case of the English participants) or Scottish (in the case of the Scottish participants).

The children responded to this task in a similar way irrespective of their age and national group. When they were presented with a pair in which one of the people was 'born in England/Scotland', the children typically chose this person. However, if birthplace information was absent, then the children tended to choose the person who 'speaks English/Scottish'. If there was no information about either birthplace or language, then the children typically chose the person who 'has English/Scottish parents'. Finally, if there was no information about birthplace, language or parentage, then the children tended to chose the person who 'lives in England/Scotland'. Interestingly, the children paid very little attention to either the religion or the race of the people when making their decisions – they seemed to regard these two characteristics as being largely irrelevant to people's national group memberships (they tended to choose on the basis of religion and race only when these were paired with one of the two distracters, '8 years old' and 'goes to school').

Notice that the first four criteria are similar to those obtained by Carrington and Short. In addition, this study shows that children as young as 6 years of age are able to make systematic judgements about people's national group memberships, and that the criteria which they use for making these judgements do not change across the course of middle childhood.

3.2 Children's beliefs about people who belong to different national groups

Children's beliefs about the people who belong to different national groups have now been investigated in a number of interview studies (for example, Piaget and Weil, 1951; Jahoda, 1962; Lambert and Klineberg, 1967; Barrett and Short, 1992). These studies have found that national stereotypes start to be acquired at about 5 years of age. And during the following years, children's knowledge of, and beliefs about, the people who belong to different national groups expands (see Table 2). Initially, at 5 or 6 years of age, children simply report the typical characteristics of just a few major national groups. At this early age, the characteristics they talk about are primarily the physical features and traits of the national group concerned. However, by 10 or 11 years of age, children very willingly produce detailed descriptions of the characteristics exhibited by the members of many different national groups, including their physical features, clothing, language, traits and habits, and sometimes their political and religious beliefs as well (Piaget and Weil, 1951; Lambert and Klineberg, 1967).

Table 2 **Attributes ascribed by English children to French, German, Spanish and Italian people by 50 per cent or more of the children within each age group**

Age group	National group			
	French	German	Spanish	Italian
5–7 years	brown/suntan hardworking		brown/suntan tall thin happy	
8–10 years	brown/suntan strong speak French clean peaceful clever hardworking	white tall speak German happy aggressive hardworking	brown/suntan brown hair dark eyes strong speak Spanish happy clean peaceful	brown/suntan strong speak Italian smart clothes poor eat spaghetti/pasta happy peaceful

Source: Barrett and Short, 1992.

3.3 Children's feelings about people who belong to different national groups

Children's feelings about national groups have also been extensively investigated, using a number of different measures. Some studies (such as Piaget and Weil, 1951) have used open-ended questioning, while others (such as Barrett and Short, 1992) have asked children to rate how much they like particular groups on scales running from 'like a lot' to 'dislike a lot'. Other studies have used tasks in which children are asked to assign positive and negative traits (for example, 'friendly', 'lazy') to national groups, and an overall positivity–negativity score is then calculated (for example, Barrett *et al.*, 2003). And finally, some studies (such as Verkuyten, 2001) have asked the child the question 'What would you think about having X friends', where X refers to a particular national group.

Despite these variations in the method used, a common finding has emerged. Children generally prefer their own national group over all other national groups. This bias has been found to occur at all ages from 6 to 15 years. It has also been found to be present in most countries in which children have been tested. This includes England, Belgium, Holland, Austria, Spain, Italy, Israel, America, Russia, Ukraine, Georgia and Azerbaijan (Barrett, 2005).

That said, there are occasional exceptions to this general rule. For example, Tajfel *et al.* (1970, 1972) found that although ingroup favouritism was present in English, Dutch, Austrian, Belgian, Italian and Israeli children aged between 6 and

12 years, Scottish children who were of the same age did not display a preference for their own national group. Notice that the Tajfel *et al.* studies were conducted in the late 1960s. More recent studies, such as Bennett *et al.* (1998), have revealed a different picture, with Scottish children now exhibiting ingroup favouritism (on a 'like/dislike' scale) in much the same way as children living in other countries.

In addition, it is worth noting that different findings can sometimes emerge depending upon the specific measure which is used. For example, Barrett *et al.* (2004) assessed English, Scottish, Spanish and Italian children aged between 6 and 15 years using both a 'like/dislike' scale and a positivity/negativity trait attribution task. Ingroup favouritism was present in all groups of children on the 'like/dislike' scale. However, it was less prominent on the trait attribution task. In addition, the latter task revealed different developmental patterns in different countries: Scottish children did not show ingroup favouritism on this task until 15 years of age, whereas Italian children showed ingroup favouritism at 6 years of age but did not exhibit it at later ages. The fact that this kind of cross-national variability occurs poses a serious problem for universalist accounts, such as Piaget's cognitive-developmental theory, which propose that children develop in a similar way irrespective of their specific location or national context.

Although ingroup favouritism is a common phenomenon, this is not to say that all national outgroups are disliked – quite the contrary, in fact. Children of all ages do typically like most national outgroups, but just to a lesser extent than the ingroup. Outgroup denigration (that is, either negative feelings or negative trait attributions to an outgroup) is a comparatively rare phenomenon which tends to be exhibited only in relationship to those national groups which are the traditional historical enemies of the child's own country (as illustrated by Hilary's comments about Germans quoted in Section 1). For example, English children typically display significantly more negative affect towards German people than towards any other national group (Barrett and Short, 1992), as do Greek children towards Turks (Buchanan-Barrow *et al.*, 1999), and Azeri children towards Russians (Bennett *et al.*, 2004). In all three cases, the outgroup concerned is a historical enemy of the child's own nation.

As a general rule, children's attitudes towards national groups tend to be the most polarized at the age of 5 or 6, when they express the most positivity towards their own national group, and the least positivity towards outgroups. Across the course of middle childhood, their attitudes tend to become less polarized, with attitudes to the ingroup becoming less positive and attitudes to outgroups becoming more positive (Barrett *et al.*, 2003; Barrett and Short, 1992). However, once again, exceptions have been found to this general rule. For example, Lambert and Klineberg (1967) assessed the attitudes of children living in 10 different countries. They found that children living in many different countries did indeed become more positive towards national outgroups with age. However, Bantu children living in South Africa did not show any changes at all in their national attitudes between 6 and 14 years of age. More recently, Reizábal *et al.* (2004) also found no changes in Basque children's national attitudes between 6 and 15 years of age. Hence, once again, we have evidence that there is cross-national variability in the development of children's national attitudes.

3.4 The relationship between national attitudes and national identification

An important issue, and one relevant to the evaluation of Tajfel's social identity theory, is whether the strength of children's national identification is related to their feelings and attitudes towards national groups – in other words, whether those children who have the strongest sense of national identity are also the most biased in favour of the ingroup and the most prejudiced against outgroups. Barrett *et al.* (2004) examined this issue, using data from British, Spanish and Italian children aged between 6 and 15 years. They found no evidence of a relationship between the strength of the children's national identification and their attitudes towards national outgroups (irrespective of whether these attitudes were measured using 'like/dislike' scales or trait attributions). Neither was there any relationship between the strength of national identification and children's trait attributions to the ingroup. Strength of national identification was, however, related to how much the children liked their own national ingroup, at all ages. Section 5 of this chapter will return to this point.

3.5 The sources of children's beliefs about other nations and national groups

Children derive their beliefs about other nations and national groups from a number of different sources. In their study, Lambert and Klineberg (1967) found that 6 year olds reported that they had learned about foreign groups from their parents, direct contact with foreigners, television and films. Children aged between 10 and 14 years reported that they had acquired their information primarily from television, films, books, school course work, textbooks and magazines. For the English children aged between 5 and 10 years interviewed by Barrett and Short (1992), television was an especially prominent source, with parents, holidays and books also being mentioned.

Using a different method, Holloway and Valentine (2000) asked 13-year-old British and New Zealand children to e-mail each other with descriptions of what they thought the other country and its people were like. They found frequent references to media images from soap operas (such as *Coronation Street*) and films (such as *Crocodile Dundee*) in the children's descriptions. For example, two comments from the New Zealand children were:

> I assume your house is like the ones off *Coronation Street* as these are the only British houses I have seen.
>
> (Holloway and Valentine, 2000, p. 351)
>
> The houses are old and of an older style than seen in New Zealand. They often have two storeys and no front or back gardens like *Coronation Street.*
>
> (*ibid.*, p. 348)

And two comments from the British children were:

> We think you probably dress like Crocodile Dundee in Bermuda shorts and a hat with corks dangling.

(*ibid.*, p. 344)

> New Zealanders look like us but have more of a tan and they speak Australian English.

(*ibid.*, p. 342)

Notice the conflation of New Zealand and Australia by the British children. Holloway and Valentine found that the British children frequently confused the two countries, drawing not only upon movies like *Crocodile Dundee* but also soap operas such as *Neighbours* and *Home and Away*, and advertisements such as those for Foster's lager, for their images of New Zealand.

Figure 4 Do we hold an implicit belief that people who belong to different national groups have different physical appearances?

Evidence that television does indeed influence children's beliefs about national groups is reported by Himmelweit *et al.* (1958). They found that the beliefs of children aged between 10 and 14 years who had watched television programmes about other national groups over a period of a year matched the way that these national groups were being portrayed in those television programmes to a greater extent than did the beliefs of children who did not watch these programmes.

When the child's own nation is either currently, or has historically been, in conflict with another nation, then the mass media within that country tend to present negative images of the enemy people (English and Halperin, 1987; Hesse and Mack, 1991). It is therefore perhaps not surprising that children often come to display negative beliefs and feelings about enemy countries and national groups.

3.6 Is children's understanding of people's national group memberships historically specific?

It is worth bearing in mind that some of the research discussed in Section 3 is quite old, dating back to the 1950s and 1960s in some cases. This raises the interesting question of whether, if identical studies were to be conducted today using similar populations of children, the findings would be the same (we have already noted one case, involving Scottish children, where the findings of an older study by Tajfel *et al.* and a more recent study by Bennett *et al.* differ). There have been many significant changes over the past half-century, not least in the opportunities which some children now have to travel to other countries, to encounter people from other cultures, and to watch television programmes and films which are set in other countries. Given the influence of media representations upon children's views of national groups, it is plausible to suppose that replications of the early studies would yield different findings. However, recent studies have identified deeper underlying patterns in their data which are actually very similar to those of the early studies (such as the common, although not universal, occurrence of ingroup favouritism and the display of less positive affect towards historical enemies). Hence, it might only be the superficial features of children's beliefs in this domain (for example, about the specific traits which characterize particular national groups) which would differ today. The extent to which children's beliefs in this domain are historically specific is an important issue which future research will need to address.

Summary of Section 3

- Children use the following criteria to make judgements about whether or not someone is a member of a national group:
    the place where the person was born;
    the place where the person lives;
    the national group to which parents or grandparents belong;
    the language which the person speaks;
    the legal citizenship of the person.
- In making judgements about national group memberships, children do not take account of race, ethnicity, or religion.
- National stereotypes start to be acquired at about the age of 5 years and during middle childhood stereotypes become increasingly elaborated and detailed.
- With some exceptions, children and adolescents usually display a systematic preference for their own national ingroup at all ages. However, most national outgroups are also positively liked at all ages, although to a lesser extent than the ingroup.
- Outgroup denigration is comparatively rare, and is usually only exhibited in relationship to national outgroups which are the traditional historical enemies of the child's own nation.

- Attitudes towards other national groups tend to become more positive during middle childhood, and to level out during early adolescence. However, there are some groups of children who do not show any age-related changes in their attitudes to national groups.
- No clear relationship exists between the strength of national identification and attitudes towards national outgroups. However, the strength of national identification is related to how much the child likes the national ingroup, at all ages.
- Children appear to derive their beliefs and feelings about national groups from television, movies, books, school work, parents, and holidays in other countries.

4 Other aspects of the sense of national identity in children

Very little research has been conducted into either children's knowledge of national emblems, or children's national emotions (such as national pride, national shame, etc.). Children's knowledge of national emblems clearly does increase with age (Jahoda, 1963b; Weinstein, 1957) but little is known about the processes or factors involved. It is possible that children's emotional responses to national emblems vary according to their ethnicity. For example, Moodie (1980) found that Afrikaans-speaking children in South Africa had a stronger preference for national emblems (such as the South African national flag and the national anthem) than English-speaking children who were growing up in the same country.

However, none of these studies assessed the emotions that children experience in response to national emblems or to events with a national dimension (such as winning gold medals at the Olympic Games). And very few studies have attempted to examine whether or not children might sometimes feel negative emotions in connection with their own nation or national group. One rare exception is a study by Hengst (1997), who found that whereas English children aged between 9 and 12 years commonly thought that their fellow nationals were liked abroad, German children of a similar age sometimes acknowledged that their fellow nationals were unpopular abroad, either because of the neo-Nazis or because of the two world wars. But this study failed to provide any concrete information about individual differences, or even age group differences, in the extent to which the children expressed these kinds of judgements.

Activity 5

Allow about
30 minutes

What are the principal phenomena which require explanation?

This activity encourages you to revisit the factors which characterize the development of national identity, and think about how these might fit into a theoretical framework.

Before reading Section 5, go back to the beginning of Section 2, and skim read Sections 2 and 3 once again, noting down the principal phenomena which characterize the development of national identification and national attitudes. Pay particular attention to those phenomena which you yourself think it is vital for any theoretical framework to explain.

What type of theory do you think is required to explain children's development in this domain?

Comment

There are two main types of theoretical approach to explaining these developmental phenomena. Section 5 below describes them.

Summary of Section 4

- Future research will need to examine children's knowledge of national emblems and children's national emotions.

---

5 Theoretical explanations of the development of national identity in childhood and adolescence

The two main theoretical approaches to the development of national identity during childhood and adolescence have their roots in rather different psychological traditions. One stems from the cognitive-developmental theory of Piaget, while the other comes from Tajfel's social identity theory.

5.1 The cognitive-developmental explanation

Piaget himself is relatively reticent about how to explain the development of national identity in children. However, his descriptive account of the developmental changes in this domain (Piaget and Weil, 1951) locates discontinuities in children's understanding at the ages of 7–8 and 10–11 years of age. The first discontinuity involves the child achieving (concrete-operational) understanding of the spatial inclusion relationships between cities and nations, while the later discontinuity involves the child achieving (formal-operational) understanding of the more abstract concept of national group memberships, and of the (decentred) notion that foreigners can be emotionally attached to their own nation in the same way as the child is attached to his or her own nation. Thus, implicit within Piaget's descriptive account is the idea that the child's understanding of national identity is dependent upon the child's general cognitive capacities at any particular point in development; as the child's cognitive capacities change, so too does the child's understanding of nations and national identity.

Although Piaget's own descriptive account was significantly undermined by Jahoda (1963a, 1964), who showed that many of the details in Piaget's description were incorrect, Piaget's underlying view, that children's understanding in this domain is dependent upon their more general cognitive capacities, has continued to the present day, albeit in a different guise. The most prominent advocate of the cognitive-developmental position today is Aboud (1988; Aboud and Amato, 2001).

Like Piaget, Aboud also argues that there is a discontinuity in development. She places this discontinuity at about 6–7 years of age, rather than at 7–8 years, but she also ties this discontinuity to the acquisition of concrete operations. She maintains that, at about 6 years of age, children's ingroup favouritism reaches a peak. In her own studies (which typically examine ethnic rather than national attitudes), she has found that, at the age of 6, children attribute mainly positive characteristics to members of their own group, and more negative characteristics to members of other groups. Between the ages of 6 and 12, this polarization in the attribution of traits to ingroups and outgroups decreases, as children gradually come to attribute more negative characteristics to the ingroup and more positive characteristics to outgroups. The overall result is a reduction in ingroup favouritism during middle childhood. Aboud argues that this change is driven by the development of the child's cognitive capabilities in middle childhood. The key cognitive changes, she suggests, are the onset of conservation, the ability to use multiple classifications, the ability to judge the deeper similarities between superficially different groups, and the ability to attend to individual differences within groups (Aboud and Amato, 2001). In other words, the developmental changes observable in this domain across middle childhood are a consequence of underlying domain-general cognitive changes.

Cognitive-developmental theory is clearly able to explain why there is a reduction in national ingroup favouritism, and an increase in positive regard for national outgroups, across middle childhood. However, there are several other phenomena which this theory cannot explain. For example, it does not explain why, within individual countries, there are differences in the development of children's national identifications as a function of their geographical location within the nation, their ethnicity, and their use of language. It also does not explain why national groups which are the traditional national enemies of the child's own nation are evaluated significantly more negatively than other national outgroups.

Even more problematically, Aboud's theory cannot explain why there are some populations of children who do not show ingroup favouritism at 6 years of age.

Nor does it explain why there are some populations of children who do not exhibit any changes in their national attitudes across the course of middle childhood. Notice that these particular findings run directly counter to the predictions of this theory.

5.2 The social identity explanation

Although Tajfel (1978; Tajfel and Turner, 1986) did not formulate social identity theory in order to explain developmental phenomena, attempts have been made by other researchers to apply his theory to the development of national identity in children. Social identity theory is based on the idea that individuals belong to many different social groups (such as gender, ethnic and national groups) and that these social group memberships can sometimes become internalized as part of an individual's self-concept. The theory suggests that, when this occurs, the individual strives to obtain a sense of positive self-worth from that group membership. In order to achieve this, the individual constructs their view of the ingroup and their views of comparison outgroups in such a way that the ingroup appears superior to the comparison outgroups (in other words, dimensions of comparison are chosen in such a way that the ingroup appears better than the outgroups). Positive self-esteem is then derived from the perceived superiority of the ingroup over the outgroups. However, for this to occur, the individual must have internalized the social group membership as part of his or her self-concept, that is, the individual must subjectively identify with that category. If an individual's subjective identification with the group is weak or absent, then ingroup favouritism will not occur. (The theory additionally proposes that, under certain circumstances, it may be difficult to achieve a positive image for the ingroup. When this occurs, other strategies may be used instead, such as changing one's social group membership, or changing the existing social order to try to improve the status of the ingroup.)

If subjective identification is indeed a precondition for ingroup favouritism to occur, then the strength of subjective identification with the ingroup should be related to the individual's attitudes towards either the ingroup, or salient outgroups, or both. However, this prediction is not well supported by the available evidence. No relationship has been found to exist between the strength of national identification and attitudes towards national outgroups. And as far as attitudes to the ingroup are concerned, the strength of national identification is only correlated with how much children *like* the national ingroup, not with the positivity–negativity of their trait attributions to the ingroup. Finally, and most pertinently of all, the strength of national identification is not correlated with the discrepancy between ingroup and outgroup attitudes either (Barrett *et al.*, 2004). Hence, social identity theory is not well supported by the existing evidence.

In recent years, social identity theory has been given a more explicitly developmental slant by Nesdale (1999, 2004). He argues that there are four phases in the development of national and ethnic identities:

1   In the first undifferentiated phase, which occurs prior to 2 to 3 years of age, racial and national cues are not yet important to young children.

2   In the second phase, which begins at 3 years of age, ethnic and national awareness starts to emerge, with children gradually acquiring the ability to identify and distinguish members of different groups. This process can continue up to 10 or 11 years of age. At this second phase, self-identification as a member of the ingroup occurs.

3   In the third phase, which begins at about 4 years as a direct result of self-identification, a focus on, and a bias towards, the ingroup emerges. Outgroups are not disliked during this phase, and negative attributions to outgroups are not yet made. Instead, the ingroup is merely preferred over all other groups, with ingroup favouritism thus prevailing.

4   In the fourth phase, which starts at about 7 years of age, children's focus shifts from the ingroup to outgroups. It is during this period that prejudice and negativity towards outgroups can emerge. However, not all children enter this final phase. Whether or not they do depends upon three factors: their level of identification with the ingroup; the extent to which other members of the ingroup hold negative attitudes towards those outgroups; and the extent to which the ingroup believes that its status or well-being is under threat in some way.

However, Nesdale's attempt to recast social identity theory also faces problems in accounting for the evidence on the development of national identity in that, for example, preference for the ingroup (ingroup favouritism) does not always occur, even at relatively young ages. Then there is the fact that children's attitudes towards national outgroups usually become more (rather than less) positive between 7 and 11 years of age. And, again contrary to the theory's predictions, national groups which are the traditional enemies of the child's own nation are often liked significantly less than other national outgroups, and this phenomenon can already be present at the age of 5. Why this phenomenon should occur at such an early age, when the child's focus is supposed to be upon the ingroup rather than outgroups, is not explained by the theory. Hence, Nesdale's social identity development theory is not well supported by the existing evidence on the development of national identity.

5.3 Towards an empirically adequate explanation

It appears, then, that none of the existing theories can explain all the different phenomena. A key finding which any theory must be able to explain is the variability which occurs in development in this domain, both across different nations and within nations. Research has shown that most children and adolescents display a systematic preference for their own national ingroup at all ages; however, ingroup favouritism is not universal. Also, there are different developmental patterns in the importance ascribed to national identity by children living in different countries: in Spain, children already ascribe very high importance to national identity at 6 years of age, whereas in many other countries, national identity is not important to young children, but increases significantly in its importance through middle childhood up to early adolescence. Another example is the commonly occurring developmental pattern for attitudes towards other national groups to become more positive through middle childhood, and to level out during early adolescence; however, there are some groups of children who have been found not to show any age-related changes in their attitudes to national groups between 6 and 15 years of age.

In addition to this variability in children's development from country to country, there is also variability in children's development within individual countries. Differences in development occur depending upon the geographical location of the child: children living within capital cities have an enhanced sense of their own national identity compared with children living elsewhere. The sense of national identity also varies depending upon the child's ethnicity: ethnic minority children and adolescents display different patterns of national identification from majority-group children and adolescents. Development also varies as a function of the use of language: children and adolescents living in Catalonia and in the Basque Country in Spain exhibit different patterns of development depending upon whether they speak only Catalan/Basque in the home or they speak Spanish in the home.

In addition to this variability in development, an empirically adequate theory must also address the likelihood that development in this domain is affected not only by cognitive-developmental and social identity factors but also by media, school and family influences. For example, television almost certainly impacts upon children's representations of other nations and national groups: children themselves commonly cite television as a major source of their knowledge about other countries, and there are systematic differences between the representations held by children who have watched television programmes about other countries and the representations held by children who have not watched these programmes.

Sense of national identity in children and young people is also likely to be affected by their schooling. Over the years, various authors (such as Gellner, 1983 and Smith, 1991) have argued that States often harness the State-regulated educational system in order to transmit culturally dominant representations of nations to children. Hence, in the case of children who are exposed to a common educational system the content of which is tightly constrained by a prescribed national curriculum (particularly in school subjects such as history, geography and literature), common representations of the national ingroup may be acquired as a consequence of exposure to this formal educational input. However, the impact of the school curriculum upon children's subjective sense of national identity has not been studied extensively to date. This is likely to be a fertile field for investigations in the future.

In addition, parents' attitudes and practices are likely to have a significant impact on children's sense of national identity. Family trips to national museums and national monuments, family holidays to other countries, personal contacts or kinship relations with people living in other countries, are all likely to vary as a function of the family's geographical location within the nation, and as a function of family ethnicity. It is therefore not surprising to find intra-nation differences in the development of national identity as a function of location and ethnicity. So even though young people may be exposed at school to a uniform national curriculum, there is likely to be a great deal of variability in their patterns of national identification as a consequence of the variability in their families' national attitudes and practices.

In other words, it seems highly likely that media, school, family, cognitive-developmental and social identity factors *all* play a role in shaping young people's sense of national identity. Given that the balance between these different factors will vary from nation to nation, and from one social group to another within a nation, and the fact that the content of national representations to which children are exposed via the media, the school and the family will also vary according to children's social, geographical and national location, it is only to be expected that considerable variability (rather than universal patterns) will exist in the development of national identity.

Summary of Section 5

- Cognitive-developmental theory proposes that developmental changes in the sense of national identity are a consequence of changes to the child's general cognitive capacities. However, it does not explain differences in the development of national identity as a function of location, ethnicity and use of language, or why some children do not show any changes in their national attitudes during middle childhood.
- Traditional social identity theory proposes that, when the child identifies with the national group, national ingroup favouritism will occur as a consequence of the need for positive self-esteem, but it does not explain why the strength of national identification is not consistently related to national attitudes
- Social identity development theory proposes that national identity develops through a sequence of four stages: undifferentiated, group awareness, ingroup preference and outgroup prejudice. However, it cannot explain why outgroup prejudice towards traditional enemy nations sometimes occurs early in development, why ingroup preference does not always occur, or why national outgroup prejudice typically declines with age.
- An empirically adequate theory is needed to account for the variability that occurs in the development of national identity, both across countries and within countries, and to explain how the development of national identity is affected not only by cognitive-developmental factors and social identity processes but also by the media, schooling and the family.

6   Conclusion

This chapter has examined some of the research which has been conducted into how children's and adolescents' sense of national identity, and their attitudes to national groups, develop. Findings indicate great variability in the way these views develop, not only between one country and another but also within individual countries. At present there is no empirically adequate theory to explain development in this domain, largely because existing theories have overlooked the extent of the developmental variability that occurs. These theories have probably also underestimated the extent to which the mass media, the school and the family impact upon the development of national identifications and national attitudes in young people.

Future research needs to examine in much greater detail exactly how family attitudes and practices, the school curriculum, and media representations – such as those available on television and in films – impact upon children's and adolescents' national identifications and national attitudes. In addition, there are several aspects of the subjective sense of national identity which still require much closer scrutiny. For example, little is currently known about young people's knowledge of national emblems, or about their emotional responses to them. The development of emotions such as national pride and national shame is another area that warrants further research.

The psychological study of how the subjective sense of national identity is acquired and develops is not merely of academic interest. Because of the pace of technological change over the past 50 years, in the modern world national identities and national attitudes can have very significant consequences, on a global scale. Developmental psychologists have a vital role to play in understanding how these identities and attitudes are acquired, and in contributing to the formulation of effective educational curricula that will prepare children to live in an increasingly international and culturally diverse world.

References

Aboud, F. (1988) *Children and Prejudice*, Oxford, Blackwell.

Aboud, F. and Amato, M. (2001) 'Developmental and socialization influences on intergroup bias' in Brown, R. and Gaertner, S.L. (eds) *Blackwell Handbook of Social Psychology: intergroup processes*, Oxford, Blackwell.

Barrett, M. (2000) 'The development of national identity in childhood and adolescence', inaugural lecture presented at the University of Surrey, Guildford, March 2000.

Barrett, M. (2002) 'Children's views of Britain and Britishness in 2001', keynote address presented to the Annual Conference of the Developmental Psychology Section of the British Psychological Society, University of Sussex, September 2002.

Barrett, M. (2005) 'Children's understanding of, and feelings about, countries and national groups' in Barrett, M. and Buchanan-Barrow, E. (eds) *Children's Understanding of Society*, Hove, Psychology Press.

Barrett, M. and Short, J. (1992) 'Images of European people in a group of 5–10 year old English school children', *British Journal of Developmental Psychology*, vol. 10, pp. 339–63.

Barrett, M., Lyons, E. and del Valle, A. (2004) 'The development of national identity and social identity processes: do social identity theory and self-categorization theory provide useful heuristic frameworks for developmental research?' in Bennett, M. and Sani, F. (eds) *The Development of the Social Self*, Hove, Psychology Press.

Barrett, M., Wilson, H. and Lyons, E. (2003) 'The development of national in-group bias: English children's attributions of characteristics to English, American and German people', *British Journal of Developmental Psychology*, vol. 21, pp. 193–220.

Bennett, M., Lyons, E., Sani, F. and Barrett, M. (1998) 'Children's subjective identification with the group and ingroup favoritism', *Developmental Psychology*, vol. 34, pp. 902–9.

Bennett, M., Barrett, M., Karakozov, R. *et al.* (2004) 'Young children's evaluations of the ingroup and of outgroups: a multi-national study', *Social Development*, vol. 13, pp. 124–41.

Billig, M. (1995) *Banal Nationalism*, London, Sage.

Buchanan-Barrow, E., Bayraktar, R., Papadopoulou, A., Short, J., Lyons, E. and Barrett, M. (1999) 'Children's representations of foreigners', poster presented at the 9th European Conference on Developmental Psychology, Spetses, Greece, September 1999.

Carrington, B. and Short, G. (1995) 'What makes a person British? Children's conceptions of their national culture and identity', *Educational Studies*, vol. 21, pp. 217–38.

Carrington, B. and Short, G. (1996) 'Who counts; who cares? Scottish children's notions of national identity', *Educational Studies*, vol. 22, pp. 203–24.

Carrington, B. and Short, G. (2000) 'Citizenship and nationhood: The constructions of British and American children' in Leicester, M., Modgil, C. and Modgil, S. (eds) *Politics, Education and Citizenship*, London, Falmer Press.

Condor, S. (1996) 'Unimagined community? Some social psychological issues concerning English national identity' in Breakwell, G.M. and Lyons, E. (eds) *Changing European Identities: social psychological analyses of social change*, Oxford, Butterworth Heinemann.

English, R. and Halperin, J.J. (1987) *The Other Side: how Soviets and Americans perceive each other*, New Brunswick, NJ, Transaction Books.

Gellner, E. (1983) *Nations and Nationalism,* Oxford, Blackwell.

Giménez, A., Canto, J.M., Fernández, P. and Barrett, M. (2003) 'Stereotype development in Andalusian children', *The Spanish Journal of Psychology*, vol. 6, pp. 28–34.

Hall, S. (1999) 'Un-settling "the heritage": re-imagining the post-nation', keynote address presented to the conference on Whose Heritage? The impact of cultural diversity on Britain's living heritage, The Arts Council of England, Manchester, November 1999.

Hengst, H. (1997) 'Negotiating "us" and "them": children's constructions of collective identity', *Childhood*, vol. 4, pp. 43–62.

Hesse, P. and Mack, J.E. (1991) 'The world is a dangerous place: images of the enemy on children's television' in Rieber, R.W. (ed.) *The Psychology of War and Peace: the image of the enemy*, New York, Plenum.

Himmelweit, H.T., Oppenheim, A.N. and Vince, P. (1958) *Television and the Child: an empirical study of the effect of television on the young*, Oxford, Oxford University Press.

Holloway, S. L. and Valentine, G. (2000) 'Corked hats and Coronation Street: British and New Zealand children's imaginative geographies of the other', *Childhood*, vol. 7, pp. 335–57.

Jahoda, G. (1962) 'Development of Scottish children's ideas and attitudes about other countries', *Journal of Social Psychology*, vol. 58, pp. 91–108.

Jahoda, G. (1963a) 'The development of children's ideas about country and nationality, Part I: The conceptual framework', *British Journal of Educational Psychology*, vol. 33, pp. 47–60.

Jahoda, G. (1963b) 'The development of children's ideas about country and nationality, Part II: National symbols and themes', *British Journal of Educational Psychology*, vol. 33, pp. 143–53.

Jahoda, G. (1964) 'Children's concepts of nationality: a critical study of Piaget's stages', *Child Development*, vol. 35, 1081–92.

Karakozov, R. and Kadirova, R. (2001) 'Socio-cultural and cognitive factors in Azeri children and adolescents' identity formation' in Barrett, M., Riazanova, T. and Volovikova, M. (eds) *Development of National, Ethnolinguistic and Religious Identities in Children and Adolescents*, Moscow, Institute of Psychology, Russian Academy of Sciences (IPRAS).

Kipiani, G. (2001) 'Ethnic identification in the structure of personal identifications and sociocultural conditions of development' in Barrett, M., Riazanova, T. and Volovikova, M. (eds) *Development of National, Ethnolinguistic and Religious Identities in Children and Adolescents*, Moscow, Institute of Psychology, Russian Academy of Sciences (IPRAS).

Kumar, K. (2003) *The Making of English National Identity*, Cambridge, Cambridge University Press.

Lambert, W. E. and Klineberg, O. (1967) *Children's Views of Foreign Peoples: a cross-national study*, New York, Appleton-Century-Crofts.

Modood, T., Berthoud, R., Lakey, J. *et al.* (1997) *Ethnic Minorities in Britain: diversity and disadvantage*, London, Policy Studies Institute.

Moodie, M. A. (1980) 'The development of national identity in white South African schoolchildren', *Journal of Social Psychology*, vol. 111, pp. 169–80.

Nesdale, D. (1999) 'Social identity and ethnic prejudice in children' in Martin, P. and Noble, W. (eds) *Psychology and Society*, Brisbane, Australian Academic Press.

Nesdale, D. (2004) 'Social identity processes and children's ethnic prejudice' in Bennett, M. and Sani, F. (eds) *The Development of the Social Self*, Hove, Psychology Press.

Parekh, B. (2000) *The Future of Multi-Ethnic Britain: the Parekh Report*, London, The Runnymede Trust/Profile Books.

Pavlenko, V., Kryazh, I., Ivanova, O. and Barrett, M. (2001) 'Age characteristics of social identifications and ethno-national beliefs in Ukraine', in Barrett, M., Riazanova, T. and Volovikova, M. (eds) *Development of National, Ethnolinguistic and Religious Identities in Children and Adolescents*, Moscow, Institute of Psychology, Russian Academy of Sciences (IPRAS).

Penny, R., Barrett, M. and Lyons, E. (2001) 'Children's naïve theories of nationality: a study of Scottish and English children's national inclusion criteria', poster presented at the 10th European Conference on Developmental Psychology, Uppsala University, Uppsala, Sweden, August 2001.

Phoenix, A. (1995) 'The national identities of young Londoners', *Gulliver*, vol. 37, pp. 86–110.

Piaget, J. and Weil, A.M. (1951) 'The development in children of the idea of the homeland and of relations to other countries', *International Social Science Journal*, vol. 3, pp. 561–78.

Reizábal, L., Valencia, J. and Barrett, M. (2004) 'National identifications and attitudes to national ingroups and outgroups amongst children living in the Basque Country', *Infant and Child Development*, vol. 13, pp. 1–20.

Riazanova, T., Sergienko, E., Grenkova-Dikevitch, L., Gorodetschnaia, N. and Barrett, M. (2001) 'Cognitive aspects of ethno-national identity development in Russian children and adolescents' in Barrett, M., Riazanova, T. and Volovikova, M. (eds) *Development of National, Ethnolinguistic and Religious Identities in Children and Adolescents*, Moscow, Institute of Psychology, Russian Academy of Sciences (IPRAS).

Shah, S. (2000) 'Get your facts right, please', *The Guardian*, 20 October.

Smith, A. D. (1991) *National Identity*, Harmondsworth, Penguin.

Tajfel, H. (1978) *Differentiation between Social Groups: studies in the social psychology of intergroup relations*, London, Academic Press.

Tajfel, H. and Turner, J.C. (1986, 2nd edn) 'The social identity theory of intergroup behaviour' in Worchel, S. and Austin, W.G. (eds) *Psychology of Intergroup Relations*, Chicago, Nelson-Hall.

Tajfel, H., Jahoda, G., Nemeth, C., Campbell, J. and Johnson, N. (1970) 'The development of children's preference for their own country: a cross-national study', *International Journal of Psychology*, vol. 5, pp. 245–53.

Tajfel, H., Jahoda, G., Nemeth, C., Rim, Y. and Johnson, N. (1972) 'The devaluation by children of their own national and ethnic group: two case studies', *British Journal of Social and Clinical Psychology*, vol. 11, pp. 235–43.

Trew, K. (1996) 'Complementary or conflicting identities?', *The Psychologist*, vol. 9, pp. 460–3.

Verkuyten, M. (2001) 'National identification and intergroup evaluation in Dutch children', *British Journal of Developmental Psychology*, vol. 19, pp. 559–71.

Vila, I., del Valle, A., Perera, S., Monreal, P. and Barrett, M. (1998) 'Autocategorización, identidad nacional y contexto linguístico', *Estudios de Psicologia*, vol. 60, pp. 3–14.

Weinstein, E. A. (1957) 'Development of the concept of flag and the sense of national identity', *Child Development*, vol. 28, 167–74.

Chapter 7
Young consumers

Ann Phoenix

Contents

Learning outcomes

After you have studied this chapter you should be able to:

1 explain why consumption is important to the identity of young people in affluent societies;
2 describe the developmental trends in consumption identified by psychologists and the research that informs this;
3 explain how social class, ethnicity and gender differentiate young people's identities in relation to consumption;
4 evaluate the relevance of three theories of identity to thinking about young people and consumption. These are Erikson's psychosocial theory of ego identity, social identity theory together with the self-categorization theory that came from it, and positioning theory.

1   Introduction

The previous chapters in this book have discussed the developmental significance of children's relationships with other people. Chapters 2–4 highlighted the ways in which parents/caregivers and siblings are of central importance in children's social worlds. This chapter addresses another aspect of children's social development, but one that is relatively new to psychology – the issue of consumption. Psychologists have recently begun to view consumption as an important context for children and young people's development and one that involves family relationships, peer relationships and broader group identities.

This chapter introduces you to research that suggests that consumption is important to the identities of children and young people, particularly those in affluent societies, to their interactions with their peers and parents and so to their psychological development. The chapter concentrates more on young people than on children since they have been studied more. Section 2 discusses the characteristics of consumption. Section 3 considers how consumption affects young people's identities and ways in which the meanings of possessions change over the course of development. In Section 4 the ways in which young people use consumption to construct their identities is considered. It focuses on the significance of brands to young people's identities and the part played by consumption in peer relations, as well as the ways in which gender, ethnicity and social class are recognized in young people's consumption. Finally, Section 5 evaluates the usefulness of three theories to young people's consumption identities: Erikson's psychosocial theory of ego identity; social identity theory and the self-categorization theory that came from it; and positioning theory.

2   What is consumption?

Consumption is difficult to define. It is therefore important to spend some time considering what the term means. Activity 1 will help you to start thinking about this.

Activity I

Allow about
5 minutes

What is consumption?

This activity will help you to think about what the term 'consumption' means to you.

When you think of the word consumption, what comes to mind? Think about the different ways in which you use the term or have heard it used and make brief notes.

Comment

When people define consumption, they often refer to spending money on goods such as food, clothes, music, games, holidays or leisure activities. They may also include finding things, making things or receiving gifts. Some definitions suggest that consumption concerns things that can be used up (literally 'consumed') or worn out as when we consume food, although in some cases the 'consumption' does not wear out the product (e.g. books or films). The former medical usage of the word to mean tuberculosis has largely fallen into disuse.

Researchers interested in consumption use the term somewhat differently from its everyday usage. Edwards (2000) suggests that there are three interconnected elements to consumption: consumerism, which is about shopping and commodities; leisure, which is about the consumption of services as well as commodities (e.g. holidays, sport and the arts) and the activity of consuming itself, which involves eating and drinking, wearing clothes, viewing and listening. These three elements can occur together and may, but need not, involve money, traditional rituals, social groups and political policies as well as fashion. Lury (1996) uses the term 'consumer culture' to recognize that consumption is more than the using up of products and that, rather than being the end of a process, it is also about the ways in which people convert or adapt things for their own use. Many researchers refer to affluent societies as 'cultures of consumption'.

What we 'consume' does not have a fixed meaning, but is open to reinterpretation. For example, in the 1990s, a pop singer, Madonna, began to wear corsets as outerwear, although they had previously only been used as undergarments. She reinterpreted the manufacturer's intended usage and, because of her fame and influence, some women also began to wear corsets as fashionable outer garments. In this reinterpretation, Madonna and other women were active agents rather than passive consumers, who used the corsets to project a particular identity (e.g. as young, daring, innovative and not mainstream). The new meaning of the corset arose through its use and through interactions with others (including media reactions), rather than being a fixed feature of the object. This example shows that people can invest the same object with different

Figure 1   Reinterpreting
the corset.

meanings. A similar process occurred when young people began to modify the
covers of their mobile phones for reasons of fashion.

It follows from such definitions that while everybody has to 'consume' food
and drink to live, consumption involves more than simply fulfilling physical
needs. Choices of which foods, clothes or other goods we consume are affected
by the value individuals and societies place on particular items as well as their
simple financial value. Consumption therefore involves choice and is influenced
by the resources available. Moreover, it is not a one-off event, but a routine,
ordinary process in which people acquire goods or services, use them (sometimes
creatively) and sometimes dispose of them. It is not, therefore, just about
economic exchange.

From a psychological perspective, consumption is an important topic with
respect to 'self' and identities because the things people consume are related to
how they see themselves. Helga Dittmar, a psychologist who researches
consumption says: 'material goods and identity construction are closely
interrelated. This idea of people as identity-seekers is captured in the consumer
slogan ... "I shop, therefore I am"' (Dittmar, 2004, p. 209).

Activity 2

Allow about
5 minutes

'I shop, therefore I am'

This activity will help you think about the meaning of Dittmar's ideas.

To what extent do you think the statement 'I shop therefore I am', which suggests that what you buy reflects your identity, is accurate?

Comment

The statement 'I shop therefore I am' is obviously ironic. However, for young people and adults, the things they buy allow them to present themselves in particular ways and can be interpreted by other people. Dittmar herself has coined the phrase 'to have is to be'. By this she means that material goods are associated with the important psychological function of identity. This is because goods and services have social value and choices can be made both in terms of what is available, what is possible, and how we want to present ourselves.

Consumption can also allow people to imagine themselves differently by presenting themselves in new ways (Kenway and Bullen, 2001), for example by changing the clothes they wear or the objects they use. While young children clearly cannot buy goods for themselves and are not concerned with status in the ways older children and adults may be, there have long been suggestions by developmental psychologists that possessions may also be included in their self concept as an extension of the individual (e.g. Prelinger, 1959; Dixon and Street, 1975; Furby, 1978). Bronson (1975) observed the play of 1- to 2-year-olds and suggests that for these very young children: 'It is as if "I" was being defined by exploration of the notion of what is "mine" or under "my control" (Bronson, 1975, pp. 145–6).

Summary of Section 2

- Consumption is about shopping (commodities), leisure, and the activity of consuming itself.
- It is a process that can be individual or collective.
- In consumption meanings are not fixed, but can change as they are reinterpreted.
- Affluent societies can be said to be cultures of consumption.

3 Consumption, young people's identities and development

Within psychology, adolescence is seen as an important period in the development of identity. This is partly due to the influence of the psychoanalyst Erik Erikson (1968) who argued that identity formation is the most important developmental task during adolescence. It is also the period when young people in affluent societies become particularly visible because of their distinctive consumption of clothes, music and leisure activities.

Psychologists, biographers, poets and parents have a shared view that 'some degree of inner turmoil appears to be a feature of many adolescents' experience' (Barnes, 1995, p. 301). This is captured by the following accounts, which were made nearly 80 years apart. The first account was written in 1918 and is a reminiscence of the writer's mid-teens, and the other is a contemporary account written in 1994 at a similar age. Despite the different time periods in which the accounts were written, they have features in common. Both indicate an intense awareness of and interest in themselves as people, coupled with a sense that they are undergoing a significant change from what they were.

> Fifteen years old! This was indeed the most memorable day of my life, for on that evening I began to think about myself, and my thoughts were strange and unhappy thoughts to me – what I was, what I was in the world for, what I wanted, what destiny was going to make of me! ... It was the first time such questions had come to me, and I was startled at them. It was as though I had only just become conscious; I doubt that I had ever been fully conscious before ...

(Hudson, 1918, quoted in Conger, 1979, p. 9)

> Over the last few years my personality has changed drastically, mostly due to pressures from my peers to conform, although I am happier with my new 'image' than I was before. However, I now feel the need to find my true personality, if that is possible, and to define myself. It is difficult not to do this by fitting into a stereotype, as I see many people doing, where the way they dress, their way of talking and even their values are defined by something as immaterial as their taste in music. I think quite deeply about my personality. From talking to my friends I think I am fairly unusual in this. Most people seem to take the way they are for granted whereas I see myself as having to work at myself to find a state in which I am happy. I worry a lot about what people think of me so it is important to me to be complimented.

(Anna, aged 16, writing in 1994, see Chapter 4, Activity 1)

Both accounts above depict adolescence as an unsettled period and some researchers suggest that consumption gives young people one way to deal with this (Kenway and Bullen, 2001).

Before the Second World War, young people were not identified as a distinct group on the basis of their appearance, tastes in music, films or clothes. However, in the 1950s 'youth' increasingly became a focus of media attention and of identification for teenagers on the basis of their consumption (Abrams, 1959).

Some groups of young people now demonstrate their identities by wearing dramatic clothes and listening to music that marks them out as belonging to particular style groups and sometimes as opposed to socially accepted norms. In addition, as Anna says, some young people adopt music and styles of clothes because of peer pressure and can struggle to find their own styles just when they are trying to establish identities. Consumption can thus be used as a resource for young people to try on and work out particular identities for themselves at a time when they are experiencing turmoil.

Figure 2   Media images of teenagers in the 1950s and 60s.

The development of young people's identities occurs in contexts where consumption is part of their peer relations. Peer (horizontal) relationships help children to acquire skills that can only be learned among equals, particularly of how to co-operate, collaborate, participate and resolve conflicts, disputes and disagreements (see Chapter 3). Consumption highlights these issues in that young people use the interactional skills they have acquired to develop their identities through complex interactions with their peers around consumption. In addition, consumption brings to the fore wider societal influences as well as individual and peer issues (Lury, 2004).

Some developmental psychologists have suggested that rather than development occurring as a natural, unfolding process, young people have to work to show peers and parents that they are ready to fit into an older age group

(Haavind, 2003a, Korobov and Bamberg, in press). Clothes, music, mobile phones and other possessions can be seen as tools that young people can use to show that they are ready to be what Eckert (1994) calls, 'the next step older'. For example, wearing clothes associated with older teenagers allows younger teenagers to show that they are ready to be seen as older. There is evidence that there are age-related changes in preference for personal possessions that may reflect developmental processes. Kamptner (1989, 1991) studied development in what people consider treasured possessions by giving questionnaires to almost 600 Californians in five age groups ranging from 10 to over 60 years. She found that the youngest children valued toys that gave them comfort and security. Older children tended to value things that allowed them to engage in enjoyable activities and adolescents liked a range of possessions such as music, cars and jewellery. Adults identified objects that were associated with their social relationships and memorabilia as well as jewellery. In general the developmental shift was from transitional objects (objects like cuddly toys that helped children to tolerate separation from their primary caregivers) through activity-centred objects to symbolic consumption associated with identity (from about 14 years of age onwards).

There is also some evidence that culture as well as developmental processes affect age-related changes in preference for possessions. For example, Furby (1978) compared the different meanings of possessions for people in the United States and Israel and how those meanings developed over the lifespan. She showed that, across age groups and cultures, there are some common meanings associated with possessions – in particular, control, emotional attachment and utility. At every age, the most salient defining features of what possession means were 'use' and the 'right to control use'. This was most frequently mentioned by the 11 year olds. From about 8 years of age, the utility and pleasurable aspects of objects (i.e. they '*make possible some activity or enjoyment*') was 'moderately often' mentioned as a defining characteristic of ownership and became increasingly important with age. Another dimension frequently mentioned was the owner's *positive affect* for the object, that is, something was a particularly important possession because the owner liked it. These meanings appear to relate to the development of identity. In terms of developmental processes, in the sample from the United States, 16 year olds and adults (but not younger children) gave answers that suggested that personal possessions involve social power and status. They saw possessions as extensions of the individual (which seems to fit with Dittmar's (2004) idea that 'to have is to be') and as providing security. Furby (1978) explains these findings in terms of the similarity between having control of possessions and having control of one's own body. She also suggests that since possessions and consumption are socially valued, they enhance people's self-image and status. She was less clear from her findings about how possessions provide security for older teenagers and adults. However, she does suggest that it may be an emotional security (because possessions can consistently provide certain pleasures) or because the more possessions one has, the less chance there is of material scarcity in the future. Israeli children were more likely than American children to mention the right to control the use of possessions as a positive feature of ownership.

Activity 3   *The importance of childhood possessions*

Allow about
10 minutes

This activity will help you reflect on the importance you attach to possessions.

Think back to your own childhood. Can you remember any possessions you had and what they meant to you? Did the importance you attached to those possessions change as you got older? Make brief notes on their meanings for you in childhood and how you think of them now.

Comment

Many adults can remember at least one object that meant a great deal to them at some point in their childhood. Often a particular object can be a source of comfort for long periods. There is research evidence that the significance of possessions and products as well as attitudes towards them changes over the life course, from those that provide emotional security to those that provide enjoyment, and, in adulthood, to possessions that are linked with social and familial networks and personal history.

In addition to the existence of cultural and age differences in the meaning of possessions, there are also generational differences and differences in historical periods that demonstrate links between individual and social factors. Dittmar (1996) suggests that economic and consumer behaviour is inextricably bound to attitudes, beliefs, social group membership, personal history, social history, lifestyle and shared cultural understandings. In different socio-historical periods, people have different spending and saving habits. This raises a problem for most research on developmental trends in the meaning of possessions since they are cross-sectional studies of people at different ages at one time point. These are limited in their ability to identify processes because they cannot rule out the possibility that age differences result because the participants grow up in different socio-historical periods.

The findings from all this research suggest that by the middle teenage years (from about 14 years of age) young people are using possessions and clothes to construct and express identity. If this is applied to Eckert's (1994) notion that young people develop through a process of showing that they are ready to be the 'next step older', then one relatively simple way in which young people can demonstrate that they are keeping up with 'age-appropriate' behaviours is by wearing clothes and listening to music that signals this. Consumption can allow them to display (through dress, music and accessories, etc.) that they are neither like adults nor like children. In addition, youth styles allow them to present particular identities and to ally themselves with, or differentiate themselves from, other young people. This perhaps provides part of the explanation for why clothes and music become so central to many young people's lives. This issue is discussed in Section 4.

3.1 Developments in the understanding of economic processes

At the same time as the meaning of possessions is changing over the course of childhood, children's understanding of advertising, marketing, shopping and economic resources is also changing. By the time they have reached the teenage years, young people are able to demonstrate sophisticated understanding of economic processes. A review of 25 years of US research on the consumer socialization of children aged 3–16 years of age examined how children's understanding of advertising and persuasion increases with age (John, 1999). An analysis of all the studies suggested that children move through three stages of consumer socialization: the perceptual stage (3–7 years), the analytical stage (7–11 years) and the reflective stage (11–16 years). These stages match three of Piaget's four stages of cognitive development: pre-operational thought (2–6 or 7 years); concrete operations (6 or 7–11 or 12 years) and formal operations (11 or 12 to adult). The three stages of consumer development are also related to social development. John considers development in social perspective taking and impression formation particularly important:

> [the move from the perceptual to the reflective stage involves a greater focus] on the social meanings and underpinnings of the consumer marketplace. A heightened awareness of other people's perspectives, along with a need to shape their own identity and conform to group expectations, results in more attention to the social aspects of being a consumer, making choices, and consuming brands. Consumer decisions are made in a more adaptive manner, depending on the situation and task. In a similar fashion, attempts to influence parents and friends reflect more social awareness as adolescents become more strategic, favoring strategies that they think will be better received than a simple direct approach.
>
> (John, 1999, p. 187)

By about 7 years of age, children know, for example, that advertising is designed to persuade and can recognize the difference between adverts and other programmes. They can also recognize brand names, know the categories of products to which they relate and understand what shopping involves. Children under 7 years old may also sometimes be able to show some of these understandings. Young (2002) argues that 3–7 year olds who are found in research studies to think of adverts as funny and interesting think so because they often are. If, however, the entertainment function of the advert clashes with the promotional content, children aged 6 years know that the promotional content is most relevant to adverts.

As is often the case in academic literature, John, a US academic, reviewed only US literature, so it is not certain that her findings would fit children's consumer behaviour elsewhere. Her typology may not fit children in countries where many live in poverty or those from less affluent backgrounds in the USA. The anthropologist Elizabeth Chin (2001) conducted an ethnographic study in New Haven, Connecticut with black 10-year-old children (in John's 'analytical stage') who lived in a particularly impoverished neighbourhood. Chin found that the children were very familiar with adverts and the meanings of brands but learned *not* to 'pester' their parents *because* they lived in poverty.

Some developmental psychologists are sceptical about stage theories. This is therefore a potential weakness of John's framework, particularly since development in knowledge need not occur at the same time that perspective taking increases. Nonetheless, her attempt at producing a developmental progression is helpful in giving some sense of the ages at which US children reported in the literature she reviewed engage in various sorts of consumer behaviour.

Summary of Section 3

- The period of adolescence involves some emotional turmoil. Consumption frequently gives young people one way to deal with this through wearing different styles of clothes and listening to music that mark them out as different from (and sometimes opposed to) adults.
- The development of identities involves consumption, particularly in affluent societies.
- There are national and cultural differences as well as similarities in the place consumption occupies in people's lives.
- The meanings of possessions change over the life course from transitional objects to activity-centred objects and later to symbolic consumption associated with identity (from about 14 years of age).
- Consumption may be one way in which young people can construct desired identities for themselves and show that they are ready to be 'the next step older'.
- Research on 'consumer socialization' seeks to explain how children develop understandings of advertising and economics. It suggests that by the age of 14 most young people have sophisticated understandings.

4   Construction of identities through consumption

This section discusses three ways in which the research indicates that young people use consumption to construct their identities. It first considers how brands give young people a relatively easy way to present themselves as high status individuals. It then considers how they manage solidarity and conflict associated with different style groups and finally, the societal differences that are both reflected in different style groups and produced as young people negotiate their style identities.

4.1 Maintaining status through consumption

In affluent societies the majority of young people are able to obtain clothes and music that are open to everyone and so most cannot claim to have an exclusive style. A research study in the US (Milner, 2004) concludes that young students are concerned with their status in the eyes of their peers because they have relatively little economic and political power. They therefore create their own status systems that are different from those their parents and teachers promote. According to Milner, peer relationships and cultures become important for young people because they spend so much time together. Dress is an important (although not the only) means of maintaining status for young people and so of maintaining identity as an acceptable member of the peer group. There is, therefore, a general pressure on young people to conform to 'rules' about what they should wear. In addition, Milner suggests that, in order to maintain status, young people have to restrict the range of people with whom they are prepared to associate. They are concerned with how others think of them and, since youth styles are continually changing and individuals can easily fail to dress appropriately to fit into their style group, many young people expend a great deal of energy on ensuring that they wear the right clothes and listen to appropriate music. Those in high-status groups attempt to keep other people out in order to maintain their exclusive high status. Associating with 'low-status' peers who are neither trendsetters nor valued for their style reduces young people's status. Consumption is, therefore, very much about the development and maintenance of identities, group relations and youth styles.

4.2 Using brands as symbols of high-status identities

Brand-name goods are of importance to many young people (as well as to adults). Sherry (1998) used the term 'brandscapes' to indicate that children and adults are surrounded with brands to which they have positive and negative reactions. Brands are important because they help some people to express particular things about themselves and so are one way in which they can construct their positions in their social worlds. For example, once young people began to wear trainer shoes as fashion items, the manufacturers promoted their particular brand as desirable fashion items. Nike, for example, promoted its trainers as brands for the attractively rebellious, young, fit and non-conventional. That image then became desirable for a wider range of people in varied age groups who, simply by wearing Nike, believe they can display and take on these identities. Trendsetters continually adapt how Nikes are worn and they are researched (and sometimes employed) by Nike in order to produce and sell new versions of their trainers. Even when groups of young people develop styles in opposition to commercialism (e.g. punk, skater or hip-hopper styles), manufacturers quickly mass-produce those styles, sometimes with brand-name labels. Those young people who are determinedly 'anti-brand' then move on to other styles, so that there is a dynamic, relational process between producers, advertisers and young people in that young people use brands to construct their identities and advertisers and producers reflect these identity positions. In turn young people draw on the themes in adverts and look at who else is wearing them to confirm their consumption decisions (Kenway and Bullen, 2001).

Since consumption has symbolic value and can be creative, the meanings of brands are never simply contained in the manufactured object itself, but are negotiated with the individual as well as with other people. This is what is meant by meanings being negotiated between advertising, the brand, the consumer and social networks over time (Higgins and Smith, 2002) and in a global context (Lury, 2004). At the same time, brands allow the achievement of consistency in a changing world since branded products sell themselves on the idea of consistent quality. The most popular brands symbolize the same identities in different countries. From his survey analyses, Lagree (2002) suggests that affluent young people in any country are more like each other than like the poor in their own countries. Wearing or using particular brands also allows the avoidance of products that produce identities that people do not wish to be associated with (known as the 'undesired self' – Hogg and Banister, 2001). In contrast, those young people who are determined to avoid commercialism also avoid branded goods – consuming branded goods would produce the 'undesired self'.

The Research summary provides an account by Anderson, who has carried out research on consumption.

RESEARCH SUMMARY

Study of young people and branded items

Forty adolescents and adults in Liverpool were asked to choose and photograph personal possessions that 'say something about you', and discuss their choices in an in-depth interview. Teenagers not only selected a larger number of branded goods than adults did, but were also much more articulate, knowledgeable and involved when talking about brands. The qualitative analysis of the interviews suggests that they embrace and use the symbolic meanings associated with brands to help with identity construction and communication. A case in point is mobile phones, heavily used by adolescents. They get a sense of affiliation and belonging through using the same brand as their peer group and shared knowledge about what the brand stands for, but at the same time express individuality through choosing a particular model that is then personally modified through ringtones, covers, glue-on 'jewellery' or logos.

Teenagers are also very skilled at 'reading' other people through their branded possessions. In a second part of the study, participants were shown sets of photographs of a person's possessions and were asked what kind of person they thought the owner was. These sets were 'fake', in the sense that they depicted a collection of highly branded goods ... chosen [by the researcher]. One example set includes Adidas Gazelles trainers, ShockWaves hair gel, Lynx deodorant and a Reebok sweatshirt. Teenagers' descriptions of the 'owner' tended to be more cohesive and comprehensive than adults', demonstrating that they are aware of, and use, the symbolic information advertising associates with particular brands: the 'brand personality' communicated in the mass media. For the example set, adolescents described the 'owner' as 'outgoing, flirty, energetic, active, young, single, image-conscious'. But they also construct their own meanings that seem to derive more from real-life interactions with the brands and the people who use them: a socially shared image of the 'typical user'. This may be more negative, such as 'unmotivated, uneducated, slow, stays in bed all weekend, laid back' for the example set.

Taken together, these findings suggest that brands are more strongly linked to identity construction for adolescents than adults.

Source: Anderson, 2004, p. 208.

Activity 4   *What do clothes say about people's identity?*

Allow about
15 minutes

This activity will help you consider the relationship between people's clothes and their identities.

Do you think that the clothes you wear say anything about you? If so, what do you think they say? Do they relate to your identity? Look at the pictures of groups of young people in Figure 3 below and overleaf . On the basis of their clothes, what do you think about them? Can you say anything about their identities from what they are wearing? Do you think that young people differ from adults in what clothes mean to them?

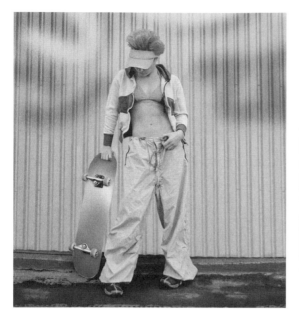

Figure 3   What do clothes say about people's identity?

Comment

You may have found it easier to think that other people's clothes styles say something about their identities than what you wear says something about your identity. When you think about how other people might view your clothes choices and how you view other people's, it may be clearer that value judgements are frequently made about consumption. It is common, for example, for people to 'read' social class and affluence/poverty from what someone is wearing – although this can be less applicable to young people. Onlookers also often make interpretations about whether people are traditional, 'trendsetting' or 'following fashion' as well as whether what they wear shows that they have things in common with some groups and not others. This can be the case whether or not people claim group identities.

It may be that you wrote down distinctions about other people's styles of clothes that relate to how you view their identities. This is in keeping with the ideas of the French sociologist Pierre Bourdieu (1984). He argued that social life is riven with struggles for social distinction, that taste is acquired and that it is often used to justify social class differences. According to Bourdieu, the middle and upper classes consider that 'taste' is natural and use it to make social 'distinctions'.

▲

In a psychological study of social class and consumption, Dittmar and Pepper (1994) gave 168 British young people (93 of whom they reported were middle class and 75 working class) one of four possible vignettes, which described the same woman or man in either affluent or less privileged material circumstances. Participants then evaluated that person's income and personal qualities, and completed a scale designed to assess materialism. Dittmar and Pepper found that both working class and middle class young people favoured the person who owns, rather than lacks, expensive possessions. Such findings indicate that people make judgements about others based on their consumption. Anderson (2004) suggests that teenagers are more likely than adults to 'read' identities from the brands on other people's clothes and possessions. This may be due to differences in their development, but is also likely to be because teenagers are growing up in a period in which brand-name goods have become more prominent than when their parents were growing up.

In discussing the importance of brands to the construction of identities, it is easy to gain the impression that they are equally important to all young people's identities. Yet, many young people cannot afford to buy original brands and some buy imitation brands. Others deliberately choose youth styles that eschew brands and construct their identities in opposition to brands as non-consumerists. Locher (1998) found this in a participant observation and interview study of two 'industrial-hardcore' bands in the United States.

> I don't have anything on that's worth over twenty dollars, and that's like if you put it in a nice little pile. I look like a Salvation Army truck threw up on me, and that's how it should be.

(Locher, 1998, p. 108)

> Well, I go out and I pick out the cheapest, most f—ed-up guitar that I can find, I take it home and I paint it black, and I put stickers on it and shit, and then it's good. I grew up with like *Guitar* magazine and Eddie Van Halen and all those c—suckers, and I was taught that it is good to play a name-brand guitar, you know? Play the Randy-Rhodes-Charvel-Bullshit, and then you're good. I subscribed to that for a little while, but it didn't make me any better or any worse, so I like playing beat-up old guitars. 'Cause it's honest. [Why not pink, or white, or yellow?] Because those colors don't emit foreboding, and they don't look like a threat. It doesn't make a statement as to what type of music we're playing. Everything has to make a statement, including the visuals. It has to make a statement. If you don't look at it and immediately think something, be it good, bad, or whatever, then what the f— is it? The stickers are a symbol of our culture. Everything in our culture says "buy, sell, good, bad," whatever. My guitar reflects my feelings on those subjects. ("F— off.") It's just a rejection of the dominant musical culture that I grew up with.

(Adapted from Locher, 1998, p. 109)

It is noticeable in both of the above quotations that despite the rejection of expensive 'name-brand' guitars, material goods are still being used to make identity statements. As Locher points out 'every musician believes the look of the instrument to be extremely important' (p. 109). In the second quotation the young man explains that he has rejected branded guitars and is explicit about the symbolic value of consumption within US culture and that he has positioned himself in opposition to it. Positioning yourself against brands does, however, influence what young people can do as much as being determined to buy brands. This is true across cultures (Miles, 2000, p. 140).

4.3 Solidarity and conflict in consumption and identities

From what is known about children's economic knowledge and what young people say about fashion and brands, most are not cultural dupes or 'fashion victims' (Gunter and Furnham, 1998; Miles *et al.*, 1998). Indeed, when talking about their style identities, many are adamant that they are individuals rather than objects of media and advertising manipulation or people who simply follow their friends (Widdicombe and Wooffitt, 1995). It may be that denying media manipulation defends young people from having to acknowledge that they are manipulated by the media or that they are not aware of how they are influenced. Nonetheless, since individuality has long been a prized characteristic of affluent societies, consumption can be used to construct desired individual identities, to ward off undesired identities and to construct group identities. Miles *et al.* (1998) argue that many young people deny that their styles are influenced by their peers because they have to deal with the contradictions between claiming individuality, wanting to 'fit in' with their peers and being afraid of 'sticking out'. Young people are, therefore, not entirely free to express their identities through consumption as the following examples illustrate.

Interviewer: Shannon, you said it's important for people to have certain consumer goods. In what ways do you think these are important to people?

Shannon: It's important to fit in with everybody. To fit in more *and* show what you are really like ...

Darren: You are influenced but I don't think anybody'd buy anything just because their mates wanted something like that.

Louise: Oh no, I wouldn't.

Tony: But if you lived on a desert island with nobody else there except a few black natives or something, you wouldn't walk around in Naf Naf coats all the time ... You'd wear a pair of jeans and a t-shirt.

(Miles, 2000, p. 145)

Interviewer: So is it important what your friends think of what you're buying then?

Jason: It's not really what you're buying. It's what they think of you. It kind of comes through in what you're buying.

Interviewer: So are you saying in some way what you buy reflects who you are then?

Jason: Well, partially yes. Well in some things. Not really in food or something like that. But if you're buying clothes or records it reflects on yourself.

(Miles, 2000, p. 136)

'Fitting in' with a particular style group can be fun, as indicated in the quotation below from a woman who had been a fan of the Bay City Rollers pop group in the 1970s:

> We were a gang of girls having fun together, able to identify each other by tartan scarves and badges ... at the concerts many [of us] were experiencing mass power for the first and last time. Looking back now, I hardly remember the gigs themselves, the songs, or even what the Rollers looked like. What *I do* remember are the bus rides, running home from school together to get to someone's house to watch *Shang-a-Lang* [the title of a Bay City Roller pop song] on TV, dancing in lines at the school disco, and sitting in each others' bedrooms discussing our fantasies and compiling our scrapbooks.
>
> (Garratt, quoted in Ussher, 1997, pp. 42–3).

Milner (2004) proposes that young people 'seek(ing) status through conformity in order to fit in, that is to gain a sense of acceptance and belonging. The paradox is that in order to be successful in the "conformity game" students must constantly change, elaborate, and complicate the norms in order to gain a competitive advantage' (p. 44). Milner suggests that, since young people can copy each other's styles, that those who are high in status hierarchies need constantly to change their styles in order to maintain their high status by keeping others out of their groups. Demonstrating solidarity with, and belonging to, particular style groups, requires effort and constant change. Paradoxically, once an individual young person becomes popular, they no longer have to try so hard to fit in and can express more individual identities without fear of exclusion. As a young woman in a Catholic school in Texas, USA, told Milner 'You had to look a certain way to become popular ... but once you became popular, you could dress sloppy and no one cared' (Milner, 2004, p. 46). Although consumption is important to popularity, having the 'right' style is not necessarily sufficient. Storm-Mathisen (1998) in Norway, for example, found that some young people were viewed by their peers as 'followers' or 'trying too hard' and so were not necessarily popular or of high status. This was the case even though they consistently made efforts to express solidarity and belonging by wearing similar clothes to those of 'style leaders'.

The importance of consumption to young people's social groups and identities mean that it is also a source of anxiety and rivalry and so can be used to hurt each other. In a study of social life in London schools, Blatchford (1998) found that clothes and music styles were one source of teasing for both 11 and 16 year olds.

Appearance: clothes

Here is the description of a 16-year-old boy:

> *P: Mainly what you look like, what you wear. You've got to have fashionable trainers. If you don't have 60 quid trainers then you're a tramp, you live in a doss.*

We see, in the next quote from a white girl, ways in which clothing and musical tastes are connected to sub-cultural affiliations that in turn affect teasing between groups.

> P: *The way music goes today like there's a lot of like hippy and grunge and the way people dress differently – dress like in clothes that don't really match ... And people think that they look like a tramp or something ... People get teased about that kind of thing. 'Cause the majority of people in this school I think are more ragga and hip-hop.*

This extract is taken from a longer account that describes two main subcultures in the school, each focused on different preferences for music and clothes. Elsewhere, the girl described how this was a backdrop against which her long-term friendship with her school friend had begun to struggle, because they were in separate groups. Though they still saw each other, the girl was clearly bemused and uncomfortable at her friend's affiliation with grunge music and the wearing of (to her) strange clothes.

(Blatchford, 1998, p. 121)

The above extracts from Blatchford indicate that school students can engage in conflicts over style at both individual and group levels. This is particularly because different groups within a school can hold each other in contempt and consider themselves of higher status than other groups – a situation that, not surprisingly can lead to conflict, including bullying. In a classic study of young people at school in a suburb of Detroit, USA, Eckert (1989) studied two competing style groups who called themselves the 'jocks' (a term from athletics) and the 'burnouts' (a term from the drug scene). According to Eckert, jocks were predominantly from the middle classes and constructed as good students while the burnouts were predominantly from the working classes and constructed as disengaged from schoolwork. Eckert found that the energy put into keeping these two groups in opposition limited their own freedom and what other people could do in the school.

Locher (1998) suggests that 'while inclusionary dynamics form the basis of attraction to an adolescent clique, it is the exclusionary nature of such groups that reinforces cohesion among the members' (Locher, 1998, p. 101). This is because young people know that the people with whom they associate have a direct impact on their own status. Who they disassociate themselves from is, therefore, as important as those with whom they associate (Milner, 2004). There is some suggestion that conformity and conflict over style groups become less marked after the age of about 16 years. Miles (2000) found that many of the British 16–20 year olds he studied felt strongly that their friends no longer attempted to pressure them into buying and wearing particular kinds of things. Although young people who say this may be denying effects that are nevertheless acting on them, Miles suggests that this trajectory is part of maturing as a teenager.

Paul: You just wear what you want, don't yer?

Don: There was more pressure at school. Fifth form at school. It's not as bad now.

Paul: You don't care at all now. You just wear what you want, don't yer?

(Miles, 2000, p. 141)

Kinney (1993) also found that young people in late adolescence are less rigid in their exclusions of those not in their style group and more tolerant of individual differences among their peers than are younger teenagers. It is important to note however that the young people in the quotation above are not just talking about a change with age but with moving from school to sixth-form college. This fits with Milner's (2004) suggestion that young people's relative powerlessness at school makes them particularly prone to focus on status hierarchies that are highly dependent on consumption. It may be that this age-related change coincides with a change in how young people are organized in the education system rather than being only due to development.

Just as some young people do not wear brand names, so not all fit into style groups. Eckert (1989) found that the majority of the US student population she studied did not fit into the two main style groups ('jocks' and 'burnouts'). Most managed identities and social relations as 'in-between', a few were isolated as 'nerds' and a very few were 'loners'. In a book published 15 years after Eckert's study, Milner also found that most students in the US high school he studied modelled themselves on the popular crowd, but did not belong to a clique. However, they were mostly not 'nerds', but were considered 'normals', 'regulars' or 'average students'. There were also some 'drifters' or 'floaters' who, although they did not have high status, managed to participate in more than one group. The fact that most young people do not belong to a clique does not mean that their identities are not influenced by these cliques. As Milner suggests, members of high-status groups go to great lengths to exclude other young people from joining their groups. Rather than engaging in conflicts around style, many young people express solidarity with these cliques by modelling themselves on the popular groups and the styles of those who resist brand-name goods is established in opposition to those of the high-status groups.

4.4 Societal differences and style identities

The previous parts of this section have dealt with ways in which young people construct individual and group identities through style and how these are interlinked. The place of consumption in young people's social groups is more complex than simply conferring identities to individuals and leading to some being teased or teasing others. It is possible to see divisions of gender, ethnicity and social class in the identities young people create through style. This part of the chapter adds a layer of complexity by briefly considering how these societal differences are represented in what young people say about their style identities.

Researchers have long pointed out that gender is a major way in which children and young people differentiate themselves and that they use sexualized and gendered behaviours to demonstrate that they have moved from childhood (e.g. Griffin, 1985; Lees, 1993, Thorne, 1993; Walkerdine *et al.*, 2001; Haavind, 2003). Gender-differentiated consumption both serves to maintain existing gender differences and to emphasize differences in gendered identities. In a study of young people and consumption carried out in seventeen schools in Milton Keynes, Birmingham and Oxford, 1,304 young people (girls and boys aged 12–13 and 16–17) filled in questionnaires on the last three items they had bought, what the items meant to them and what they thought the items said about them. One of the significant gender differences found was in the importance of brands. Boys were much more likely than girls to write that brands were very important in their purchasing decisions (Griffin *et al.*, in press). There was also an age effect in that 12–13 year old boys were most likely to report this. In the same study, 60 group interviews were held and in answer to questions about gender differences, boys consistently said that girls bought a great many things and always had to have new clothes, while girls consistently suggested that boys were poor shoppers. These differences were also mentioned in individual interviews carried out with young people and with their parents.

Already existing societal divisions of ethnicity can also be seen in consumption. The ways in which corporations and music producers have drawn on African-American and African-Caribbean young men's music and clothes as a source of cutting-edge style have been of interest to researchers (Gilroy, 1987; Klein, 2000). This produces debates and tension about whether white young people wearing clothes and making music styles originated by black young people is simply about the multicultural mixing of styles or about black styles being exploited and taken over by other groups (Back, 1996; Kenway and Bullen, 2001). The relations between ethnicized identities and consumption can cause conflicts. In a London-based study of masculinities in 11–14 year-old boys, 78 boys aged 11–14 from twelve London schools were interviewed individually and 45 group discussions – nine of which were of mixed gender – were conducted (Frosh *et al.*, 2002). Ethnicity was consistently mentioned as making a difference to young people's styles. Many boys took for granted that there are ethnic differences in styles of consumption and many agreed that 'black' styles have the highest status in their schools. Milner (2004) suggests that, at least in the US context, minority ethnic groups are often quite concerned with dressing fashionably.

> Well-to-do predominantly Jewish suburban communities ... often had groups of "JAPS" (Jewish American Princesses and Princes) who were very fashion-conscious. Similarly, the Asian cliques in a Houston, Texas, school were careful to have designer labels. Black students seem to be especially fashion conscious. In part, this has been a matter of establishing a special identity for themselves through the adoption of hip-hop clothes. But their concern seems to involve more than establishing a distinctive identity.

(Milner, 2004, p. 47)

Social class generates more debates about whether it is a useful way to think about social divisions than do gender and ethnicity. Many theorists have pointed out that social class no longer has the meanings it once did in relation to the means of production or to disposable income (Walkerdine and Lucey, 1989). In addition, young people have generally not yet acquired their own class position distinct from their parents' (Phoenix and Tizard, 1996) and the pervasiveness of branded clothes and/or uniforms in British schools means that, regardless of social class, many young people wear similar sorts of clothes. In his US study, Milner (2004) found that young people who attempted to achieve high status at school by wearing expensive clothes were often derided. Nonetheless, both access to money and social class position continue to be a feature of identities that research studies report is related to consumption.

Summary of Section 4

- Brands give young people a relatively easy way to present themselves as high status individuals.
- Consumption is important to young people's status in their peer groups.
- Young people's consumption involves them in learning to manage peer relationships of solidarity and conflict.
- Consumption includes societal differences, for example, of gender, ethnicity and social class.

5 Theories of identity and young people's consumption

A focus on consumption and identities is a relatively new area of study in psychology and so established theories of identity have little to say directly about consumption. Nonetheless, they have relevance to psychological understandings of it. This section discusses the ego identity theory first proposed by Erik Erikson, social identity theory (SIT), initially developed by Henri Tajfel and John Turner, and a social constructionist theory: positioning theory, as developed by Bronwyn Davies and Rom Harré.

5.1 Ego identity and consumption

In the 'psychosocial' theory of identity developed by the psychoanalyst Erikson (1968), identity is particularly important during adolescence. It is a period in which several life decisions have to be faced and, by the end of which, ego identity (a secure feeling of who and what one is) has to be achieved. For Erikson adolescence is a period when it is normal to experience identity crisis, although the nature of the 'identity crisis' to be faced is social in that it depends on the society and historical period in which young people grow up. Erikson saw adolescence as a period when definitive social choices could be postponed while the various elements of identity are coming together. He called the period 'psychosocial moratorium'. In this period, young people can, for a while, try out various identities without commitment before finding their own niche in society. He termed this 'moratorium', to mean a socially approved delay of adulthood when adolescents are free from adult responsibilities so that they can be helped to make the difficult transition to adulthood.

According to Erikson our communities are central to the achievement of our psychosocial identities; identity development requires solidarity with a group's ideals. Adolescent identity crisis can lead young people to fear that they are in danger of losing identity. In order to defend themselves against this possibility, Erikson argued that young people might temporarily over-identify with cliques and crowds. They may be 'remarkably clannish, intolerant, and cruel in their exclusion of others who are "different" ... in petty aspects of dress and gesture arbitrarily selected as *the* signs of an in-grouper or out-grouper' (Erikson, 1959, p. 92). Erikson's ideas about the importance of young people's 'clannishness' fits with interest in how young people use clothes, style and music to establish identities in groups.

An Eriksonian explanation of young people and consumption would suggest that young people in the period of psychosocial moratorium deal with the difficulties they experience in committing to adult identities (identity crisis) by making exaggerated commitments to some style groups and separating themselves from other style groups. They use particular kinds of clothes and music to signal that they have a unique style that differentiates them from other groups and that they use as part of the construction of their identities. According to Erikson this method of identity construction is a temporary phase before young people adopt adult responsibilities.

Evidence in support of Erikson's view comes from psychological research that suggests that many adolescents do form 'crowds' defined by style and reputation. These affect the ways they view other people and themselves and so influence adolescent behaviours (Susman *et al.*, 1994). In Box 1 the research extracts reflect the notion that young people can create their identities through 'clannishness' in their style groups.

BOX 1

Style groups and young people's sense of identity

Extract 1

Interviewer: Mmhm is being gothic very important to you?

Respondent 2: Yes

Respondent 1: Yes

[A few conversational turns omitted]

Respondent 1: It's nice being part of an identity. There's some security in it 'cos er (pause) it's (short pause) I don't know –

Respondent 2: You find people that're

Interviewer: mhm

Respondent 2: the same as you because they dress the same as you and you find they have a similar mentality so it's a very easy way of finding friends who're similar to you.

(Adapted from Widdicombe and Wooffitt, 1995, pp. 162–3, with transcription notation omitted)

Extract 2

'It's great to be in one of those groups. It feels really powerful in a horrible sort of way (...) you are accepted you know, it sounds you know really spooky, but it's like you own the city you know (...) and it's like you've joined it at last, you've joined the real world you know.'

(Hollands, 2002, p. 164)

In Extract 1 in Box 1, the two participants say that they get security, identity and easy friendships from belonging to a youth style group. In Extract 2, consumption is said to provide 'acceptance' into the 'real world' and power. In concert with Erikson then, what can be seen as 'clannishness' gives an identity of belonging. It is common for studies of teenagers to report similar findings (e.g. Miles *et al.*, 1998) although young people differ in the extent to which they consider themselves what Erikson calls 'clannish' (Milner, 2004).

In her research on youth subcultures, the social psychologist Widdicombe found that only a minority of young people who dressed in ways that would be classified as, for example, 'punk', 'rocker' or 'hippy', claimed that membership of a subcultural group was significant to their identities. Far from expressing 'clannish' views, most young people said that they saw themselves as individuals who chose their style because they liked it, regardless of what other people did. They were sometimes critical of young people within the same style group who they considered to be pretending to belong to the group rather than authentically part of it. For them, youth styles were simultaneously individual and group identities but were not necessarily combined into a coherent identity in the way spelled out by Erikson.

Erikson's identity theory explains how identity develops and there is some research evidence that there is a developmental trajectory in the 'clannishness' of those young people who become part of cliques. In keeping with Miles's (2000) research discussed in the previous section, Widdicombe found that young people were able to pinpoint when they had adopted their style. Evidence that 'clannishness' based on style is less rigid by late adolescence lends support to Erikson's ideas that exclusionary clannishness can be a phase in adolescent development.

However, Erikson's notion that adolescent 'clans' are different from 'clans' in older age groups and behave in ways that conflict with the responsibilities they will later assume is arguably too static a view of society. While Erikson emphasises the importance of history and of the social, there is no allowance for young people themselves to change society as they develop their adult identities. Yet, in the 1960s when Erikson was writing, young people in many countries contributed to changing the political and moral contexts in their societies and young people continue to do so. Some older people follow at least some of what young people do in attempting to be as young as possible and to engage in youth styles while many take up trends popularized by the young (e.g. SMS texting on mobile phones).

While Erikson conceptualized young people's groups as part of the process of searching for and finding identities, consumption can instead be seen as part of the process of constructing identities. Rather than adopting identities that already exist (albeit through an active process) as Erikson's theory would suggest, consumption allows many young people to use objects, clothes and music to project the meanings they want other people to 'read' about themselves which include being individual and showing that they fit in with particular groups. For those young people who cannot (e.g. because they lack the economic resources to do so) there can be a painful preoccupation with this and with identity that is not about inability to commit to an identity as in Erikson's theory, but about dealing with social inequality.

Activity 5

Allow about
10 minutes

Erikson's identity theory

This activity will help you reflect on what Erikson's theory contributes to explaining how young people construct their identities through consumption.

Make brief notes on what you think Erikson's ego identity theory helps to explain about how young people use consumption to construct identities.

Comment

Erikson's theory helps to explain the importance of peer groups to young people and why they may use particular kinds of clothes and music to differentiate themselves from other groups and to construct their identities.

5.2 Social identity theory and self-categorization theory

Social identity theory (SIT) was not designed to explain the process of development, but is influential because it attempts to explain the processes by which group identities become important for individuals. It is an important and influential social theory that has recently been adapted to the development of national identity (Nesdale, 1999, 2004). This section considers whether SIT can also be used to aid understanding of young people and consumption.

According to SIT, in order to develop a social identity, people have to categorize themselves as members of groups. Since group membership is important to identities, people are motivated to evaluate positively the groups to which they belong (ingroups). They do this through comparisons with groups to which they do not belong (outgroups), which they tend to evaluate negatively.

This idea was picked up and developed by one of Tajfel's collaborators, John Turner, who developed the self-categorization theory (SCT) from SIT. SCT (Turner *et al.*, 1987) is similar to SIT but places more emphasis on the cognitive processes involved in self-categorization. Social identities are context-dependent since how people categorize themselves depends on the categories they are able to think about in the context of particular social interactions. For example, people are more likely to self-categorize by age if they are the only person in their age group in a social setting, but age group is less likely to be salient if everybody is in the same age group. In that case, other differences within the group are likely to be more salient. According to SCT, at times when people perceive themselves as members of a group, they stop thinking of themselves as unique selves and become 'depersonalized'. This does not mean that they stop being individual persons, but that what becomes important in that context at that time is not their individuality, but their group characteristics. This depersonalization requires that people stereotype themselves as interchangeable members of a social category that they differentiate from other social categories. This means that it is not possible to act as, for example, a hip-hopper, if someone has not thought of him/herself as a hip-hopper. However, once people have thought of themselves as hip-hoppers, they are likely to act in ways that are consistent with their beliefs about what hip-hoppers are like.

SIT and SCT offer ways of understanding how young people's consumption of music and clothes in subcultural groups can offer a positive basis for comparison with other groups and so form the basis of a positive social identity. Andes (1998) engaged in 9 months of participant observation and interviews with punk young people. She concluded that a developmental model based on SIT could usefully account for the process of 'growing up punk'. She suggests that young people progress from rebelling against the norms and values of their parents to affiliate themselves with a punk community or lifestyle to internalizing punk ideology and behaving in accordance with its standards. Punk, she argues, is a group identity to which they have a 'commitment career'. While punk identities are clearly designed to be rebellious, other young people's identities may well exhibit similar processes of identity formation (e.g. Young Conservatives may fit this trajectory – whether or not they are rebelling against their parents' political affiliations).

Box 2 illustrates young people's commitments to particular group identities and differentiation from other groups. The extracts come from a 16-year-old British Asian young man living in Birmingham (Extract 1), a young Dutch Surinamese rapper who calls himself 'Creole' (age not given) (Extract 2) and from a member of a middle-class trio in a British city school who were 14–15 years old (Extract 3).

BOX 2

Self-categorizing in relation to social identities

Extract 1

Ashwin: I think the main way why we call ourselves rude boys is 'coz we hate authority and school and the police. We like the music and the people.
(Mac an Ghaill, 1988, p. 113)

Extract 2

Here in Bijlmer we are all hip hoppers. You don't know anyone who is not a hip hopper, at least on a part-time base. Today you have two styles: kaseko-men ... and us ... In Amsterdam we've got to develop our own style. We have guts. We are not ashamed.
(Sansone, 1995, p. 123)

Extract 3

They didn't understand it, I don't think. They thought it's something different and you don't understand and if it's in the minority I suppose, then you sort of ... to be immediately against it ... Maybe also people really didn't like our image. 'We're the middle-class rich kids. We've got brains. We've got money. We've got weird clothes', you know we're ... I think it puts a lot of people off. It did. It annoyed ... everybody!
(Hey, 1997, p. 118)

Each of the young people speaking are creating 'us'/'them' distinctions and so self-categorizing. They are also constructing themselves positively in relation to other groups by discussing the consumption particular to their styles. In doing so, they act as interchangeable members of a group through consumption. In Extract 1 Ashwin claims a black youth style identity – 'rude boys' – as oppositional to authority. In Extract 2, the teenage boy says that 'hip hopper' youth style is one that everybody claims (so it is natural that he should claim it) and further claims a specific Amsterdam hip-hopper identity. In Extract 3 the young woman names a class and socio-economic identity that she links with 'brains', clothes style and uniqueness (other people 'didn't understand it'). Her group has previously made it clear that they consider themselves elite, in comparison with other girls in their school. In each extract the young people demonstrate what Hebdige (1979) suggests – that style is multifaceted and that it is often oppositional. All the young people in the extracts above make comparisons within the contexts they discuss as important to them: in Extracts 1 and 3, the context is school, whereas in the second one it is Amsterdam. It is not being suggested that boys and girls, Dutch and British young people are identical, but it is possible to apply SIT/SCT regardless of the content of identities.

Contrary to what SIT/SCT would predict, however, it is not entirely clear that these three young people are all necessarily constructing other groups negatively. In addition, it cannot be certain that it is self-categorization that provides these young people with the idea of what are appropriate behaviours. It could instead be that the label (e.g. hip-hopper) is used because it justifies particular behaviours young people have already selected (or want to). In any case, it is difficult to analyse whether or not people are stereotyping themselves and if so, that they do so because they identify with groups.

It is also not certain that self-categorization and/or depersonalization has produced the accounts given by young people. In any case, the focus on cognitive processes means that, while SCT considers how identity arises in specific contexts, it treats the process as universal; whereas it may well be that the processes are different for each of the young people quoted above. In his work on national identities, the social psychologist Billig (1995) criticizes SCT for treating groups as if they are interchangeable. Billig suggests that the meanings associated with social groups may be more important for people's social identities than how individuals categorize themselves.

In general, stereotypes tend to be persistent (Wetherell and Potter, 1992). Yet, young people's style groups can change rapidly. Milner (2004) suggests that one reason for this is that, whereas members of a group cannot stop other people from copying their style, they can change their norms frequently and emphasize keeping up with the fashions they set in order to maintain their status. If SCT is to be able to account for this feature of young people's style groups, the notion that people self-stereotype in order to act in concert with group identities would require that people's self-stereotypes are able to change rapidly. There are constraints on this, however. In a study of 'scooterists' by Starkloff (1996) the following participant's account helps the understanding that what it means to belong to a leisure group continually shifts and is contested. As a result, it is not an easy task to know how to stereotype oneself in order to belong to particular groups. In this case, the leisure group that started out as 'Mods' has since divided and continues to change:

INTERVIEWER: Are there groups, say like mods and – ?

S3: Well you've got the mod scenes. It's like – there's two – there's two sort of mod organisations, between – friction between themselves. But that's – they're just hangin' on to like the 60's thing. You know what I mean? They just want the originality of what – what mod was, not wa [what] it is today. Well, they do – I'm not really even sure because I'm not really into the mod scene as such, you know. But they wanted some – somehow to keep the 60's thing, you know. Just the mod thing, the whole – point of what mod was. Where as the scooter scene, it basically started from mod, but it just – kept growing, kept moving with the times. And to me, I think, scootering, if it – you know – if it survives, like it has done, it's – you just gotta keep moving with the times, all the time. You know, different styles and music don't matter. You know what I mean. May be you bring in some of these other types of newer scooters, they're bringin' out, which aren't accepted for the scene at the moment, but you might have to make it acceptable – to keep the scene going.

(Starkloff, 1996, p. 33)

In this example, 'scootering' is the authentic style being alluded to. Everything else – mod style from the 1960s that gave rise to scootering, 'different styles' (meaning clothes styles) and music – are all rejected as ephemeral or insignificant. It is clear that the speaker does not self-stereotype according to already-established identity categories. Instead, he invokes 'moving with the times' and the continual reconstruction of the category. It may be then that self-stereotyping (the cognitive element of SCT) does not account for the identities that young people construct through consumption.

Activity 6   Comparing themes

Allow about
10 minutes

This activity will help you compare what SIT/SCT theory and Erikson's ego identity theory contribute to thinking about consumption and young people's identities.

Make brief notes on what you see as the points of SIT/SCT that help to explain young people's constructions of identities through consumption . Do you feel that SIT/SCT is more or less successful when it is applied to thinking about young people and consumption? Look back at the summary of Erikson's ego identity theory and your answer to Activity 5 to make your own decision about whether you think SIT/SCT or ego identity theory is the most persuasive.

Comment

SIT and SCT offer ways of understanding how young people's consumption of music and clothes in subcultural groups can give them a positive basis for comparison with other groups and so form the basis of a positive social identity. Ego identity theory also accounts for the ways in which young people compare with each other. While SIT/SCT focuses more on how a positive sense of self is created through comparing the ingroup favourably to the outgroup, ego identity theory focuses on exclusion of other groups as a means of establishing identity.

5.3 Positioning theory

Positioning theory can broadly be defined as a 'social constructionist' approach. The basic idea in social constructionist theories is that the ways in which we understand the world and present ourselves within it are constructed in particular social contexts and from the social resources available to us rather than naturally occurring. In Box 3 Woodward describes how this occurs.

BOX 3

How are identities formed?

We present ourselves to others through everyday interactions, through the way we speak and dress, marking ourselves as the same as those with whom we share an identity and different from those with whom we do not. Symbols and representations are important in the marking of difference and in both presenting ourselves to others and in visualizing or imagining who we are. We use symbols in order to make sense of ourselves in relation to the world we inhabit. This world is characterized by structures which may limit our choices, but which may also provide more opportunities.

How much constraint is exercised by social structures and how much control do we have in shaping our own identities?

Both as individuals and through collective action it is possible to redefine and reconstruct our identities. We can negotiate and interpret the roles we adopt. Through collective action it is also possible to influence the social structures which constrain us, but there are clearly restrictions and limits. The scripts of our everyday interactions are already written and at the wider level structures are deeply embedded in contemporary culture, economy and society. Identity formation continues to illustrate the interrelationship between structure and agency.

Source: Woodward, 2000, p. 39.

Woodward uses some ideas that have already been raised in this chapter. She identifies the presentation of self as important because the ways we speak and dress make us similar to some people and mark us out from others. Although Woodward was not focusing on consumption, her highlighting of dress indicates its importance to identity. Identity according to Woodward is produced through symbolic representations and we have some control (agency) in constructing ourselves, but are somewhat constrained by social structures. So although the scripts of our everyday interactions are already written, there is scope for creativity and rewriting.

Davies and Harré (1990) developed the concept of 'positioning' to recognize that people are not fixed in social locations (as suggested by the metaphor of role). Instead, 'positioning' constructs people as taking part in dynamic social relationships in which each social interaction involves taking up different positions, making assumptions about the positions that other people occupy and treating them in ways that fit with those assumptions. In each interaction people can take up, ignore or resist the positions other people assume they will (and so make available to them). One person may occupy different positions as an interaction progresses and in different interactions, but experience themselves as the same. Positioning theory suggests that people also create their own positions (Davies and Harré, 1990; Harré and van Langenhove, 1999). The positions that people choose to create for themselves and to take up can be part of their 'identity projects' – that is part of the process of trying to become who/what they envisage themselves as being (Foucault, 1977).

The idea of positioning is relevant to the construction of identities through consumption in that, as has been discussed earlier in the chapter, consumption is a relatively easy way for people to take up new identities and engage in identity projects. They can 'position' themselves through consumption. The process of identity construction that positioning theory identifies can be seen in the research process. Widdicombe and Wooffitt (1995) found that the young people they interviewed in a study of youth subcultures constructed their consumption identities in interaction with the interviewer. In the extract in Box 4 the second respondent makes this explicit by analysing the research interview situation and resisting being 'labelled'.

BOX 4

Respondents resist being categorized

Interviewer: Right. So as [I] said I'm doing stuff on style and appearance can you tell me something about yourselves... – the way you look.

Respondent I: What d'you mean like? What do you mean – about ourselves? It's a bit general.

Interviewer: Well how would you describe what you're wearing?

Respondent I: Ehm. What I feel best in – what I feel is sort of myself.

Interviewer: What about you?

Respondent 2: Uhm I just find it really offensive when people... try to label what you look like and so [Interviewer: Yeah] then go away and write a magazine article and say oh they're gothic or they're hippy or something.

Source: adapted from Widdicombe and Wooffitt, 1995, p. 106–7, with transcription notation omitted.

Positioning can also help to explain Widdicombe and Wooffitt's (1995) apparently contradictory findings that some young people simultaneously construct themselves as authentic individuals in their choice of style in contrast to others in the same style group, yet indicate that they identify with the style. They often did this by criticizing some young people who are apparently members of the same youth style group. They called them, for example, 'pseudo goths', 'mini-goths' and 'shallow' and accused them of only following what has become trendy rather than being authentic. Young people could thus position themselves both as members of groups with whom they shared dress and taste in music and distance themselves from some who dress in the same way and listen to the same music. A similar process was apparent in the account from the 'scooterist' presented above.

The other theories that have been discussed in this section (ego identity theory and SIT/SCT) are not well able to account for the fluidity in identities that consumption illuminates. Yet, young people often change their consumption to keep up with or innovate fashions or to maintain the exclusivity of their style group. These changes frequently produce new ways of constructing identity. Positioning theory can account for this fluidity since it suggests that people can experience themselves as the same person, while continually taking up and creating new positions.

In addition, positioning theory allows for contradictions in identities constructed through consumption. In a study of common culture Willis (1990) quotes one respondent who is explicit about this flexibility in the ways in which young (and some older) people can play with identity construction through style:

To me what you wear in a morning and what you wear to go out is a fancy dress, that's all I see it as because you enjoy the clothes you wear right? ... To me, fancy dress is everyday clothes, what you wear to go to college, go out to work or whatever, or what you wear to go out, it is fancy-dress costume ... I mean, you've got a costume on now, haven't you? I've got a costume on, everybody's got a costume on.

(Willis, 1990, p. 89)

Viewed in this way, it is easy to see that identities constructed through consumption can be used as resources in interactions. Styles can be changed to suit different settings in ways that allow people to negotiate different identities in different interactions. However, it is less clear how it can explain why people with similar histories and socio-economic statuses may choose different styles and different identities. Why do some positions get taken up repeatedly and so become identities? In addition, in common with all social constructionist approaches, it can be said to treat identities as too optional, rather than recognizing that some identities (e.g. of gender, ethnicity and social class) may allow people some choices, but are not optional and that not all choices are consciously made. A further and important criticism of positioning theory is its emphasis on language and conversations. This makes it unsuitable for explaining things that cannot be put into language. In addition, positioning theory does not explain why some positions that were taken up at one point might later be resisted (as happens with consumption). It is, therefore, very useful for explaining positioning and the process by which identities get formed at one time point – in this case for young people – but (as with SIT and SCT) not a developmental trajectory.

Activity 7   Applying theories

Allow about 15 minutes

This activity will help you apply the three theories above to a research finding and so to consider the relevance of each.

A study of young people and consumption found that some young people said that they were extremely careful about what they wear to school, but could wear things that would be laughed at in school when with a close friend at home. How do you think the three theories above could account for this? How well can they be applied?

Comment

Ego identity explains that young people in the period of moratorium may over-identify with cliques. The young people in the example may be over identifying with their peers at school. However, ego identity theory is less able to explain why that identification is localized to school and why these young people are able to reflect on the situatedness of this behaviour.

Of course we do not know whether or not the young people involved were in moratorium. SIT/SCT would provide an explanation in terms of self-categorization in order to belong to high-status groups. The young people therefore depersonalize and self-stereotype in order to be part of their ingroup at school. This is not necessary at home with one other person. It is not clear, however, that the young people are cognitively self-stereotyping since they realize they do not always do this.

Positioning theory would suggest that these young people are positioning themselves differently in school and out of school and possibly that they resist their school positioning when at home. It explains why it is easy for people to position themselves through consumption. It cannot explain, however, the power relations involved when many young people feel that they 'have to' wear certain things at school, but not at home.

Summary of Section 5

Erikson's psychosocial ego identity theory

- Erikson's theory is a developmental theory that views adolescence as the period when identity accomplishment is the main developmental task.
- Some support for Erikson's view comes from findings that young people often form exclusive social groups.
- Ego identity theory is less well able to explain the tension many young people express between being members of style groups and insisting that they are individual.
- Erikson conceptualized young people's groups as part of the process of young people searching for and finding identities. However, consumption can instead be seen as part of the process of constructing identities that are made, rather than found. For that reason, young people themselves may change society as they develop their adult identities rather than (as Erikson suggested) using 'clans' as a way temporarily to escape adult responsibilities.

Social identity theory and self-categorization theory

- Both theories claim that people are motivated to evaluate positively the groups to which they belong (ingroups) through comparisons with groups to which they do not belong (outgroups), which they tend to evaluate negatively.
- Both theories see people as having to self-stereotype in line with their understanding of a group in order to belong to it.
- In contradiction to SIT/SCT however, it is not clear that young people necessarily construct their own groups positively by constructing other groups negatively or that they behave in ways appropriate to their group *because* they self-categorize.
- Although SIT/SCT makes self-stereotyping central, it is difficult to analyse whether or not people are stereotyping themselves and if so, that they do so because they identify with groups.
- Unlike ego identity theory, SIT/SCT theorizes process, but does not propose a developmental trajectory.

Positioning theory

- Positioning theory is a social constructionist approach.
- The concept of 'positioning' constructs people as taking up different positions within interactions and creating positions for other people to take up. In turn, they can take up, ignore or resist the positions other people make available for them.
- Positioning theory suggests that one person may occupy different positions as interactions progress. However, people can experience themselves as continuously the same person.
- It can deal with the concept of fluidity in young people's consumption.
- It is less able to explain why people with similar histories and socio-economic statuses may choose different styles and different identities.
- Positioning theory treats identities as optional, rather than recognizing that some identities are ascribed, rather than chosen.
- It theorizes the process by which positioning occurs, but not its developmental trajectory.

6 Conclusion

This chapter has considered why consumption is an important psychological issue for children and young people's development. It argues that consumption is an ongoing individual and collective process that involves the construction of meanings. For young people in affluent societies, consumption may be a relatively easy way to construct desired identities for themselves and show that they are ready to be 'the next step older'. Brands allow young people to present themselves as high-status individuals in their peer group. Young people's consumption is therefore part of their learning how to manage peer relationships of solidarity and conflict. Young people use the interactional skills they have acquired to develop their identities through complex interactions with their peers around consumption. Consumption also involves the negotiation of societal differences, for example of gender, ethnicity and social class. Research on 'consumer socialization' suggests that by age 14 most young people have sophisticated economic understandings. The chapter also evaluated the usefulness of Erikson's psychosocial theory of ego identity, SIT/SCT and positioning theory to explaining young people's consumption identities. Each provides some useful explanations but has some shortcomings. The research available consistently shows that consumption is important to children's and young people's identities and to their relations with their peers and parents.

References

Abrams, M. (1959) *The Teenage Consumer*, London, Press Exchange.

Anderson, N. (2004) 'Brands, identity and young people – ongoing research', *The Psychologist*, vol. 17, p. 208.

Andes, L. (1998) 'Growing up punk: meaning and commitment careers in a contemporary youth subculture', in Epstein, J. (ed.) *Youth Culture: identity in a postmodern world*, Oxford, Blackwell.

Back, L. (1996) *New Ethnicities and Urban Culture: racism and multicultures in young lives*, London, UCL Press.

Barnes, P. (1995) 'Growth and change in adolescence', in Barnes, P. (ed.) *Personal, Social and Emotional Development of Children*, Oxford, Blackwell/The Open University.

Billig, M. (1995) *Banal Nationalism*, London, Sage.

Blatchford, P. (1998) *Social Life in School: pupils' experience of breaktime and recess from 7 to 16 years*, London, Falmer.

Bourdieu, P. (1984) [1979] *Distinction: a social critique of the judgement of taste*, Translated by R. Nice, London, Routledge.

Bronson, W. C. (1975) 'Developments in behaviour with age-mates during the second year of life', in Lewis, I. M. and Rosenblum, L. (eds) *Friendship and Peer Relations*, New York, NY, Wiley.

Chin, E. (2001) *Purchasing Power: black kids and American consumer culture*, Minneapolis, MN, University of Minnesota Press.

Conger, J. (1979) *Adolescence: generation under pressure*, London, Harper and Row.

Davies, B. and Harré, R. (1990) 'Positioning: the discursive production of selves', *Journal for the Theory of Social Behaviour*, vol. 20, pp. 43–63.

Dittmar, H. (1996) 'The social psychology of economic and consumer behavior', in Semin, G. and Fiedler, K. (eds) *Applied Social Psychology*, London, Sage.

Dittmar, H. (2004) 'Are you what you have?' *The Psychologist*, vol. 17, pp. 206–9.

Dittmar, H. and Pepper, L. (1994) 'To have is to be: materialism and person perception in working-class and middle-class British adolescents', *Journal of Economic Psychology*, vol. 15, pp. 233–51.

Dixon, J. C. and Street, J. W. (1975) 'The distinction between self and not-self in children and adolescents', *Journal of Genetic Psychology*, vol. 127, pp. 157–62.

Eckert, P. (1989) *Jocks and Burnouts: social categories and identity in the high school*, New York, NY, Teachers College Press.

Eckert, P. (1994) 'Entering the heterosexual marketplace: identities of subordination as a developmental imperative' [online], Working Papers on

Learning and Identity No. 2, Institute for Research on Learning, http://www.stanford.edu/~eckert/subordination.pdf (accessed 4 April 2004).

Edwards, T. (2000) *Contradictions of Consumption: concepts, practices and politics in consumer society*, Buckingham, Open University Press.

Erikson, E. H. (1959) *Identity and the Life Cycle: psychological issues*, New York, NY, International Universities Press.

Erikson, E. H. (1968) *Identity, Youth and Crisis*, New York, NY, Norton.

Foucault, M. (1977) *Discipline and Punish*, Tavistock, London.

Frosh, S., Phoenix, A. and Pattman, R. (2002) *Young Masculinities: understanding boys in contemporary society*, Houndmills, Palgrave.

Furby, L. (1978) 'Possession in humans: an exploratory study of its meaning and motivation', *Social Behaviour and Personality*, vol. 6, pp. 49–65.

Gilroy, P. (1987) *There Ain't no Black in the Union Jack: the cultural politics of race and nation*, London, Hutchinson.

Griffin, C. (1985) *Typical Girls? Young women from school to job market*, London, Routledge and Kegan Paul.

Gunter, B. and Furnham, A. (1998) *Children as Consumers: a psychological analysis of the young people's market*, London, Routledge.

Haavind, H. (2003a, unpublished) 'Contesting and recognizing historical changes and selves in development', Department of Psychology, University of Oslo.

Haavind, H. (2003b) 'Masculinity by rule-breaking: cultural contestations in the transitional move from being a child to being a young male', *Nordic Journal of Women's Studies*, vol. 11, pp. 89–100.

Harré, R. and van Langenhove, L. (1999) *Positioning Theory*, Blackwell, Oxford.

Hebdige, D. (1979) *Subculture: the meaning of style*, London, Methuen.

Hey, V. (1997) *The Company She Keeps: an ethnography of girls' friendship*, Buckingham, Open University Press.

Higgins, M. and Smith, W. (2002) 'Engaging the commodified face: the use of marketing in the child adoption process', *Business Ethics: A European Review*, vol. 11, pp. 179–90.

Hogg, M. and Banister, E. (2001) 'Dislikes, distastes and the undesired self: conceptualising and exploring the role of the undesired end state in consumer experience', *Journal of Marketing Management*, vol. 17, pp. 73–104.

Hollands, R. (2002) 'Divisions in the dark: youth cultures: transitions and segmented consumption spaces in the night-time economy', *Journal of Youth Studies*, vol. 5, pp. 153–71.

John, D. R. (1999) 'Consumer socialization of children: a retrospective look at twenty-five years of research', *Journal of Consumer Research*, vol. 26, pp. 183–213.

Kamptner, N. L. (1989) 'Personal possessions and their meanings in old age', in Spacapan, S. and Oskamp, S. (eds) *The Social Psychology of Aging*, pp. 165–96, Newbury Park, CA, Sage.

Kamptner, N. L. (1991) 'Personal possessions and their meanings: a life-span perspective', in Rudmin, F. (ed.) *To Have Possessions: a handbook on ownership and property*, special issue of the *Journal of Social Behaviour and Personality*.

Kenway, J. and Bullen, E. (2001) *Consuming Children: education-entertainment-advertising*, Buckingham, Open University Press.

Kinney, D. (1993) 'From nerds to normals: the recovery of identity among adolescents from middle school to high school', *Sociology of Education*, vol. 66, pp. 21–40.

Klein, N. (2000) *No Logo*, London, HarperCollins/Flamingo.

Korobov, N. and Bamberg, M. (in press) 'Positioning a "mature" self in interactive practices: how adolescent males negotiate "physical attraction" in group talk', *British Journal of Developmental Psychology*.

Lagree, J-C. (ed.) (2002) *Rolling Youth, Rocking Society: youth take part in the post-modern debate on globalization*, Paris, UNESCO.

Lees, S. (1993) *Sugar and Spice: sexuality and adolescent girls*, Harmondsworth, Penguin.

Locher, D. (1998) 'The industrial identity crisis: the failure of a newly forming subculture to identify itself', in Epstein, J. (ed.) *Youth Culture: identity in a postmodern world*, Oxford, Blackwell.

Lury, C. (1996) *Consumer Culture*, Cambridge, Polity.

Lury, C. (2004) *Brands: the logos of the global economy*, London, Routledge.

Mac an Ghaill, M. (1988) *Young, Gifted and Black: student–teacher relations in the schooling of black youth*, Milton Keynes, Open University Press.

Miles, S. (2000) *Youth Lifestyles in a Changing World*, Buckingham, Open University Press.

Miles, S., Cliff, D. and Burr, V. (1998) '"Fitting in and sticking out": consumption, consumer meanings and the construction of young people's identities', *Journal of Youth Studies*, vol. 1, pp. 81–91.

Milner, M. (2004) *Freaks, Geeks, and Cool Kids: American teenagers, schools, and the culture of consumption*, New York, NY, Routledge.

Nesdale, D. (1999) 'Social identity and ethnic prejudice in children', in Martin, P. and Noble, W. (eds) *Psychology and Society*, pp. 92–110, Brisbane, Australian Academic Press.

Nesdale, D. (2004) 'Social identity processes and children's ethnic prejudice', in Bennett, M. and Sani, F. (eds) *The Development of the Social Self*, pp. 219–45, Hove, Psychology Press.

Phoenix, A. and Tizard, B. (1996) 'Thinking through class: the place of social class in the lives of young Londoners', *Feminism and Psychology*, vol. 6, pp. 427–42.

Prelinger, E. (1959) 'Extension and structure of the self', *Journal of Psychology*, vol. 47, pp. 13–23.

Sansone, L. (1995) 'The making of a black youth culture: lower class young men of Surinamese origin living in Amsterdam', in Amit-Talai, V. and Wulff, H. (eds) *Youth Cultures: a cross-cultural perspective*, London, Routledge.

Sherry, J. F. (1998) 'The soul of the company store: Nike Town Chicago and the emplaced brandscape', in Sherry, J. F. (ed.), *The Concept of Place in Contemporary Markets*, Chicago, IL, NTC Publishing.

Starkloff, P. (1996) *Scooterists* [online],http://paeps.psi.uni-heidelberg.de/starkloff/pub/Scooterists.pdf (accessed 21 January 2004).

Storm-Mathisen, A. (1998) *Buying pressures – what is that? A preliminary project on the meaning of clothing among 13-year-olds*, Report 4:96, Oslo, Statens Institutt for Forbruksforskning (SIFO).

Susman, S., Dent, C., McAdams, L., Stacy, A., Burton, D. and Flay, B. (1994) 'Group self-identification and adolescent cigarette smoking: a 1-year prospective study', *Journal of Abnormal Psychology*, vol. 103, pp. 576–80.

Thorne, B. (1993) *Gender Play: girls and boys in school*, New Brunswick, Rutgers University Press.

Turner, J., Hogg, M., Oakes, P., Reicher, S. and Wetherell, M. (1987) *Rediscovering the Social Group: a self-categorization theory*, Oxford, Blackwell.

Ussher, J. (1997) *Fantasies of Femininity: reframing and the boundaries of 'sex'*, London, Penguin.

Walkerdine, V. and Lucey, H. (1989) *Democracy in the Kitchen*, London, Virago.

Walkerdine, V., Lucey, H. and Melody, J. (2001) *Growing up Girl: psychosocial explorations of gender and class*, Basingstoke, Palgrave.

Wetherell, M. and Potter, J. (1992) *Mapping the Language of Racism: discourse and the legitimation of exploitation*, Hemel Hempstead, Harvester Wheatsheaf.

Widdicombe, S. and Wooffitt, R. (1995) *The Language of Youth Subcultures: social identity in action*, Hemel Hempstead, Harvester Wheatsheaf.

Willis, P. (1990) *Common Culture: symbolic work at play in the everyday cultures of the young*, Milton Keynes, Open University Press.

Woodward, K. (2000) 'Questions of identity', in Woodward, K. (ed.) *Questioning Identity: gender, class, nation*, London, Routledge/The Open University.

Young, B. (2002) 'The child's undersanding of the intent behind advertising: a personal story', in Hansen, F., Rasmussen, J., Martensen, A. and Tufte, B. (eds) *Children, Consumption, Advertising and Media*, Copenhagen, Copenhagen Business School Press.

Chapter 8
Themes and issues

Karen Littleton

Contents

After you have studied this chapter you should be able to understand the key themes and issues which have emerged from this book as a whole.

1 Introduction

The chapters of this book have all addressed areas of psychological enquiry that have grown rapidly in recent years: the study of children's personal and social development. Each chapter has focused on a specific key issue or topic, such as parenting or gender identity, and has discussed associated theories and research. However, when the book is considered as a whole, a number of overarching themes and issues emerge.

Activity 1

Allow about 15 minutes

Looking back over the book as a whole

This activity will help you consolidate the material you have read.

This chapter considers some of the key themes that have arisen in the course of the book. To begin this process, and before reading on, briefly note down the themes and issues which you feel have emerged from your study of this book. Then, as you read through the rest of the chapter, elaborate or annotate your notes to add any further points that are raised.

2 Levels of analysis

One overarching theme of this book concerns the various levels at which psychologists now investigate children's social development. Social development was once studied primarily at the level of the individual child, with psychologists asking questions about the emergence of particular social behaviours – such as the age at which children first begin to smile, become capable of imitation, or can recognize themselves. Examples of such work are mentioned in Chapter 4. While this remains a valid and valuable level of analysis, the work reported in this book illustrates how psychologists interested in social development are increasingly studying children *in interaction with others*. It also shows how they are investigating children's social development in and through interactions and relationships that are embedded and constituted in particular social contexts, framed by culture-specific goals for development. The importance of understanding child development in a social context thus emerges as a key theme that recurs throughout the book. Chapters 1 to 3 characterize relationships and interactions as contextually situated, while Chapters 4 to 7 clearly highlight the importance of studying identity 'within a social context which takes full account of the transactional relationship between children and their environment' (Chapter 4). The significance of social context is highlighted particularly through the consideration of behaviour 'problems' in Chapter 2. Here the authors explain that there are 'several respects in which problems can be seen as context-embedded and normatively defined' and draw attention to the fact that difficulties arise when 'the behaviour and goals of the child lack "goodness of fit" with the social environment to which the child is expected to adapt' (Chess and Thomas, 1984).

As shown in Chapters 1 and 2, much attention has been paid to the importance of children's relationships with their parents, and the developmental significance of the mother–child relationship in particular. However, the notion that children are simply 'shaped' by their parents' rearing practices has given way to research that argues for seeing children as 'agents' who make sense of their worlds (that is, negotiate meanings) rather than being passively subjected to socialization. This emphasis on children as active meaning-makers, negotiating and constructing their understanding of the social world, highlights how 'children as well as parents play an active role in the process of development; interactive patterns of influence will apply in all cases. The relative influence of parenting behaviour versus child behaviour will vary, according to the characteristics of the child, the characteristics of the parent and the circumstances affecting both' (Chapter 2).

A dynamic transactional model of development, such as that described in Chapter 2 (and revisited again in Chapter 4), offers a way of encapsulating these processes such that psychological development – including disturbed development – can be understood in terms of complex, continuous transactions between the child and social processes.

3   Processes and products

This characterization of development as involving the negotiation and construction of meaning, knowledge and understanding sits at the heart of the work reported in Chapter 3. In this chapter, the emphasis shifts away from attempts to understand children's early relationships with their parents, to consider the nature and developmental significance of interactions between siblings and peers. The chapter draws heavily on research work that involves analysing ongoing social interaction between children. By emphasizing the importance of such analytic work, the chapter underscores a theme emerging from the previous two chapters, namely that developmental psychologists are increasingly seeking to understand the processes (the 'how') as well as the outcomes, products and end results of development (the 'what'). As you read the account of such interaction-based research you will probably have developed a strong sense of the complexity and multifaceted nature of children's interactions and relationships with others. Chapter 3 also makes it clear that not only do children interact with others in face-to-face settings, but many, particularly those in affluent societies, also communicate with others using the telephone, mobile phone, internet, and e-mail. The use of technology can thus sustain and extend children's relationships, in ways which need to be understood. Furthermore, taken together with the research reported in Chapters 1 and 2, the work in Chapter 3 shows how different kinds of relationships and interactions afford different kinds of experiences which each have significance for social and personal development.

4 Methodological issues

The research reported in the different chapters illustrates the wide range of methods used by psychologists to study and assess aspects of children's social development (including examples of diverse observational, interview and questionnaire-based approaches). It also highlights some of the thorny issues encountered when attempting to study and interpret children's behaviour in both laboratory and more naturalistic settings. For example, how can psychologists measure or index 'problem' behaviour? How can they assess gender development or beliefs about national group membership? How is the avoidant response of a child in the Strange Situation to be interpreted – as evidence of an insecure attachment relationship or of growing independence? When are chasing and 'fighting' indicative of playfulness and when do they constitute conflict and dispute? All the chapters present details of how psychologists set about studying different facets of social development, to enable you to understand the methodological choices and challenges faced by researchers working in this broad field of enquiry. Through the descriptions, and the associated critiques and evaluations of the research studies that have been presented, you can see that designing and interpreting research work can be a challenging process, requiring rigour and careful consideration of both the demands placed on the children who participate and of what constitutes a valid and reliable study.

Throughout the book you have heard the voices of children and young people and what they themselves say about their family and social lives, consumption and their sense of national identity. This reflects an important shift in social research, one which views children's own accounts as central and valuable. As children and young people are the central 'stakeholders' in the developmental process it is vital that their voices and experiences are heard. The contemporary literature is thus beginning to reflect increased involvement of children as active, engaged participants and co-researchers in research work and there is increasing recognition of the need to ensure that methods play to children's strengths rather than weaknesses. The inclusion of discourse analytic and ethnographic work within the book in part reflects this concern. Some researchers, however (such as Kellett *et al.*, 2004), believe that it is important to empower children and young people to undertake, not just participate in, research of significance and importance to them. In this way children and young people would potentially be in a position to make a distinctive and valuable contribution to the study of social development, through researching and presenting work motivated by their concerns and conducted and interpreted from their perspective.

5   Complexity and diversity

Schaffer (1996, p. xvi) characterizes the child as 'an inhabitant of a heterogeneous social world' and the work reported in this book is undoubtedly a testament to his description. You have read how, from a very early age, children are active, engaged participants in diverse kinds of interaction and they form and sustain multiple relationships. Much of the work reported in this book, in the first three chapters in particular, attempts to understand the nature and significance of certain kinds of relationship and interactions – for example, mother–child, father–child, peer and sibling relationships. However, the authors also acknowledge the limitations of studying each type of relationship in isolation. In doing so they point to the importance of understanding what Schaffer (1996, p. xv) describes as 'the interconnectedness that characterises social life and social behaviour' and the associated need to understand the nature and developmental significance of the interconnections between the child's different relationships. Similarly, the links between the different contexts or 'sites' for development, such as home, school and peer group, also need to be investigated and theorized and their developmental significance explored. This is because being sensitive to the 'joined-up' nature of children's experiences of life leads to an understanding of the impact of, for example, the significance of continuities and discontinuities between children's experiences at home and at school. The book also raises the issue of whether early childhood experiences have an enduring impact on, or significance for, our lives as adults – notably whether the close relationships of adults are influenced by their attachments as children (see Chapter 1). The difficulty and the necessity of understanding and theorizing complexity and diversity thus emerge as key themes within the book.

Throughout the book questions arise as to how far psychologists' theorizing is generalizable beyond the immediate context or contexts being studied. In particular, it is recognized that a description of developmental processes observed in one particular cultural context should not become a prescription regarding development in another. In studying this book you have been introduced to work that has been conducted in diverse cultural contexts, including cross-cultural research, and this is because the consideration of such work enables an evaluation of the associated theorizing in terms of its universality or relativity. In Chapter 2, for example, you saw how 'Adopting a cross-cultural perspective has important implications for the clinical assessment of "disturbed" behaviour. Behaviour that is adapted to one social or cultural context may be maladjusted in another ... solutions to the tasks of growing up may vary at cultural, sub-cultural and individual levels'.

The limitations of theorizing about the significance of peer and sibling interactions from research conducted primarily in Western industrialized settings were noted in Chapter 3. It was suggested that care must be taken not to over-generalize from patterns of relationship observed in a particular society at a particular moment in time. The issue of universality and relativity also emerged in Chapter 4, with the idea that, seen from a Western perspective, identity development is often regarded as the 'long process of becoming a self-aware individual'. However, through the discussion of the work of Tobin *et al.* (1998), it became clear that 'the ideas about individuality are not universal, but instead are culturally bound. ... To consider, even briefly, the ways in which different cultures view the self helps individuals put their taken-for-granted views into perspective – to see them as theories, as assumptions'. Thus, it is argued, notions of what constitutes a self should be regarded as culturally constituted constructions – theories or assumptions – rather than universal experiences. This is a stance that also pervades the chapters in the second half of the book where the plurality of childhood experiences, both within and between cultural contexts, is recognized.

6   Identity in question

The first three chapters of the book focus on understanding the nature, scope and developmental significance of children's relationships and interactions with others. In the later chapters the emphasis shifts to a detailed consideration of children's identities, specifically how children develop a sense of who they are, including their gender and national identities, and how consumption is implicated in identity work. The material discussed in these four chapters, however, resonates with the work discussed earlier in the book. Again the image emerging from research is of a child who is active in the developmental process. Strong emphasis is placed on the significance of children's negotiation and re-negotiation of meaning, not only in interaction with but also in relation to other people – with symbols and representations being used by children and young people to produce meanings and make sense of themselves in relation to the world they inhabit. While the work presented within the chapters on gender identity, national identity, and consumerism emphasize different theoretical perspectives and highlight different developmental phases, the authors demonstrate that, particularly as children get older, identity becomes increasingly 'dependent on meanings which have been formed through comparison or interaction with others' (Chapter 4). Social and cultural environments are seen to have a profound impact on children's sense of identity. It is also the case that these environments are shaped by the child and, as noted previously, there is a transactional relationship between children and their environments.

7   The interrelationship between the socio-emotional and the cognitive

Research conducted in 'everyday' settings such as those described in this book can both highlight and address immediate practical concerns. At the same time, however, it can also contribute to contemporary theoretical debates and discussions regarding children's development. One of the key issues that has come to the fore, partly as a consequence of researching children in 'real-life' contexts, is the extent to which it is possible to consider the cognitive, social and emotional realms of development individually. Recent years have seen researchers with an interest in social development advocating the need for a more integrated perspective on familiar topics. For example, the idea of an 'internal working model' addresses cognitive dimensions of attachment; studies of early social relations are clarifying the capacity for perspective-taking; the links between language disorders and behavioural difficulties are being recognized, as are the reciprocal relationships between social sanctions and gender conceptions. At the centre of these perspectives is a belief that social and emotional development does not just happen in parallel with cognitive development, but that all three may be closely interlinked and mutually dependent.

Perspective-taking
The child's capacity to comprehend points of view different from his or her own, either in relation to other people's interests, feelings and so on, or even others' perceptions.

8   Problematizing development

Towards the end of the book, in Chapter 7, the notion of 'development' itself is problematized and subject to critical scrutiny. Perhaps controversially, the notion of development as a natural, unfolding process is challenged, the suggestion being that it is something that has to be accomplished through display. Seen in these terms, development does not result from children and young people's resolution of developmental tasks, but rather it is 'performative', being accomplished in everyday practices. 'Childhood is among other things learning to be the next step older. Participation in kid communities requires a continuous learning of new age-appropriate behaviour and age appropriateness changes rapidly. Social status among one's peers requires growing up and it requires demonstrating new mature behaviours' (Eckert, 1994, p. 3).

This issue, among many others, will continue to be debated by researchers and those who are concerned to understand and promote children's development. Having studied this book you will be well placed to follow and contribute to these debates as they emerge and unfold in the years to come.

References

Chess, S. and Thomas, A. (1984) *Origins and Evolution of Behaviour Disorders*, New York, NY, Brunner Mazel.

Eckert, P. (1994) 'Entering the heterosexual marketplace: identities of subordination as a developmental imperative' [online], *Working Papers on Learning and Identity No. 2*, Palo Alto, CA, Institute for Research on Learning, http://www.stanford.edu/~eckert/subordination.pdf (accessed 18 January 2005).

Kellett, M., Forrest, R., Dent, N. and Ward, S. (2004) 'Just teach us the skills, we'll do the rest: empowering ten-year-olds as active researchers', *Children and Society,* vol. 5, pp. 329–43.

Schaffer, H.R. (1996) *Social Development*, Oxford, Blackwell Publishing.

Tobin, J.J., Wu, D.Y.H. and Davidson, D.H. (1998) 'Komatsudai: a Japanese preschool' in Woodhead, M., Faulkner, D. and Littleton, K (eds) *Cultural Worlds of Early Childhood*, London, Routledge.

Acknowledgements

Grateful acknowledgement is made to the following sources for permission to reproduce material within this book. Every effort has been made to contact copyright holders. If any have been inadvertently overlooked the publishers will be pleased to make the necessary arrangements at the first opportunity.

Chapter 1

Figure 1: Science Photo Library; *Figure 3:* © Hugh Threlfall/Alamy.

Chapter 2

Figure 1: © Ace Stock/Alamy.

Chapter 3

Figure 1: © Bubbles; *Figure 2:* © Bob Ebbesen/Alamy; *Figure 3:* © Jeff Morgan/ Alamy; *Figure 4:* © Photofusion Picture Library/Alamy.

Chapter 5

Figure 1: © Photofusion Picture Library/Alamy; *Figure 2 left:* © Bubbles; *Figure 2 right:* © Janine Wiedel Photolibrary/Alamy; *Figure 3:* © Bubbles; *Figure 4:* © Bubbles.

Chapter 6

Figure 1 upper left: PhotoDisc Europe Limited; *Figure 1 upper right:* © Image State/Alamy; *Figure 1 lower left:* © Travel Shots/Alamy; *Figure 1 lower right:* © David Sanger Photography/Alamy; *Figure 2 left:* © Worldwide Picture Library/ Alamy; *Figure 2 right:* © Black Star/Alamy; *Figure 3:* © Alamy; *Figure 4 left:* © Alamy; *Figure 4 right:* © Alamy.

Chapter 7

Figure 1: Associated Press Ltd; *Figure 2 left:* The Advertising Archives; *Figure 2 right:* The Advertising Archives; *Figure 3 lower left, p. 235:* Jean-Louis Bellurge/ Powerstock; *Figure 3 lower right p. 235:* © Homer Sykes/Alamy; *Figure 3 upper left p.236:* © Alamy; *Figure 3 upper right p. 236:* Rex Features.

Cover photographs

© Getty Images.

Name index

Subject index